CW00766303

PILGRIM OF THE VOID

PILGRIM *of the* VOID

KENNETH WHITE

TRAVELS *in* SOUTH-EAST ASIA *and the* NORTH PACIFIC

EDINBURGH AND LONDON

First published in France as *Le Visage du Vent D'Est* (1980) and *Les Cygnes Sauvages* (1990)

First published in Great Britain 1992 by
MAINSTREAM PUBLISHING COMPANY (EDINBURGH) LTD
7 Albany Street
Edinburgh EH1 3UG

ISBN 1 85158 473 0 (cloth)

The publishers wish to acknowledge grateful thanks to the Scottish Arts Council for their financial assistance in the production of this volume.

A catalogue record for this book is available from the British Library

Book design by James Hutcheson
Typeset in 10/11½ pt Garamond by Blackpool Typesetting Services Ltd
Printed in Great Britain by Mackays of Chatham Plc., Chatham

'I decided to go away into foreign parts, meet what was strange to me . . . Followed a long vagabondage, full of research and transformation, with no easy definitions . . . You feel space growing all around you, the horizon opens.'

Nietzsche,
The Wanderer and his Shadow

'. . . unlike you, Joyce, I am more concerned
With the East than the West and the poetry I seek
Must be the work of one who has always known
That the Tarim valley is of more importance
Than Jordan or the Rhine in world history.'

Hugh MacDiarmid,
In Memoriam James Joyce

'He's inside the house, and yet he hasn't got off the road. He's on the road, and yet he hasn't left the house. Is he just an ordinary fellow, or is he into something else? Who can say? There's not a man living could define him. As soon as you try to grasp him, he's gone — he's on the other side of the mountain.'

Rinzai,
on 'the real man without situation'

CONTENTS

PREFACE

This is a book of 'travels in Asia'.

Cultural history (the terms are heavy, but they can mean something live and enlightening) tends nowadays to get so sliced up — ten years of this, five years of that — perspectives have dwindled to such an extent, that it is no doubt necessary, in the present context, to make it clear that 'an attraction to the East' is not confined to a particular period of the fifties and sixties of this century. That period was only one moment in Western culture's deep-grounded preoccupation with its other half.

Ever since the encounter between Alexander's Greek philosophers and the gymnosophists (i.e. yogi) of India, the opening East has been a constant channel, sometimes evident, sometimes latent, in Western thought. To give only relatively recent examples, think of the Chinese influence in the eighteenth century, most interestingly with that partisan of Eurasia, Leibnitz. Think of the Eastern reference in Thoreau, Nietzsche ('I could have been the Buddha of the West'), Schopenhauer, Hesse, Yeats (looking for a 'half-asiatic masterpiece'), Heidegger, as well as in the thought of more than one twentieth century physicist, once the conventional world-picture had disintegrated and a radically new vision of things appeared, at least nebulously, on the mental horizon. There is, then, a long line of sporadic effort that can be seen comprehensively as an attempt to heal the split between East and West, an attempt to get at something like a whole way of being. It's a way that has been rarely fully explored (it's only maybe nowadays the means for it are available) and even more rarely followed right through expressively, most literature being still based on false notions of substance, simplistic notions of psychology, and a very limited aesthetics.

My own awareness of what Pindar calls 'Asia's great space', which

I saw from the start as an area of potentiality, goes back to my adolescence in a small village on the West Coast of Scotland, where I had access to a private library fairly well endowed with Indian and Chinese texts such as the *Upanishads* and the *Tao te ching*. Those texts gave me a sense of mental expansion like nothing I had read before. Running underground for a while, this early acquaintanceship came back to the surface and became more concentrated when, living in Munich, in the years 1955–56, I came across certain Japanese texts (those of Dôgen, Bankei, Hakuin) that hit my brain like lightning. Back in Glasgow, I was reading David Hume, so close at times to Buddhist thought, and in particular to its conception of the void, that it makes his *Treatise on Human Nature* sound like a Scottish version of Nagarjuna. Hume blasts the notion of identity, seeing in its place a series of perceptions held together, if at all, by desire and intention. And Kant continues Hume who, he says, woke him up from his 'dogmatic slumber'. I remember discussing Kant's ideas with a German assistant at Glasgow University while swimming about in the Whiteinch baths. In Glasgow too, I was deep in existentialism; Sartre's *néant* is next door (the back door, yes) to the void — ontological vacuity, making for liberty. These early studies were continued for years in Paris (the years when I wrote *Incandescent Limbo*) where, again, I had access to a private library that had in it practically everything, not an Orientalist scholar (to be that had never been my aim), but a late-modern Western writer, that is, a mind-traveller looking for new ways of thinking, writing and being, could want. I have never ceased working this material, following up those paths.

All this is to say that when I started, in the early seventies, a series of Asian trips that were to continue right up to these last few years, it was in no way to look for a guru or a doctrine, it was with a sense of the *extreme* areas of Eastern thought in my mind, with the desire to plunge myself into a total field of sensation and experience, and with the idea of pursuing the logic of an already quite extensive 'work in progress'. That's what this book, *Pilgrim of the Void*, is about. It begins between West and East, in Hong Kong's floating world, moves out from there into the South China Sea, to Macao and Taiwan and thereafter to Thailand, before going still farther out, to Japan, with a 'haiku-journey' from Tokyo, up through the northern provinces, to the Hokkaido. It's neither a book about the East, nor a book about Buddhism, it's a book about a landscape-mindscape in which you no longer feel the need to talk about Buddha or whatever at all, you just live it in and for itself.

Don't let's confound 'the void' with nothingness, blankness or any kind of excessive purity. The Void isn't empty in an absolute sense, it's empty only of confused imaginings and constricting (because over-constructive) ideas. In fact, it's full of live realities, complex movement, flashes of light and insight. Which is to say, again, that to be a 'pilgrim of the void' is not to be blind to, or oblivious of, social reality or psychological complication, it's just not to get bogged down in them, not to get all fankled up in discussion about them. Voidness means absence of blockage, and blockage comes ultimately from mistaken ideas (illusions) as to substance and identity. You don't get rid of these by ploughing over them (human science) or playing about with them (so much literature). Let's look at it therapeutically. If you consider somebody's ill because of his diet (that's often the *basic* cause), you don't simply describe the symptoms (maybe with wailing and gnashing of teeth), nor do you provide new recipes within the old diet, you suggest a *change* of diet. Let's say, to extrapolate, a new way of conceiving things and consuming life. That's what the theory and practice of the Void does. It's not out to set you apart from life, it's out to make you live life differently and enjoy it differently. There's a phrase quoted somewhere in this book that says this: 'What's the use of talking about enlightenment to someone who hasn't fully lived?'

What's life lived to the full? What's a complete life-path?

As I write this Preface, I'm thinking back to that time when, having left the Great Western Road of Glasgow, I was living in Munich, in a shack at the edge of the Englischer Garten, on the banks of the Isar. I'd just spent two years at a Scottish university studying languages and philosophy, and there in Munich I was officially also a university student, but if I was still a student, it was no longer, except obliquely, at the university. One of my few acquaintances was an American, a student like myself (we met from time to time at the university *mensa* where we had our meals), who had left the States and was making, by a long and devious route interrupted by nervous breakdowns, for the

East, saying he wasn't going to stop 'till he got to the place where the sun comes up', that is, till he got right back into the depths of the East, where we came from.

That American is in my mind, as a kind of *alter ego*. But there's another image, going deeper perhaps than any *alter ego*, and that's a girl's face. It was in Paris, a winter evening years ago, in a theatre, that I saw that face, a very fascinating one. I find it very hard to place it ethnically. It wasn't Chinese, nor Indochinese. I think I'd place it higher up, on the Mongolian steppes maybe. But this is vague, or maybe after all not so vague, it's maybe just a way of suggesting that this face was not on any map, that it was the face of the unknown. Anyway, what was far from vague was the impression it made on me. But 'impression' is wrong. Rather a quickening, an awakening, something that awakened an idea in the mind even before it awoke desire in the senses. I thought of that face immediately as the Face of the East Wind, and had locked it away under this name in the depths of my mind when, years later, with one of those jolts of recognition that are the delight of the intellect (the whole way is sensual and intellectual at one and the same time), I learned that the 'face of the East wind' is an ancient Chinese expression for the realisation of Tao. 'If you once recognise the face of the East wind,' says Chu Hsi, 'every flower is the Spring.' And, referring to the region where the East wind blows, Lao Tzu says 'impossible to define, it is called the form of the informal, and the image of what is imageless'. The face of the East wind takes on various forms as I travel the roads of this book. In the final phase, it's a flight of wild swans.

So, a book of travels? Yes, no doubt — but more, a book concerning a certain (and uncertain) way of being in the world. Hsüan-chüen gives a pleasant description of the *tao-jen*, the man-on-the-way:

> *Take a look at that easygoing fellow, out on the way*
> *Who has given up all striving*
> *Neither avoiding the false nor seeking the true*
> *For ignorance after all is really enlightenment*
> *And this changing body is the body of deep reality*

It looks like there may be something beyond the strict categories of true and false, something beyond the heavy notions of spiritual and material — maybe a space in which these notions and categories are no longer seen as contradictory. Maybe the girl I saw was the body of the Dharma, maybe she was just a figment of my excited imagination. Who can say? Maybe the thing is, not to ask yourself so many questions, but to get out on the road, the life-road, and live it, taking it all as it comes, the up and the down, the sordid and the marvellous, the tough and the gentle.

When the monk asked the master: 'What is Tao?', the answer came like a shot: 'Go!'

Wherever we go, we're going home.

K.W.

IN THE FLOATING WORLD

My old desire
T'ao Ch'ien

1. Hotel Confucius

I hit the hotel at the same time as a couple of film-makers, a Frenchman and a Belgian, and in the lobby of the hotel the Belgian says to the Frenchman:

'Do you think this is a hotel where you can get girls?'

and the Frenchman answers:

'You can get girls if you've got the cash'

to which the Belgian rejoins:

'Well, it isn't lollipops I've got in my pocket.'

Hong-Kong — gateway to the Orient, pleasure-town of South-East-Asia.

What gives its name to the hotel is a gilt portrait of Confucius on the wall, under it a plaque with the following text:

Born in the 21st year of Lin Wang, died in the 41st year of Kin Wang, of the dynasty of Chou, or 551–479 B.C., Confucius lived in the age in Chinese history known as the Spring and Autumn period, 723–481 B.C. He was a native of Lu, in what is now Chufu County, Shantung Province. He advocated Jen, humanitarianism, and Yee, righteousness, as the supreme principles of morality, and spent thirteen years teaching these principles among the states. His philosophy and wisdom has been so great that since ancient times he has been — and still is — revered as The Teacher of Ten Thousand Generations. He travelled so extensively in his day that we also consider him as the Father of Tourism.

Confucius, the father of tourism . . .

When I get into what's to be my room, I'm accompanied by the white-jacketed floor-boy who busies himself folding down the bedspread while I take a look around. I'm quietly contemplating a diminutive pair of brown knickers hanging on the peg of the bathroom door when the boy, with a puzzled expression on his face, standing in front of a vase of carnations, six white and one red, says:

'Did you buy flowers?'

'No. But,' I continue, indicating the little brown knickers, 'there was a lady here last night. Maybe she bought the flowers.'

The boy looks more puzzled than ever and his gaze goes from the knickers to the carnations, from the carnations to the knickers, till his puzzlement becomes amusement:

'Velly beautiful lady. You should tly her. Maybe she lose flower.'

Well, thanks to the knickers and the carnations, Chan Kin Wo and I are on intimate terms, so that when he leaves, he says:

'Velly fliendly'

and I continue my exploration of the room, finding in the bed-table drawer a Holy Bible thoughtfully placed there by the Gideons and reading the fire instructions:

'If you are unable to get downstairs, go up the roof.'

2. Nathan Road in the Morning

A Chinese philosopher I read years ago said Chinese learning was for substance, Western learning for function. He was refuted some time later by another philosopher who said there was a learning for substance and function in China, and a learning for substance and function in the West — different substance, difference function. Leaving the philosophers to their quarrel, it's certainly substance that interests me: matter, the sheer delight in matter (it seems to me that if you get the matter really related and radiating, you have no functional problem, you have a living reality, something to go on). For years too, I considered that the 'East', as the limit of a certain orientation, that orientation which for me began high up in the North-west, was in my own substance, within my own six feet and seventy-two kilos — and that still goes. But now I have, to some extent, found that East within myself, as a result of long quiet study interspersed with fracture zones, I'm avid for a sheer plunge into open, flowing life, with nothing to refuse and no holds barred. Because, where I am now, there's no difference at all between Nirvana and Samsara and, as I think Nietzsche says somewhere, it is possible to be superficial — out of depth. All the problematics — psychological, philosophical, sociological, you name it — come from people tying themselves up in knots in halfway houses. The whole world is a halfway house. It's time we got into the field of living life.

Nathan Road in the morning! I buy a red-and-black-printed newspaper, which I can't read, for that very reason — newspapers which

I *can* read I never buy, and with this newspaper, which is more a kind of musepaper, in my hand, I walk down the street in a sea of yellow faces amid sounds of Cantonese.

At a dusty corner, under the big ideogrammatic signs glinting now in the morning sun, dead, but waiting their turn, like snakes in winter, two beggars, one beating a drum, the other scraping a two-string fiddle, provide a thin ancient music, while from disc-shops come the opulent sounds of rock'n'roll. Further on, another beggar, but is he begging, a long-haired, Mongolian-looking character in black rags, is sitting up against one of the old banyan trees that line the road, smiling on the scene. A half-wit, or a sage? A man passes with a little green bird in a cage — another man passes with a little green bird in a cage. Is there somebody round the corner selling little green birds in bamboo cages, or do the Chinese take their birds out for a stroll the way people in the West do their dogs?

Nathan Road in the morning. Did you see that pretty girl? What is it again Nietzsche says (if I refer to Nietzsche so much, it's because he's *at the limit of the West*, and would have actually 'gone East', in his own way, if he hadn't gone mad): 'Progress of the idea: it becomes subtler, more captious, more unseizable — it becomes female!' Ah, my idea of China, my lovely yellow idea . . .

I'm really in Asia, I'm really in China. How often, holed up in some room in the West, I dreamt of it — dreamt of Mi Fu's junk on the Blue River, or the colours and smells of India. I'd open a book, and the mention of Shiva, or the photo of some corner of a temple would be enough to set me going. I'd go from North to South. I'd be up in the Himalayas, among the rhododendron, the giant rhododendron of the Himalayas, and then I'd be away down South at Mahabalipuram, a lotus growing in my brain, a thousand-petalled lotus, and my feet beating the dark red earth. Then I'd leave India for China, for *Mahacina*, and I'd be over on the Blue River again, evening coming down, dragons running along the banks, herons silent at the water's edge, the water lapping up against their legs. Imaginary extravaganzas: my mind a cauldron of images and memories, my heart a drumbeat monotonously insisting on a distant unknown past, and my body a desire.

And now, Nathan Road, Hong Kong — real Asia, real China. All

I'd had to do was take a plane in Paris, another in London, eating and sleeping in the clouds — and then, when I woke up, it was India: red earth, green rivers, and the ocean a great calm blueness; thereafter Burma, Bangkok, Laos, Hong Kong. Each place as it came was like a *chakra* opening up in my body. It was like making love to the planet. And Hong Kong — it might seem a forlorn hope, a certain disappointment, but in a queer kind of way, how to put it, I'm beyond all hope and all disappointment, and *everything is good for me.* I expect nothing, I have no expectations — at last, to have got rid of expectation! Isn't the whole of Western civilization a compound of expectation, whether it be for the Messiah, the Future or God knows what all else? Even when it's given up waiting for anything else, doesn't it keep on waiting for Godot? Well, I'm expecting nothing, I'm waiting for nothing. I'm not even a nihilist. I'm nothing at all. I'm out of Western terms altogether; my being's an ideogram.

Nathan Road in the morning.

3. Crossing the Ferry

If things get too hot and noisy for you in Hong Kong, either Hong Kong-side or Kowloon-side, you can always take the Ferry and enjoy a few minutes of coolness and space, with an occasional whiff of the South China Sea (comes out of the subconscious via Conrad). Now to say that you enjoy the Ferry in Hong Kong is like someone who's just been to Paris enthusing about the Métro — and I'll admit that, just as the Métro hardly concentrates all the interest of Paris, there are other things in Hong Kong besides the Ferry. But for an old Whitmaniac like myself, whose adolescence crossed Brooklyn Ferry time and time again:

> *I too many and many a time cross'd the river of old,*
> *Watched the Twelfth-month sea-gulls, saw them high in the air floating with motionless wings, oscillating their bodies,*
> *Saw how the glistening yellow lit up parts of their bodies and left the rest in strong shadow*
> *Saw the slow-wheeling circles and the gradual edging toward the south*

the Ferry has meaning, the Ferry is a place of meditation that gathers memories and lets the mind breathe, lets it 'go up into the sky in broad daylight.' How often I crossed the Ferry in Glasgow too, not only the one beyond Scotstoun that allowed me to get clear of the city and walk (thirty miles or so) down to the wind-and-wave coast, but the small Kelvinhaugh Ferry, the wee, tarry, oily, mucky ferry that used to ply between the banks of the dirty old Clud there at Kelvinhaugh in the heart of town. *Out of the cradle endlessly rocking . . .*

Here in Hong Kong it's January, a bright, clear January. As the marine forecast said: *Pressure high over China. Hong Kong harbour and approaches, northeast force 4 fine and dry.*

Fantastic weaving, criss-crossing movement on the bay. Several cargos at anchor, and sampans clustered around them; launches foaming their way across the crisp blue waves; lighters piled high with goods; and junks, broad-beamed ancient teak junks, magnificently slow, with sails of many colours from white to rust-red, moving out to the fishing grounds.

On the ferry itself, the faces: Chinese faces, Japanese faces, Cambodian faces, Korean faces — faces that, while facing the skyscrapers of Hong Kong, face back also (is this not the month of January, the month that faces both ways?) to what quiet island, to what back street in Shanghai, to what barge-filled Osaka. The spectacle and the source, the function and the substance — the seagull, pure life, knows nothing of this dialectic.

I have been in love with many faces.

4. *Over in Aberdeen*

It's well seen that Hong Kong was started up in the first place by Scots adventurers with a nose for commerce when you discover that the name of the main fishing village there is Aberdeen. Back where I come from, I mean up in Scotland, I always had less sympathy for the citizens of Aberdeen, who can get on very well without it (they're among the most 'getting on' people in the world) than for that Eskimo — I keep coming back to him — who, in the eighteenth century drifted down from the North in his kayak and was fished out, half dead, offshore of the town. I've always considered him as one of my spiritual ancestors . . . Well, anyway, this Aberdeen is a different kettle of fish: a floating population of twenty thousand people living on, and making a living off, three thousand boats, from the massive junk to the flimsy blue-hooded sampan.

'Sampan! Sampan!'

One of the ways of making a living here is to offer sampan-trips round the floating town at so much the quarter-hour. So that any Eskimo in the vicinity is going to be hassled all along the waterfront, with sampan-women clutching at his clothes and practically dragging him into their embarcation:

'Sampan! Sampan!'

— the cry rings out from differently-pitched voices all over Aberdeen. I'll take one of the little trips maybe later on tonight, but for the moment, all I want to do is wander round the harbour and in among the narrow, smelly streets.

Here's a street-barber, working in a little ramshackle booth, serving himself a meal he's just cooked up on a primus stove — the steam and fumes rise in the clear air as he pours the pan's contents into the bowl that lies on the board he's placed across the arms of his barbershop chair. Here's a street-doctor, with nothing but a chair as premises, and a woman having her foot seen to. Here's a fortune teller; here's an orange seller (look at the neat way he's laid out samples on their peel) — and there, God help me, is it the same man, or is there a whole band of them, crouches that black ragged Mongolian beggar I saw the other day on Kowloon-side, with the *self same smile* on his face, staring apparently into nothing.

Why do I suddenly think of that English opium-eater with the French name who finally settled in Scotland and died there — I've duly visited his tombstone in the Princes Street graveyard: Thomas de Quincey, and that strange book of his, the *Confessions*, which I've had for years in the Bodley Head edition given to me one bleary New Year's morning in the 'sma' oors' by a sympathetically drunken school-teacher? It must be because it was one such as that black-ragged beggar who first introduced de Quincey to opium, having come off some Cantonese ship maybe at Liverpool and wandered up into the Lake District. And also because, walking alone here in these back-streets amid this sea of yellow faces, I'm thinking of the illustrations in that edition, particularly that one illustrating the author's search for the lost Ann in Oxford Street, and that phrase printed in red on the rice paper leaf protecting the drawing: *I have looked into many myriads of female faces*. And the whole thing becomes a descent into the underworld, to the womb-world, to the kingdom of the mothers, the yellow sources. And is not Asia that for us Eskimos — we Hyperboreans? Do we not need, to complete our initiation — our millenial initiation — to go back down to the yellow sources?

Let's take to the water now. I'm intrigued by that floating world of the boat people whom the townspeople call by the derogatory name of Tanka (*taan ka*), but who refer to themselves as *soi söng ian* ('the people of the water'). Nobody knows exactly where they came from. Some say the original nucleus was a survival of ancient, non-Chinese, Yüeh tribes. Whatever their origins, they were outcasts from landed society. Their traditions, totally at variance with those of the landlubbers, are sea traditions. Every day on their junks they burn incense to the Sky Spirit and the Sea Surface Spirit. And certain fish to them are sacred: the sturgeon, the sawfish, the manta ray, the turtle, the whale, the white porpoise — fish that are out of the ordinary, marked by some peculiarity, fish with an aura of the strange and the marvellous. They believe that white porpoises swim up rivers to temples, and they tell weird stories of whales: 'Once a woman was sitting on a rock. A whale came up. She offered it tea. It drank the tea, thanked her, made a little bow, and swam away. . .'

Aberdeen at midnight. The floating restaurants are closing down, the mahjong players are spitting their last spit and putting away their blocks, there's a thin mist drifting over the harbour. I'm on a little sampan with an old woman, chug-chug-chugging along the winding water-lanes between the junks. In one junk — massive, its dark red glistening hulk — there's a family mending nets, visible through the window in its hull. As we chug past, a young girl looks up from the net, and it's all like a myth, an ancient myth — a night in eternity.

5. Letting it Drift

The evening began in Wanchai, in a Szechuanese restaurant. I was with Chang, a poet, well known in Hong Kong literary circles for a long poem he wrote on rice wine, or rather a certain kind of rice wine, *kua diao*, of which he is inordinately fond. He has just completed a long political allegory based on a scene of boys playing at marbles — but more of that, I mean literature, later. For the moment, let's eat.

We're in a Szechuanese restaurant, which is to say that the food is hot, very — viciously seasoned with hot peppers, black pepper, and with a dish of hot sauce on the side just in case any hot-mouthed diner wants the hot food hotter. Szechuan has no opening on the sea, and there are few workable rivers and lakes, so there's no cool fish on this menu, it's all hot-blooded meat: beef stew and then 'cloudy pork' (pork in such thin slices it's 'as light as cloud'), with noodles and egg-plant to accompany them. If your mouth really begins to feel too much like a furnace, you can calm it with one of those little dough-puffs, that's what they're there for. And, of course, there's the wine. Tu Fu, says Chang, spent the last years of his life in Szechuan, and he particularly appreciated beef stew and noodles (along with strong, cheap rice wine). It's a good substantial beef stew we have here tonight. Chang points with his chopsticks at some fatty lumps in it. 'Maybe penis,' he says, 'make you fuck fuck.'

Some time later, the food gone, but the wine still well to the fore, Chang is telling me about his poetry. As I said, his main works are long poems, but he likes 'relaxing' with what he calls 'Zen things', and it's these he is talking about and quoting now. He wrote a poem once on the problem (hah hah!) of time: past, present and future. It went like this:

I wear a white shirt
Enter a white room
Open the door
And see whiteness . . .

Then a few months ago he was in Japan, at Kyoto, and he spent a lot of time looking at a stone garden there, and that gave rise to the following:

I look at you from the West — you say nothing
I look at you from the East — you say nothing

I look at you from the North — you say nothing
I look at you from the South — you say nothing
I look at you from the Centre — you say nothing
I'm bored
Then suddenly you laugh!

— the 'laugh', he says, laughing, was a sudden flight of swallows.

'You like? You like Zen, huh?' He'd met a professor of American literature once who said he was 'interested' in Zen. 'How heavy can you get?' he says. '*Interested* in Zen, my God!' He drains his cup: 'I know you, you know me — we are not professors of literature!'

There's another bottle empty. We ask for a new one to be brought up. Meanwhile Chang is contemplating the old one, with one eye closed, and he contemplates, and he better contemplates (we are . . . slightly . . . drunk). Suddenly he announces: 'I say you a bad poem':

There is a jar sitting there
just sitting there
for no reasons

silent
a silent existence
remembering nothing joyful
nothing sad

maybe just wondering
how empty yesterday's tomorrow
and tomorrow's yesterday

feeling
a little
lonesome
a little cold.

After the new bottle's become old ('yesterday's tomorrow, tomorrow's yesterday'), he suggests we go down to the bay and hire a sampan and spend some time there floating drunk under the stars. Like Tu Fu:

By bent grasses
in a gentle wind
Under straight mast
I'm alone tonight

And the stars hang
above the broad plain
But the moon's afloat
in this Great River

Oh, where's my name
among the poets?
Official rank?
'Retired for ill-health'

Drifting, drifting
what am I more than
A single gull
*between sky and earth?**

So we go down to Causeway Bay and hire a little boat festooned with Verey lights, with a diminutive TV set flickering bluely in the back, manned by an old woman and a young girl, and move out in an easy rocking sampan rhythm ('you should write a poem to this rhythm,' says Chang), over the dark waters. Dark, but lit up here and there with lamps — rosy, blue, yellow — for we are far from being alone in the bay. There are food-sampans (with fruits and wines, fish, shellfish and meat) looking for trade, and music sampans ready to entertain. We buy some pears ('Mao's pears,' says Chang, 'from mainland China'), and listen to a piece from a Chinese opera followed by *'Rose, Rose I love you'*. Thereafter we pull further out, and there's just the rocking of the boat, the stars, the sound of the oar in the water and not much talk. I found myself thinking, naturally enough in the context, of Shen Fu's *Six Chapters of a Floating Life*, autobiographical and travel notes ('Conjugal felicity', 'The Little Delights of Life',

* Chang spoke the poem in Chinese. I give here Arthur Cooper's translation, in *Li Po and Tu Fu* (Penguin Classics, 1973).

'Pleasures of Travel') written 'with a careless brush' (Shen Fu hadn't passed through the mill of the literary examinations, so that his style is fresh and natural): 'At that time we lived, you and I, in the Residence of Solitude and Light . . .'

These thoughts are interrupted by a quiet phrase from Chang:

'Do you want a girl?'

and he points to a sampan about ten yards away, not a food-sampan or a music-sampan this time, but a sampan with a 'wild flower' in it.

'Let's take a closer look.'

Autumn night rain is the perfect time for love . . .

6. Train to Sheung Shui

It was a morning as cool as green tea. I felt like a quiet little trip on the Kowloon–Canton Railway. The KCR.

I spent my earliest childhood beside the tracks of the G.B.&K., which is the Glasgow–Barrhead–Kilmarnock line. And when, later, we moved down the coast, my father being a signalman, we lived beside the tracks of the West Coast line, out of St Enoch, Glasgow, terminal Largs. So that railway tracks have always had a peculiar kind of attraction for me.

The sleepers reeking of creosote . . . In Spring we'd follow the tracks out of the village, beyond the High Station (Fairlie, the village, had two stations: the High, and the Pier Station), past the faded yellow signalbox, making for Primrose Bank where we'd gather in those furry little yellow flowers that were the beginnings of the long, long Summer.

And the rust of old, disused tracks. There was a set of these in the Wilderness, a waste patch of ground between the working line and the boatyard, full of bramble bushes, wild raspberries and strawberries, and crabapple trees. Saturday mornings we used to sit at the end of them, looking down at the boatyard, full of yachts and fishing smacks in for repair, and over the bay, wondering what to be up to next, how to get the utmost enjoyment out of the great free day.

I know signalcabins. I know the smell of black tea brewing on the stove. I know the glint of levers, the reek of paraffin. I know the tick of the wall clock, that big, significant tick, and its door inscribed on the inside with the names of all the signalmen who've worked in the box. I know the ledger, with the train data and the observations. I know the flags, the detonators (for use on the tracks in time of fog), and the lamps — lamps with green and red shutters. I know the smell of them and the feel of them. I've gone over this knowledge before, I'll go over it again, for it's the going over intimate knowledge of this kind that gives satisfaction. Is the world not dying for lack of such intimate knowledge?

In some sense my writing began in a signalbox. For it was a slate that had hung on the walls of the box that my father gave me to write on, I think before even I went to school. For years you could see the mark left on the signalcabin wall by the removal of the slate, and when I was in the box, as I was often, my father would point to that mark and say: 'Do you remember that slate?' I remember that slate, and the smell of creosote, and the taste of black tea brewed on the stove . . .

Now it's a railway in China. I've been thinking all the above, or rather just letting it all rise in my mind ('let the mind breathe'), as the train has pulled out of Kowloon station and moved up to Mong Kok, Sha Tin, the Chinese University, Tai Po Kau, Tai Po Market (a horde of women with poled baskets get off here), and Fanling. Sheung Shui is the next stop, and that's as far as I can go. The station after, Lo Wu, is a closed area, for which you need a special permit, not easy to obtain. After that, it's the frontier of the People's Republic.

Sheung Shui. My idea in coming up here into the New Territories was to get closer to Chinese earth. So when I get off the train at the little station, I don't make for the village itself, but take the road leading out of it.

About two miles out from Sheung Shui, I go into a field and pick up a handful of Chinese earth, wrapping it in a paper I've brought along with me for that purpose. It'll go back to the West with me, and will stand on the shelves of my workroom beside my Chinese books.

Now let's just look at the blue hills there shimmering in the noonday sun:

Drinking tea, eating rice
passing my time as it comes:

looking down at the stream
looking up at the mountain —
how relaxed and serene!

— that was Ch'an master Pao-tzu Wên-ch'i.

7. *Meet Bossie Wong*

For the French, he's 'Edouard', head of 'Edouard Services'; for the Chinese, he's Boss Wong (pronounce it Possee Wong). He's a Chinese from the island of Mauritius, which explains both his French tongue and his British passport. Chinese-French-British, that is only one combination of the many that make up the life of Bossie Wong. Defining himself, he says: '*Je suis une tomate*' (I'm a tomato), and he explains '*Je suis à toutes les sauces*' (I'm in all sauces).

I met him for the first time in his cluttered little premises in Mody Road, Kowloon: about five feet tall, round-nosed, and bald, with a humorous twinkle in his eye which might indicate that he isn't taken in by his own '*personnage*'. He's in that little office of his, piled with goods and correspondence (he displays the many letters of recommendation and thanks, and the articles written about him in newspapers and tourist books), which is preceded by two other rooms, equally chock-full of goods. In one of these rooms, the one you enter once you've negotiated the heavy, barricaded door (like so many doors in Hong Kong), a handful of young men — innocuous employees of Edouard, henchmen of Bossie Wong? — are watching colour television.

The leaflets of Edouard Services for French tourists offer, in particular, night-trips in Hong Kong, including a super-real Chinese meal in a radically Chinese restaurant (at the end you'll see living serpents, the venom of which, after the snake-man has slit them with a pair of scissors, will be presented to you as a pick-me-up), a look at the Forbidden City (completely lawless, ruled over by the Triads, where no white man can enter), and a visit to the Flower Boats (only one girl per boat, who has the right to invite to her private residence, otherwise it's prostitution). And Edouard concludes: 'We've got all you want. All you have to do is ask.' If he doesn't have the goods you want on the spot (suits, shirts, kimonos, handkerchiefs, sheets, cases, jewels, jade, cameras, radios . . .), he'll send you to one of the shops he has an arrangement with. He has an arrangement with about ninety shops, and the arrangement is not that he receives a percentage, no, he receives a modest monthly salary from each of them, which is the method he figured was most convenient. It's only one of the conveniences he's thought up in his time. He's all for convenience and arrangements. As he says himself: 'In Hong Kong, everything's organised.'

Although I'm not a good buyer (what would I want with a suit, or a radio, or a camera?), but only a curious writing bum, a kind of wave-and-wind man, economically paleolithic, Edouard suggests that we have dinner the next evening — it's possible he thinks he may still be able to sell me something, or that I may somehow further his plans, it's possible also, and I incline to this hypothesis, that Edouard really believes in sheer disinterested friendship, just simple human communication, and he wants it.

So, next evening, we're dining in a restaurant in Mongkok (which Edouard translates as something like 'full house district'). There's a night market (with a lot of goods from dubious sources) in that quarter, and as we pass through it on the way to the restaurant Edouard says he knows his presence has been remarked and that the news is running from barrow to barrow: 'Bossie Wong is here.' He says the same thing happens when the police appear, as they feel obliged to do now and then, for the sake of appearances ('The police open one eye and close the other,' he says), and sure enough word like that must have got around like lightning because we're hardly clear of the market when there's a clatter of boxes being shut and a trundling of barrows moving off into side streets, and in no time the place is bare — with a police car just showing its nose at the corner of the street.

In the restaurant, whether because he actually likes it, or whether because he's got so used to putting on the little act — and it's probably a bit of both — Edouard goes through his shrimp routine, which consists of dipping a live shrimp in a glass of whisky till it's drunk and incapable, though still twitching, then shelling it and swallowing it. It's supposed to be good for the health and strength — like rat wine, shark's fin, and other imaginative delicacies. Let it be said too that Edouard carries his own personal drink about with him: a bottle of whisky, a bottle of cognac, and a bottle of mineral water which he keeps in a little cloth case. He's really organised.

It's a one and only Chinese restaurant, this, with not a word of English spoken by anyone, and nothing much to look at (tiled walls, nondescript furniture), a place where you can spit on the floor to your heart's content — and the food is excellent.

The whisky's been going down at a very commendable rate (my old friend in Edinburgh could hardly have done better), and Edouard goes on and on in his French-tongued mystery-Chinese voice — I let him talk, because I enjoy listening (well, sometimes). By and by he gets round to opium, saying it's encouraged by rich men who don't want their sons to leave the family fold. They keep them docile at home with opium and girls — two girls: one to hold the pipe, the other to light it. The smoker has his hands on the breasts of the pipe-holder, and everybody's happy.

It's almost midnight. Edouard's old ivory face is rosy, and his eyes are sparkling. He concludes his evening talk the way he started it:

'I'm a tomato.'

8. *Mid-Autumn Moon*

Moon-gazing has always been a favourite Chinese pastime. What do they see in it? All kinds of things. For example, a woman called Ch'ang O who stole from her husband, the famous archer Hou I, the Elixir of Immortality (given him by the Queen Mother of the West who controls the furies from her residence in the Great Wilderness) and after the theft fled for refuge to the moon, where, to her consternation, she was changed into a three-legged toad. Another thing they see, or used to see, is a hare busy pounding the drug of immortality — but that's a hare seen through Taoist eyes; if the eyes are Buddhist, it's the hare that offered his body to the Buddha when he was cold and lost, and was rewarded by residence on the moon. There's also an old man, in China he's the God of Marriage (Yüeh Lao, Old Yüeh), who ties people together with loving red thread. For more abstract minds, the moon is the essence of the female principle in nature which is maybe why the poet Li Po tried to embrace it when he was out on a boat one drunken night and got himself drowned in the moony water.

It is the fifteenth day of the eighth month, which is the celebrated Moon Festival. The bakery shops are full of moon-cakes, and tonight the moon will be bright, very bright and full in the sky.

I was out at one of the city parks in the Causeway Bay district still very early in the evening, intending to be in on things right from the start. Bird-sellers and bird-fanciers are airing their pets, hanging the cages in trees. Stalls are being set up and loaded. Rehearsals are in progress: flag wavers going through their evolutions; folk dancers; singers; comedians.

The crowd begins to arrive around eight o'clock — families with children, every child carrying a lantern, mainly red, but all colours, and all shapes: globes, concertinas, fish, hens, even ships and tanks. These dot and bob, their candles flickering, all over the landscape. Things are beginning to hum. The fortune-tellers are doing a roaring trade — there's a whole row of them over there at tables, using their various techniques. A young man, stolidly indifferent, is having the wings of his nose examined and explained — while his girlfriend listens all agog; another client watches as the fortune-teller scribbles signs with chalk on a felt blackboard (will he get rich, be happy in love?). The families have begun to stake out lots for themselves on the green, hanging their lanterns on the branches of the trees, and laying out cloths or newspapers spread with goodies. The moon is out in style — perfect up there on the Hong Kong heights, above the skyscrapers and the shanty towns. I sit under a tree myself and gaze on it, maybe I even doze off a little . . .

I'm not sure what time it is, but it's the end of the Festival: little lanterns are floating up to the sky attached to balloons. Must be midnight or after. Going through Wanchai, I pass by a bunch of American sailors, one of them saying to his mate: 'Did you get it?' and the other replying: 'Yep, I got it, man.' Further on, I come across two startingly white M.P. angels, one murmuring with a puritan accent: 'Steambaths, huh.' Further on again, an old woman comes up to me and whispers in my ear: 'Nice young girl?'

It was the night of the mid-Autumn moon.

9. The Day of the Green Dragon

A fine blue morning, and I'm up in Central. I've just stopped in front of a little book-and-curiosity shop, and I'm looking at old wooden seals, their faces thick with ancient wax, their ideograms looking like crows in a red dawn . . . A young man inside the shop who's seen me through the cluttered window comes out, and looks at the seal I have in my hand:

'Chop for marriage,' he says. 'Chinese poem hard reading.'

Seeing I'm interested, he invites me into the shop. There on a shelf I see a book, looking very old, and in writing that attracts me.

'Pakistani,' says the young man, then, seeing I don't look too convinced, he calls out a name and another man, older, appears from the backshop. He's sturdily built, with black cropped hair, but hardly any teeth — only two or three on the right side, one of them huge and gold. It's easy to make the dental inventory, because he's always smiling, and it's not a smirky, commercial smile, it's openhearted, full of fun. The young man indicates the book:

'Tibet,' says the other. 'Long way North China. Little people — few. Sometimes talk Turkey language. Funny religion. Hah! hah! Not South China.'

After a short discussion as to prices, I buy the seal and the book. And I leave. But outside my eye is attracted by more seals. And I'm fingering them when the Laughing Man comes out to talk. As I pick up seals, big ones, small ones, thick ones, thin ones, he translates what's written on them:

'Hong Kong West Scholar — chop of learning shop'

'One Hundred Flower Room'

'Wild Game House'

— these seals are marked four dollars each. 'Three for ten,' he says, smiling. I pick out four. 'Four for eleven,' I say. 'OK!' he says, laughing.

With that, I make to go on my way, but just a few paces further along the pavement there's another shop, exactly like the first, but this time it's not chops and snuff bottles and books that are conspicuous, but opium-smoking materials. I stop in front of the window, and in no time at all Laughing Man is at my side.

He points to a crude wooden figure in the window:

'Tin Hau,' he says. 'Mother of Heaven. Prayer to her. Get opium every day. Very funny.' And while he's on statues he comments on a small Buddha: 'Buddha under ground. When people dead, they think still alive. Funny religion, hah hah!'

After that he points out the weighing scales and the special tea pot — 'for thick tea'. He says there's too much water in ordinary tea, that is, too much for opium smokers: 'They want the tea thick,' and he continues: 'Opium man different from common man. All different.'

We go into the shop.

Inside, in the semi-darkness — outside, Hong Kong is blazing with high morning sunlight — he tells me that it is still possible to smoke in Kowloon, but expensive. Two years ago, opium was still to be had for two to five dollars a pipe, now it's 50 dollars:

'Very expensive. Criminal to smoke.'

While Laughing Man has been talking, my eyes have fallen on the weirdest pipe I've ever seen: about two feet long, black wood, twisted like the devil, with a small metal bowl and knobs right along the stem, the mouthpiece a couple of inches of very cool green jade. A marvel! I pick it up.

'Green dragon pipe. Old men smoke. Old scholar!'

At that moment, an old man passes in the street, dressed, like Laughing Man, in baggy black pants and jacket. Laughing Man hails him. He comes in. They talk. The old man looks at me handling the green dragon, and makes a remark. Laughing Man translates:

'He says very interesting to smoke'

but he hasn't smoked in twenty years. They continue talking, the old man with a kind of embarrassed nostalgia, Laughing Man with laughter. When the old man goes away, making a little bow, with a quiet smile on his face, Laughing Man says:

'Old man. Long life persons. They have the knowledge.'

10. Rain on Wanchai

Walking in Wanchai, under the rain, a soft warm rain that is easy on the skin. Seen against the bursts, the sheets, the floods of electricity in the main thoroughfare here, the moon, way up in the sky, looks poor — definitely non-commercial. It's an old beat-up moon, came out of a ballad or a love-song a long time ago, now unemployed, at most an object of study. Old beat-up moon, you're like that remnant of Genghis Khan's horde, the black ragged beggar I keep seeing here and there.

I've talked of being nothing, and of a density that means you can do without identity — your being's an ideogram. What that signifies maybe is that I've pushed my identity so far back that most of what's called reality — reality being here defined as that in which we feel ourselves implicated — is quite simply unreal to me, mere spectacle.

What fascinates me is some body-mind breaking into the light, or the light breaking into the body-mind.

The moon behind the rain is like the face of a woman in pleasure.

Dance of ideogram, orgasmic moon, ah, Wanchai, Wanchai.

My reality is cosmo-demoniac. I can *walk* myself into ecstasy. Just give me a little rain — or a little wind, or a little sunlight.

And tonight it's rain.

Rain over Wanchai, rain over Tsimshatsui — I like to let these words turn over on my tongue.

I don't feel like going back home yet, to the Hotel Confucius I mean. I think I'll take a tram out to *Shau ki wan* and see what the night still has to offer.

In the rainy night, a green tram full of yellow faces making for *Shau ki wan* . . .

11. The Boys from Okayama

It's the Bar of the Asia Hotel, one or two in the morning. Not many customers left. The Belgian film-man and his French partner we met at the beginning of these pages have just departed, the Belgian shouting, somewhat enigmatically: *'Je suis un grand garçon, je ne viens pas du Texas'* (I'm a big boy, I don't come from Texas), and the Frenchman saying (each of them is apparently pursuing his own inner monologue): *'Je suis sûr qu'elle va me proposer la botte'* (I'm sure she's going to go to bed with me). That leaves only myself and an Australian with whom I've been talking about films ('Yes, I saw it in Sydney'), and three Japanese.

The Nipponese have their eyes on the little Hong Kong serving-girl, pretty enough, her slit-skirt offering inviting, or so might it seem, glimpses, and they obviously think it will be easy enough getting her, just a matter of arranging the price. The one who speaks the best English, that sounds as if it came from 1930s' American gangster films, shouts over to the waiter:

'Hey, boy!'

and when the waiter, a young fellow of about twenty-five, roughly the same age as the Japanese, comes over, the man from Yamato points with his thumb over to the girl, and says:

'How much?'

The waiter just looks at him for a moment, then says quietly:

'You have already paid your bill, sir.'

The Japanese doesn't take the hint, but comes back to the attack:

'The girl, I mean the girl.'

At this, the girl, looking disgusted, walks out of the bar. The waiter repeats, just as quietly:

'You have already paid your bill, sir. And it's closing-time now, sir.'

The Japanese, who's pretty drunk, is about to start up again when his two companions, by word and gesture, tell him to give over. And with that they collect their things and leave. I also leave, with the Australian. But the night is young.

There's a late-night coffee-shop down at street level. We go in there. It's pretty crowded, and there's a fog of blue smoke, but we find a table all right, and it's there we come up against the Japanese again. They're at the table next to us.

The Australian is tucking into a plate of ham-and-eggs, and I'm half-heartedly playing with a whisky, more than half regretting I've come, when the Japanese spokesman leans over and says:

'Where you come home in Hong Kong?'

'The Confucius,' I say.

'What is your big home?' he then asks.

'Paris,' I say.

At this, the Japanese beams, points to his bashed nose, and says:

'Belmondo!'

and, right enough, he does look a bit like the French actor.

This little gesture of his, and the clownish expression he puts on his face, makes me laugh, and I say: 'Right. Belmondo!' and the others laugh too. We're all laughing, except the Australian who's wholly engaged in blottily transferring ketchup from the bottle to another plate of ham and eggs and maybe doesn't like those yellow-peril Japanese anyway. I've kind of taken a liking to them: Belmondo, the fat one who looks like a wrestler, and the quieter, more handsome one, who turns out to be a school-teacher.

'On business?' says Belmondo.

'Just travelling. And you?'

'Pleasure. Three days.'

I ask Belmondo where they came from in Japan, and when he answers:

'Okayama'

the fat one echoes:

'Okayama'

and the quiet one smiles and nods his head.

'You know Okayama?'

'No. I've never been to Japan.'

'Tokyo!' says Belmondo, 'Kyoto!'

'But I love Japanese literature: Tanizaki, Akutagawa, Kawabata . . .'

At this, Belmondo looks to the other two, as if this isn't his domain, and the other two look at me, a bit astonished. The quiet one says:

'You read Japanese books?'

'Yes,' I say, 'many.'

'*Yukiguni*?' says the school-teacher.

'*Snow Country*? Yes,' I say, 'very beautiful.'

The three Japanese look at each other.

'Mishima?' says the school-teacher, as though he were putting me through a quiz.

'Yes. But I don't like him so much. Too militaristic.'

The school-teacher smiles, looks over to the wrestler, and they talk between themselves.

'They give up,' says Belmondo.

'What's that?'

'They give up. Happy you know so well Japan.'

'Oh, I don't know it, I just like what I know of it, a few books.'

The other two turn back smiling.

'You like *old* books?' says the school-teacher.

'Oh yes,' I say, and spin off a sequence of names:
'Kojiki, Genji Monogatari, Manyoshiu, Chōmei, Kenko, Matsuo Bashō . . .'
'You are beautiful!' says the school-teacher, looking absolutely delighted.
The wrestler says something. Belmondo translates.
'He asks if you are born in Japan.'
'No.'
'Where are you born?' asks Belmondo.
'Scotland,' I say.
'Scotland,' repeats Belmondo, then he turns to the others, and says:
'Karewa Sukotsutorando de umareta.'
The wrestler again says something in Japanese, Belmondo translates:
'What is your name?'
'White Kenneth.'
'Hoshina Sadahiro,' says the wrestler, pointing to himself.
'Masamitsu Kitagawa,' says the school-teacher, slightly bowing.
'Katumi Inoue,' says the third, and, pointing to his nose again, adds:
'Belmondo!'

12. Beyond the 10,000 Buddhas

On a warm and humid afternoon, I took the train again at Kowloon Station, making this time for Shatin, where the 10,000 Buddha Temple is located. There was a little beauty in the carriage, one of these beauties that grace South China, only sixteen years old, the kind of girl described in the beautiful Cantonese phrase *ham bao doi fong* (flower blossom waiting open). Ah yes, lovely, perfect loveliness — *ni ho lei*, little girl, *ni ho lei, ni ho lei*!, shall I say it a hundred times under my breath, like a prayer?

At Shatin, I asked the way to the temple and was directed to the far end of the village where it dwindles away into a huddle of shacks: first, vendors' booths (fruit, shellfish, cookies, fritters), then dwelling shacks full of the click of mahjong pieces and the flicker of little TV screens. After that, there was only the path, up through the thick green bamboo, and by now a thin rain was falling.

At weekends and in fair weather, quite a lot of people visit the 10,000 Buddhas, but that day the path was deserted, given over completely to the green bamboo silence. I enjoyed the path, I was in no hurry to reach the Buddhas.

Further up, there was a notice which began rather aggressively:

TEMPLE OF TEN THOUSAND BUDDHAS
Visitors are not welcome

then specified the limits of the aggressivity, indicating times:

before 6.30 a.m.
and after 8.30 p.m.

and ended on a general warning note:

Beware fierce dogs

After the green-bamboo-silence path it was like getting a punch in the face. The Buddhist content was low, and I was prepared for the worst, but I went on nonetheless.

A few yards further on, you reach the temple, and you get another punch in the face, this time not with aggressive words, but with garish colours. This, you think, isn't a temple, it's a bloody fairground. The courtyard is adorned with huge images of Sakyamuni's ten disciples, each riding his mount: Samantabhadra on a grotesque white elephant, Manjusri on a blue lion . . . It's all very ugly. In the temple sits Buddha himself, ten thousand little metal replicas of him on shelves from floor to ceiling. But there's a large presence of him also, a great Buddha of shiny metal flanked by the Earth God on the one hand and the Goddess of Mercy on the other. Offerings are laid out on the altar, mostly oranges, and on a table, eight pots of different-coloured fortune sticks, so eight people can work out their fortune at the same time.

I talk with the caretaker, a little bob-haired no-nonsense woman in a frock, with navy blue woollen stockings pulled up to the knees. From the way she talks about the people who come here — 'they bring cooked chicken sometimes, offer it to the god, then go home and eat it' — I gather she's not a believer herself. No, she is not: 'I work here.' She works here for the nephew of the monk who founded the temple and left it on his death to him; he comes at weekends. She says if I want to see the old monk, I can, he's in another temple further up the hill.

So he is — in a glass case, and all gilded over. Dying, he sat in a big wicker chair (there are photos on display) and, dead, he still sat in that big wicker chair, just sat there decomposing. But not too much, indeed hardly at all. In fact, in a word, it's a miracle. Old Yuet Kai wrote 96 books on Buddhism, preached numberless times, founded the temple of 10,000 Buddhas — and is now a gold Buddha himself. What a career! I salute Old Yuet with a wink, and I'm not sure if he doesn't wink back.

This second level of the temple grounds has three buildings, one of which houses the monk, the second being his former dwelling house (the caretaker there, an old woman, is watching opera on TV), the third, a dormitory with four bunks.

A path leads on from right behind the dormitory. I take it, still curious. It brings me to a kiosk beside a waterfall, and I think, ah, here we are beginning to get somewhere. The first level was pop-Buddha, the second level was daddy-monk, now there's no temple any more, just contemplation, and Buddha is a waterfall.

Whatever may have been the piety of Old Yuet Kai, he had no sense of aesthetics, his kiosk is on a par with the rest of his constructions. But he must have had a feeling for this waterfall, otherwise he wouldn't have built the kiosk at all, and this is the place where, at least in his own mind, he de-constructed: 'I know you builder of the building. From now on, you'll build no more.'

The water falls from about fifty feet, hits a rock and splits into two streams that come to fill a sandy pool. I find myself at first thinking of other waterfalls: the one on the moor above Fairlie which was one of my favourite haunts as a child; the one at Gourgounel, in the Ardèche . . . But time and place gradually get lost. This isn't even China any more. It's just water falling into water.

QUIET DAYS IN MACAO

A nice quiet paradise
Ezra Pound

1. Typhoon

Macao, the oldest European colony in Asia, is situated just across the estuary of the Pearl River from Hong Kong: a short boat trip away. Macao — the sound of the name was enough, when I was fifteen or so, to set my mind racing: a den of corruption, an Oriental hell, a perverted Paradise. Macao the myth . . . When you get there, the myth fades, it goes out like a light, and what you have in its place is a sleepy, Mediterranean-type township, all blue, pink and yellow pastel, a quiet, stagnant backwater that looks absolutely inoffensive.

At one time I had the impression that there was something that didn't want me to go to Macao at all.

Obtaining my boat ticket had been easy enough. I'd just gone down one rainy morning — that warm lush rain you can get in Hong Kong, with the Peak veiled in mist — to the Macao Travel Service in Star House, Tsimshatsui, and booked with the *Agencia da Compania de Navegacâo*: twenty dollars each way and eight dollars Embarcation Fee levied by the Hong Kong government. I was organised, all set. The cosmos wasn't. In fact it was damned *up*set.

I'd heard vaguely in the hotel that they'd hoisted the No. 1 tropical cyclone signal, and even that later in the evening they'd put it up to 3, but that had only crossed my mind, it hadn't sunk in. So that, on the following morning, according to plan (*my* little plan), with dawn breaking rainily through the grey-blue cloud, I was walking, rucksack on back, along Connaught Road Central, past the Jordan Ferry and the Yaumati Ferry, to the Macao Wharf, just beside the open-air market that is called the Poor Man's Night Club. Newspapers were being laid out, men were moving around in shorts and singlets with umbrellas, and some, in the pier hall, were doing *T'ai chi* exercises — but none of the offices were open yet, so I sat on a bench to wait alongside a couple of old streetsweeper Buddhas. I waited, I waited. Coming on eight o'clock, I began to wonder. Wondering, I wandered over to a ticket office window, tapped on it and showed my ticket. Without a word, the woman opened the window, then opened a brown envelope of cash and began counting out forty-eight dollars. It looked as if the trip was off, but in case it still depended on me (I might have knocked at the refund window), I say I don't want a refund, I want to make the trip. She tells me the boat's not running, there's a Force 3 cyclone, going by the name of Sara, playing around Hong Kong, and at Macao it's Force 8. Force 8, that is a lot of wind. Once I did get to Macao, I saw just what it meant, but I wasn't in Macao yet, and God knows when I'd get there — because of dear Sara. Sara in fact turned into a tropical depression the following day and dissipated herself, the drunken bitch, over mainland China. But by the time I'd turned my mind Macao-wards again, Anna had turned up. After dancing up the South China Sea, she was just strong enough in Hong Kong to stop the boats running, but she created all hell in the Ryukyu archipelago and Japan.

That's when I began to think that something didn't want me to go to Macao. But I finally made it. Between typhoons.

2. *Troubled Waters*

Macao had a dazed look about it that morning — a dazed look with little patches of bedazzlement. The typhoon had heaved up the depths of the sea, and the waters were brown. Though they were now sunlit — the sun was shining fitfully through scattered cloud — they still looked troubled, and the gurly waves had a sluggishness to them, a sultry opacity.

In the town itself, there were many signs of the typhoon times: trees mutilated, roofs and shutters torn away, and tarmac ripped up off the streets. Ruin and havoc was evident, but everything was fantastically clean, and the whitewashed, bluewashed, pinkwashed walls had a shine to them despite their stained decrepitude.

Macao. Morning in Macao.

The streets are called *'avenida'*, *'estrada'*, *'rua'*, *'calçada'*, *'largo'*, *'travesso'*. I'd come along the avenues that skirt the harbour, then I'd cut up the Estrada do Repouso to the heart of town. After that I just followed my nose from street to street, from patio to patio, in an atmosphere of Saints (Santa Rosa, Santa Maria) — Macao is called, on its escutcheon, the *'cidade do nome de Deus'*, the City of the Name of God — among Sino-Portuguese shops like *'Chiu's Sapatos'*, *'Mercenaria da Hui Teng'*, *'Casa de pasto Cheong Heng'*, *'Loja de vinhos Chineses Üt Long'*. What a mixture! And everywhere colours as various as sweets in a poke. I stopped at a *casa de pasto* for some tea and buns (very yellow buns, one flaky and stuffed with meat, the other doughy and sweet), then continued my peregrinations past dozing bodies, street letter-writers, and schoolgirls saying 'bye-bye' to one another with a Chinese accent. In the name of God, is it real?

Having come up against a hotel — the Hotel Esmeralda — I get myself a room and settle in. Half an hour later I'm lying on my bed with a new-bought notebook, and I write on the first page:

Macao's an old banyan tree
and a man sleeping
a pink wall stained with damp and fungus
a warm silence
a memory of rolling seas

— I'll have to be taking it further than that I suppose, but '*festina lente*' (I'm remembering my Latin here, if I nasalise it a bit, it might pass for Portuguese), let us hasten slowly.

3. Camoens

Blue seas, with monsters of the deep staring and spouting — and a tiny caravel sailing gaily under the sun . . . The captain was maybe one-eyed, the sailors were rotten with scurvy and gangrene, but history seemed to be opening a new page in its book, a page of ocean and gold (and spices and dusky maidens!). Conquest was the word, *conquistador* . . . It's hard for us to think back into those times, and if we do, the religious ideology and the political blunderbussing turn us off, but there's a freshness at least about the maps, and there must have been, in some minds, abstracted from the all too human mixture of bombast and boredom, that sense of opening space, the blue and the gold, the flash of an eye, and the curve of a breast or a turning wave.

All I've read of the *Lusiads* is a prose version in English, and it was tedious (I'm willing to concede that in verse, and in Portuguese, it may be otherwise), but I have an *idea* of Camoens and the least I could do was take it up to the Grotto named after him. Camoens was in

Macao in 1556–57. He had a job there as Trustee for the Dead and Absent, which maybe doesn't sound very exciting, but it was a job (Camoens couldn't afford to spit on jobs), and it may even have been lucrative. It certainly got him into trouble, for in no time at all he was being sent back to Goa, his old place of exile from Portugal, in chains (as the story goes). And whatever wealth he had scraped together went down with the ship he was on at the mouth of the Mekong — he was lucky to escape with his life and the manuscript of the poem he was working on, his epic to the glory of Portugal and the Renaissance. My idea of Camoens is not that of a man who sings the praises of a nation, and has his head full of Renaissance mythology, but a man who had weathered the Cape of Bad Luck and kept his eyes skinned (or rather his eye, the left one — he lost the right one in a fight) over waves and rocks. This Camoens doesn't get much into the poem, what gets into the poem is a loud colonial-imperialist mouth, but he was real. He was real in Lisbon, Goa, Macao, Mozambique and a few other places. If only he had kept a journal! Maybe he did. But it was probably burnt in a fire. That was what Luis Vaz de Camoens' life was like.

So, in Macao, not far from the seafront, between the Rua da Patane and the Rua dos Colonos, lies the *Jardim de Camôes* (The Camoens Garden), and in the *jardim* there is a *gruta* (a grotto), called the *Gruta de Camôes*.

The grotto is . . . grotesque. If certain well-intentioned people had been content to leave it with a bust of Camoens and the first few lines of his poem engraved in the rock:

As armas e os barôes assinalados
que da occidental praya lusitana
por mares nunca de antes navigados
passaram

it would not have been too bad. But the *'principe dos poetas portugueses'* has inspired other 'poems' in and around the silent rocks, and they really have to be seen to be believed. Here's one in English by Sir John Somebody:

Gem of the orient earth and open sea
Macao — that in thy lap and on thy breast
Hast gathered beauties all the loveliest
Which the sun shines on in his majesty

The very clouds that top each mountain crest
Seem to repose there, lingering lovingly.
How full of grace the green cathayan tree
Bends to the breeze . . .

You've had enough of that? I'm not surprised. But don't go away yet, I have another offering, a change of language. A certain Louis de Rienzi (*'Français d'origine romaine voyageur religieux soldat et poète exile'* — 'A Frenchman of Roman origin, soldier, traveller, man of religion, poet in exile') dates the following 30 March 1837:

Patane lieu charmant et si cher au poète
Je n'oublierai jamais ton illustre retraite.
Ici Camoens au bruit du flot retentissant
Mêla l'accord plaintif de son luth gémissant
Au flambeau d'Apollon allumant son génie
Il chanta les héros de la Lusitanie . . .

(Patane, charming place, so dear to the poet's heart
I shall never forget your illustrious retreat.
Here Camoens mingled his lute's plaintive words
With the wild roar of the ocean's billows
Lighting the lamp of his genius at Apollo's torch
He sang the heroes of Lusitania . . .)

The Grotto of Camoens, believe me, can be written off as a bad job.

As for the Gardens themselves, they are pleasant, not trim, neat and pretty, but dark and chthonian, more wood than garden, full of big elephant-hide banyan trees with hulking, uncouth gnarled roots. The citizens of Macao — the 'unimportant' citizens — know how to make use of them. From where I'm standing here, under a 'green cathayan tree', I can count fifteen men, fifteen stalwart men of Macao, all fast asleep.

I think I'll follow suit.

The memory of rolling seas . . .

4. The Shrine of the Sea Goddess

If the cognomen of Macao is 'City of the Name of God', its name actually derives from the name of the sea-goddess: A Ma. When Europeans first arrived on the scene, the Macao Peninsula was known to the Chinese as 'Water Lily Peninsula', but the first edifice encountered by the Portuguese on entering the inner harbour was the shrine of A Ma — hence they named the place that was to become their settlement: *A-Ma-gao* (Bay of A Ma). The fact of their seafaring obviously meant more to these first settlers than any ideology they carried with them — otherwise they might have christened the place 'St Joseph's Mount' or patriotised it into 'King's Town' or something of the like. One can only be grateful to them. 'Water Lily' is probably even better for the rosy quiet of Macao, but 'Bay of A Ma' is a good next best.

According to Chinese legend, A Ma was born into a poor family in Fukien province. Her father, Lin-Wei-chiu, had had a son and five daughters from his wife, but since the son was weak in constitution, they prayed to the goddess Kwan Yin for a stronger successor. On 23 March, in the first year of Chien Lung (Sung dynasty), another girl was born. Initial disappointment of the family, but from an early age this girl showed outstanding ability. By the time she was eight, she was studying Buddhism, and then, when she was thirteen, an old Taoist priest initiated her into the mysteries. At the age of twenty-eight, she burnt incense sticks, chanted a sutra, and left on a long sea-voyage. All along the South China coast are spots were she is supposed to have landed. The story as told in Macao is that she was seeking passage to Canton but, being poor, was refused by all but the very humblest of fishermen. While at sea, a great storm blew up, and all the rich men's ships were wrecked — only one boat reached safety in the harbour of Macao, the one on which A Ma was sailing. Whatever be the spot at which she is supposed to have landed, what she did on her arrival was to climb the nearest hill from which she disappeared into the sky accompanied by strange music.

But she continued to make appearances here and there, to save good people from the dangers of the sea. So one shrine after another was consecrated to her. Emperor Kao Tsung conferred on her the title of 'Madam'; Emperor Kuang Tsung gratified her with the title 'Concubine'; while Emperor Sheng Tsu designated her 'Queen': Sky Queen, Queen of the Sea, Controller of the Elements. She has two attendants: Chian Li Yan (Thousand Mile Eyes) and Shun Feng Er (Fair Wind Ears). These two, again according to the legend, were brothers, and generals of King Chou of the Yin dynasty — one noted for his keen sight, the other for his extraordinary hearing. Both of them were killed fighting against Wu of Chou, but their souls, even when they'd reached Mount Peach Flower, were restless, so that they still made distressing apparitions on earth. One day when A Ma was passing by Mount Peach Flower, the two brothers jumped out on her, claiming her as their bride. A Ma persuaded them that it would be better to decide the issue by fighting. If they won, she would be their wife; if she won, they would be her servants. She won. And the brothers became not only servants, but (at least in the illustrations I've seen) female servants. Translated into less colourful terms, it might signify that if you want to have a chance of survival at sea, you had better have with you a telescope — and a wireless?

There are A Ma temples all along the coast. Every junk is furnished with her image, and a lamp burns perpetually before it. Every fisherman consecrates his nets to her, and worships her daily. But her big festival is on the 23rd day of the 3rd moon, her birthday, when candles are lit and incense and golden papers burnt in her temples, and offerings made of chicken and roast pork.

The first thing that strikes you as you enter the precincts of the A Ma temple at Macao is a bas-relief carving on a rock of the junk on which A Ma arrived from Fukien — it is painted in several colours, and the painting is refreshed once a year. To my feeling, this rock with the painted junk is all that is necessary by way of a shrine — but there's more, a lot more. Beyond the rock is a wall, painted red, with a moon-gate leading into a hall that contains the wooden model of a junk with the goddess on deck. Above this first level, winding paths run up the hillside among boulders and banyan trees. The rocks are spattered red with verses to the goddess, surrounded by little dark red forests of spent joss-sticks. And every few steps one comes across a little pavilion — its guardian in pants and singlet dozing in the hot afternoon — dedicated to A Ma or to Kun Iam (whom I referred to before in this text, in more mandarin form, as Kwan Yin), or yet another god or goddess.

From up on the hillside, in the shade of a banyan tree (not extraordinary enough to become a god, this one, but affording pleasant shade nonetheless) you have a good view across the inner harbour and the junky waters: shores and hills in a blue haze; multicoloured sails (many of them patched and repatched — I get the impression that the boat folk here are poorer than those in Hong Kong) and, closer at hand, as the eye runs from one *ponte* (pier) to another, the broad decks festooned with washing out to dry. If you listen close, you can maybe even hear the low *lap-flap-aslap* of the slow Macao tide.

5. The Dead and the Absent

A white marble plaque above the entrance, wasting no words, provides the following brief information:

East India Company OLD PROTESTANT CEMETERY 1814

Before that date (or rather until the cemetery really got under way a few years later), Protestants who happened to meet their death in Macao were buried, along with other non-Catholics, on the hills outside of town, Catholic Macao having no place for heretical corpses within its holy walls. Once this plot had been purchased, however, and the cemetery was in working order, many of the older graves outside the city walls were removed to this new haven, so that there are tombstones bearing dates that go back further than 1814.

You have to ring a bell at the door to gain admission. A Chinese woman came to the gate and let me in, then went about her business among the flowers while I went over to take a look at the chapel, more out of a sense of 'seeing it all while I was at it' than from any feeling of reverence. For if I have an unholy attraction for graveyards, I have no inclination whatever towards churches and chapels. There can be an existential starkness in a cemetery, allied to all kinds of grotesquery, whereas in church and chapel one is rarely aware of anything more than a stale odour of sanctimoniousness. The stale odour was there as usual, but the smallness of this chapel spoke after all in its favour, and my eye was caught by two plaques, one to a certain

Henry Davies Margesson who was drowned when the steamer *Hayomaro* sank off Yokohama, the other commemorating a Mr James B. Endicott: *'American buried in Hong Kong'*.

From the chapel a sloping path leads you down into the cemetery, and it really is a beautiful place. It's a sunken garden, well protected, but at the same time it's high up here on the hill overlooking the sea. Then there are flowering trees galore — frangipani, bohin-flower, and others of which I do not know the names. I sat down for a while under a tree, just enjoying the silence, then strolled around reading the tombstones.

There are famous tombs in this graveyard, tombs of famous men such as Robert Morrison, the first Protestant missionary to China, who compiled the first English and Chinese dictionary and translated the Bible into Chinese; George Chinnery, the artist who painted so many scenes along the China coast; and the ancestor of Sir Winston Churchill *'The Right Honourable Lord Henry John Spencer Churchill, 5th Duke of Marlborough, Captain of Her Britannic Majesty's ship* Druid, *and senior officer in the Canton Seas, Departed this life in the Macao Roads, 2nd June 1840.'* But my attention is held much less by these stones than by those of totally unknown figures such as Samuel Proctor (d. Macao 1792) whose stone states simply and starkly:

Under this
lieth the body
of
Dr Samuel Proctor
of Boston

or that of the Dutchman Pieter Kintsius:

Ter gedagtenisse
van der
Weleden Heer
Pieter Kintsius
Eerste super cargo opperhoofd
der Neederlandsche Oost Indische
Compagnie int Ryk van China

gebooren te Amsterdam
en
overleeden te Macao
den 25 Iuny 1786
in den Ouderdom van 53 Iaaren

— one sees a dry Yankee with a sniffing nose and a burly gin-soaked Amsterdamer with a belly laugh.

After the Protestant cemetery, I was still hungry for stones, so I continued on to the Parsee cemetery, in the Estrada dos Parses, on Guia Hill. Here, the dates are given both in Western terms and according to the ancient Persian calendar, so that we find: *'Here lies the remains of Dhunjee Bhoy Framjee Cassna, a Parsee and Merchant and Inhabitant of Bombay, who quitted this world on the 2nd Day of September 1848. Corresponding to the 11th Day of the 12th Month in the Year of Yazedezierd 1217. Aged 40 years.'*

So many of these people died young. The tropics in those days must have taken a terrible toll, foreign colonials and merchants dying off like flies in the *Ryk van China*. And whatever it was their lucrative trade was in: tea, opium, cotton, tobacco, silk, whatever the fortunes they amassed, they must have lived with the thought that death was working in their body. The oldest stone in the Parsee cemetery, *'Sacred to the memory of the late Cunsetjee Framjee (Native of Bombay)'* has this text engraved on it:

The light is sweet, and a pleasant thing it is
For the eyes to behold the Sun; but if a man live
Many years, and rejoice in them all,
Yet let him remember the days of darkness
For they shall be many; all that cometh is vanity.

6. *Wenceslau de Moraes*

If you look at the map of Macao, away up in the northern part of town, you'll see a street, stretching roughly from the Lin Fong temple to the Kun Iam temple, called Avenida de Venceslau de Moraes. Wenceslau de Moraes is far from being the most famous of the renowned inhabitants of Macao — Camoens and Sun Yat Sen (who worked here as a doctor) no doubt take precedence — but he is, for me, the most interesting. This was the man who, in his book of notes *Bon Odori em Tokushima*, written in Japan, and according to the style of the Japanese *nikki* (fragments, scattered notations) wrote: 'so far as social activity is concerned, I am this — Zero!'

It had not always been so. Born in Lisbon, in 1854, into a solid bourgeois family, Moraes became a naval officer and eventually arrived in Macao as Harbour Master. There he married a Chinese woman, Atchan, and had two sons by her, but by the end of the 1880s he was visiting Japan on official trips, and the country fascinated him: 'When I arrived in Japan, I loved it with an overwhelming emotion, I absorbed its beauty as if it were a nectar.' Within the next few years he realised that he wished to live permanently in Japan, and still a man of 'importance', got himself appointed Portuguese Consul to Kobe in 1899. One year later, he married, by Shintoist rites, a twenty-five-year-old geisha, O-Yone Fukumoto, and lived with her till her death in 1912. Thereafter Moraes abandoned his Consular post, resigned from the Navy, and went away to live in retirement in the little town of Tokushima. It was there he wrote his books on Japan, general works on Japanese history and culture (*Relance da Alma Japonesa, Relance da História do Japão, Cartas da Japão*), but also more impressionistic works, sharp with the sensations of a man's individual life, such as the already quoted *Bon Odori em Tokushima* and *O-Yone e Ko-Haru*.

In Tokushima, Moraes lived in a wooden house, definitively alone after 1916 (he had lived for a time with a niece of O-Yone), knowing solitude, poverty and trying to know simplicity. 'I live poorly but I do not need anything.' He had no easy time with his neighbours: Japanese civilisation, he found, also had its aggressive moments. During the First World War, children would throw stones at him, calling him 'Mr Savage with the long beard', and the police felt free to insult him and treat him as a spy. But the Japan he saw in his mind was not ruffled by these manifestations, and, no longer living in his 'little ego', he himself did not suffer from them unduly. Life went on: he continued to break his coal, light his fire, cook his meal of rice and fish, and write his book. To a missionary who brought him some bread and butter, he replied: 'I do not eat bread, I am a Japanese.' And when a friend wanted to make him the gift of a chair, he answered that he would 'live and die on the *tatami*, like a Japanese'.

There's something pathetic about it, something desperately pathetic in the figure of this old European scarecrow trying to be Japanese. But once we get behind the conflict of civilisations and cultures, once we see into the mind of the old scarecrow, there's nothing pathetic about his sense of life and his delight in the presence of the things: stone, water, daybreak, winter mist, June rain, he saw about him. The old scarecrow seems to have achieved a consummation, a realisation of his life, and he is therefore beautiful.

7. The Macao Book of Hours

There are times when it's enough, perfect and all-inclusive, just to be lying flat on your back under the sun. It's like that with me now, here on the Macao waterfront. I've had an excellent meal, in a restaurant called The Fat Buddha, a meal accompanied by a very fine rosy wine, and there's still an after-glow of that wine in my head as I lie here at my ease, among the drying fish. Yes, all along the waterfront there are fish laid out to dry, and I'm stretched out beside them, my sweat mingling delectably in the air with their fishy stench. A junk makes slowly out of harbour with a great sputtering ruckus at its bow. They're letting off squibs and crackers for good luck — *rat-tat-tat*, puffs of smoke and flashes in the warm blue air. Then it's all over, the stillness comes down again, and I can just see, from my reclining position, the junk disappearing down the roads, its stern high and mighty, like a palatial wardrobe.

I go through the Museum, old colonial house, smelling of polish and mothballs, heavy with silence: ox blood pottery, a collection of fans, scrolls piled in a glass case, and a Belgian machine-gun dating from 1872.

Going over to the island of Taipa in the blue evening haze, there were only two of us passengers, myself and a Chinese girl — which is why we'd been transferred from the regular boat, where we'd been waiting, to a much smaller one. She was dressed, that girl, in black high-collared jacket and baggy black pants, and was carrying with her a basket of vegetables. Not pretty, but good-looking and solid. The boat chug-chugged over the water, I exchanged a smile with the girl, and there was a kind of quiet communication between us. Over on the other side, where the girl was met by her mother, I walked around the island for a bit, then came back to Macao over the bridge.

Sitting on a red bench looking at a lotus pond; sunlight filtering through green bamboo; rocks being as grotesque as can be: afternoon in a Chinese garden.

Away up in the bamboo grove at the back of Kwan Yin temple, four men are playing cards and an old man is gathering the firewood with which the ground is littered after the passage of the typhoon.

All the hills around Macao are Red. Macao fishermen may pray to A Ma, but they get their meteorological information from the Red China weather station. In Macao town you can't miss the Red China Bank and the Red China Hospital, and there are Red China slogans on the walls. If you take the road that leads up to the northern end of the Istmo Ferreira do Amaral, up to the place called Porta do Cerco (the Border Gate), Red China itself is not far away. There's a market up there, or rather there used to be a market, where China goods were laid out for sale to local Macao merchants — nowadays it's little more than a souvenir bazaar. I wandered along the stalls nevertheless and was offered 'the Mao book' by a young vendor (told him I preferred the Tao). Beyond the bazaar, a hundred yards of no-man's-land where trucks pass (with two licence plates: black and white for Macao, yellow and black for China), but no one walks. If you squint along these hundred yards, you may just see the tiny figure of a guard of the Chinese People's Liberation Army. And it's just possible he may be squinting along at you.

A ferocious blue dragon leaps in the clouds at the Lotus temple, Avenida do Almirante Lacerda. What a dragon 'is' depends on your system of representation. For me, I suppose it means cosmic power, going back to the tides of fire at the beginning of the universe. Appreciating Lao Tse's 'power', Confucius is said to have called him a dragon. In other minds, though, it represents nothing but religion and imperialism (ever since the reign of Kao Tsu in the Han dynasty, the dragon has been the emblem of imperial power), and if a dragon means that to somebody, you can understand why that somebody would rather get rid of it . . . This could lead us into a long debate, but it's too hot for dialectics. The old dragon doesn't give a damn anyway.

Yellow baroque mass of the Hotel Lisboa. I go down to the gambling hall, drink a coffee at the bar:

'Gamble for pleasure. Don't bet more than you an afford to lose. No one can win all the time.'

I change a pataca into two 50 cent pieces, play them in the slot machines, and lose.

Saved!

MEDITATIONS ON A CHINESE ISLAND

Old Yellow Man burst out laughing and said: Subtle! Deep! Use meditation! That's the way to go up into the sky in broad daylight!

Chen jen nei Chuan,
Biography of the Realised Man

1. Hegel and Chang San-feng

Hegel, if I remember rightly, recommended that one's first 'important' task on waking (he presumably allowed for an insignificant little shit before) should be the reading of the morning newspaper — to make sure that one was in tune with world events, and in a real political frame of mind. This seems to me the worst of alienations. To the historical waking of Herr Hegel I much prefer the attitude of Chang San-feng's Sleeping Immortal:

> *Sleeping on a pillow of stone*
> *Forgetting the calendar, the seasons*
> *When the* ch'i *sinks to the abdomen*
> *The spiritual nature will be complete.*
> *The* ch'i *rises to the mysterious cavity*
> *Every breath, inhaling, exhaling, natural and easy,*
> *Not confused, not separate.*
> *A quiet man, I seem crazy, I sleep all day*
> *But I sleep without sleeping*
> *I learn the real Ch'an . . .*

In other words, I prefer *t'ai chi* (great absolute) to the daily paper.

It was Chang San-feng who invented the system of exercises (known as *t'ai chi ch'uan*), performance of which brings one's body-mind in touch with *t'ai chi*. A magistrate in the district of Chung-san (a post which he later gave up in order to become a mountain hermit), Chang San-feng was sitting quietly in his house one day when he heard a ruckus going on beneath his window. Looking out, he saw a snake fighting with a crane. Their movements fascinated him. He noted them as best he could, and they lead him to take notice of other similar movements: clouds in the sky, flowing water, trees in the wind. These movements he codified into a system of exercises. Which is why, on my way down to the piers this morning, I passed a man in a parking lot performing *White Crane Spreading Wings*, and another, just a couple of steps away, doing *Snake Creeps Down* — while on a pier, outlined against the morning sky, a little group of workmen were engaged in *Waving Hands like Cloud, Golden Cock on one Leg, Riding*

Tiger to the Mountain. Apart from anything else ('these exercises will lead practitioners to health, happiness and longevity'), it's a lot pleasanter to look at than a square head puffing at a cigar behind the Daily Shriek, even if that head, which is not always the case, is the godly head of Hegel . . .

2. Lantao

The island of Lantao is known as the 'lung' of Hong Kong: this is where the population of the congested colony comes to breathe. But this exodus is restricted more or less to weekends and holidays; on weekdays the island is practically empty. After some time in Hong Kong, I felt the need to 'breathe' a little myself.

'Lush and green, the serene, unspoiled island of Lantao basks in the warm blue waters of the South China Sea west of Hong Kong . . .' I'm reading this in a guide-book as the boat moves out of Hong Kong Bay, the blue sea dotted with islands opening out before it.

Island, I-land — narcissism? Yes, but not to admire the self, to work with it, to let it radiate (not just become entangled with other selves), to let it become aware of fundamental connections, to let it disappear in the pulsing cosmic field, that field of correspondence which renders superfluous all search for an 'answer' to questions concerning the meaning of life . . .

We're approaching Silvermine.

3. Silvermine

Mui Wo (Silvermine Bay) is a bridge, a muddy river bed with junks and sampans, shacks on stilts, and a huddle of little shops. Fish on all sides, on trays, in baskets, drying in the sun: bream, plaice, mullet, eel . . . Alongside the black little fishy village that straggles off into a patchwork of vegetable plots lies a beach lined with tamarisk trees.

It was a fine Autumn morning when I arrived, but the enormous number of blue and green dragonflies flitting here and there might indicate that there was a storm in the offing . . . No signs of it yet other than the flies, but just as I left the village, a wind sprang up, tousling the tamarisks, sending leaves flying, raising a wisp of sand, and it was accompanied by this wind that I struck out on the South Lantao Road, passing on my way the powerhouse of the China Light & Power Company.

Power and light . . .

Somewhere in the hills a cock crew.

'Following the example of the ancient priest who is said to have travelled thousands of miles caring naught for his provisions and attaining the state of sheer ecstasy, I left my broken house on the river Sumida in the August of the first year of Jyokyo (1684), amid the wails of the Autumn wind . . .'

That was Basho, in his *Records of a Weather-Exposed Skeleton*.

Basho's rules for 'poetic wandering':

— Always go on foot.
— Eat simple food.
— Don't sleep twice at the same inn.
— Don't engage in senseless chatter.
— Look deep into yourself.

Walking rhythmically, face to the wind, I feel more and more 'crazy' as I walk that South road (now skirting the shore, now in the hills, with only brief glimpses of the sea), and shivers of ecstasy are running from the soles of my feet to the top of my skull. Somebody reading this may think I'm exaggerating, all I'm doing is walking along a shore road, and that's no cause for ecstasy. Well, all I can say is that you don't get to ecstasy by piling up causes, it comes from reduction rather than reason, and I was 'empty' and walking, with the wind around me, and those blue glimpses of the sea.

Along the coast road
goes no one
this October morning

— that was the first of the 'haiku' that were to grow like weeds all along the way.

4. The End of the World

To go to the end of the world, on the 'path going nowhere', as the Sanskrit puts it (*lokanirodhagaminipatipada*) . . .

My first 'end of the world' on that Lantao trip was a beach which was, to me, nameless. I left it that way.

I'd been walking for about two hours when the road, that had been winding for a while among the hills, broke seawards again, and the landscape opened out onto the blue of water, with a cluster of blue islands.

I took off my clothes and, making myself comfortable on the sand, gazed out at the sea and the islands, into the blue. But pretty soon I was aware of living presences around me. Big crabs, with fierce claws and antennae, were scuttling over the sand at incredible speed, appearing from and disappearing into holes — suddenly one turned up not far, looking like a nightmare with a shell on. I found it harder to concentrate on the blue, with all that scuttling going on around me . . . So I turned my attention to the crabs. The big fellows weren't alone, I noticed. As I looked closer, I saw there were little grey invisibilities also scurrying over that greywhite sand.

For some reason or other, maybe it had become too hot for them, at one point the crabs settled down, retreated into their holes, and I got back to the blue.

In no time I was breathing slower than the tide . . .

After a few more miles more walking, I was back on another beach. This one had a name: *Cheung Sha*.

At the entrance to the beach there was a wooden store. Since I was hungry, I went in there first to get some food. I was eyeing some eggs when the storekeeper, by signs, offered to boil them for me. So it was that when I came back out of the shop a few minutes later, it was with three boiled eggs and two cans of Japanese beer.

I made my meal with my back against a rock and the sea tumbling dreamily at my right.

There were a lot of dragonflies and butterflies.

Having satisfied my hunger, I lay in the shade of the rock, and watched the sea — a blaze of light out there, the blue-green undulations, and the crash of spray:

Who has not observed it
the primal movement
the play of wind on water
the undulation
the glassy membrane
lifted
excited
and energised
by insisting air
the curving
the deliberate inflection
the flurry of whiteness
the bright cast of spray
the long falling rush
and the hundredfold ripple

The sea and I never get tired of each other.

5. A Temple in the Hills

About six o'clock, I was moving towards the centre of the island. A misty cloudiness had come down over the hills — every now and then a plane loomed through them, to remind me that the world wasn't all pedestrian — and I felt like a little figure in some landscape painting, say Fan K'uan's 'Travellers among Mountains and Streams'.

At a crossroads (one road going down to Tai-O, the other up to Sham Wat), I caught a glimpse of the monastery. I say 'the' monastery, because when I started out for Lantao, I'd only heard of one, and I knew roughly where it was situated. This site corresponded in every way. So when I saw the yellow roof and the red gates up there in the hills, I was sure this was Po Lin, where I intended to spend the night.

I climbed further up into the hills. When I'd got to the level of the temple, and had left the road for the track leading to it, I put down my rucksack and sat there on the hillside for a while — the wind cool, the long grass swaying — before covering the last two or three hundred yards.

Passing through the red gates, I was surprised to find the place deserted: only a monk sweeping leaves, and a cat with little bells round its neck that tinkled as it moved.

By signs, I gave the monk to understand that I would like board and lodging for the night. He nodded, went to fetch a fellow monk who maybe had more to do with this kind of thing, and it was all arranged.

A quarter of an hour or so later, after the sweeping monk had shown me my quarters and I'd deposited my things on the bunk and lowered the mosquito net, I was seated at a table in the refectory, in front of me a big bowl of noodles with mushrooms, celery and bamboo shoots, and a pot of tea.

There were two paintings on the wall, one of Buddha in meditation, the other of a mountain hut with a pine tree, and several calligraphy scrolls.

Outside the wind was rising, setting the temple roof-bells ringing.

I'd made a big hole in the noodles, and was sitting back drinking tea when the refectory monk, with the idea of completing my pleasure, brought in a transistor radio. To please him, and not to show myself ungrateful, I turned it on, learning that a tropical depression (hence the dragonflies, hence the wind) 880 miles East of Manila had been moving NNW at a speed of 10 knots, but when this information was followed by a 'happiness programme' — 'this is your Happiness Programme!' (horrible variety voice) — from Hong Kong, I turned it off, and, leaving the refectory, went out into the courtyard.

It was green darkness out there, the wind whooming through the pine trees, and a moon shining fitfully through the cloud. The little cat came tinkling up, its yellow eyes gleaming.

I went up on to the roof above the sleeping quarters, sitting in the green darkness, listening to the wind in the pines.

When I came back down into the courtyard, the sweeping monk was all for showing me the temple proper, where Buddha was enshrined. I accepted, the way I accepted the transistor. He put on the lights, lit an incense stick, and told me (pointing to his ring-finger) that the Buddha was of gold. I made as if I admired it. As we came away, the monk asked me if I was '*Amelika*'?, I shook my head and said '*Sugulan*'. But I knew I wasn't that either.

I was waves breaking on a beach, wind in pine trees . . .

6. *The White Rain at Tai-O*

That morning began with my leaving the temple-in-the-hills, accompanied by wind and a hawk, after a meal of rice gruel, noodles and beans. I'd begun to suspect, since I'd been told that the Po Lin temple was much frequented, with a monastery of many monks, that I wasn't in Po Lin at all. Not that it mattered. But I'm curious about names after all, so, making a circular movement of my arm to take in the premises, I said to the refectory-monk: 'Po Lin?'. He made negative gestures with hand and head. 'Luk Wo,' he said, and pointing over the hills, added, 'Po Lin.' Well, maybe I'd go to Po Lin that night, for the moment I intended to make for the village of Tai-O.

The wind blew and a hawk hovered and it was morning on the Tai-O Road.

Tai-O is a little fishing village, reputed to be the one that has best retained the traditions of the South China boat people. When I got there that morning, it was to find fish laid out on trays to dry, a girl playing peever (using a bead bracelet), people making and repairing nets, and women washing blue and black clothes.

I was walking through the village when suddenly rain began to fall, what in Japanese is called a 'white shower'. The fish trays were hurried indoors in a twinkling, and I myself took refuge in a little cakeshop, watching the rain pit the estuary and pass over the village like a silver cloud. It left as suddenly as it came, leaving in its place a steaming rainbow. Ah, that rainbow, that body of light!

7. *Po Lin*

Walking, walking — enjoying the walking, I was in no hurry. But I found myself at Po Lin around midday rather than evening.

Po Lin turned out to be a very busy place indeed. As I covered the last lap of the hill-road, through a drifting mist, I was passed by a bus.

And when I finally stood in the monastery grounds I saw there were *two* buses, and people all over the place, Chinese, Japanese, Westerners, taking photos, listening to transistors, waiting for the monastery meal.

The monks themselves were already at table, black robed, chanting.

I took it all in, followed the wall-painted life of Shakyamuni Buddha in a small temple behind the refectory, then sought out a quiet place to eat the bananas I'd bought for my midday meal in Tai-O. A dog came to lie down beside me, and went to sleep. A group of girls passed, amused at my banana-eating; I was to make their acquaintance later.

My meal over, I climbed up a hill beyond the monastery. A good way up the hill stood a brightly-coloured *stupa* and a young man was refreshing the paint. Further up there was only rock, and the drifting mist, with glimpses of a sunlit sea and islands.

Up there, I'd like to be able to say I engaged in a thorough meditation concerning the non-permanence of things and the not-self of being, but I fell asleep, like the dog.

As soon as I was awake, I started downhill again, and had arrived at the monastery gates when a bus passed. I hopped on it. It was probably quite late on in the afternoon now, but if I could gain some time with this bus, I might still be able to reach the beach at Tung Chung before darkness. I'd thought while eating my bananas of staying the night at the monastery, but had decided I'd rather be on the beach.

The group of girls I'd seen before, five of them, were on that bus, and before long we were in conversation ('What is your country?'), one of them in particular being eager to give me lessons in Cantonese (*sin-san*, man; *so-tze*, girl), and telling me I should have offered her a banana back there in the monastery. She was good-looking, that little Cantonese girl, and fun to listen to. Among other things, she told me she'd been to Canton the year before; what had struck her was that everybody wore navy-blue, and wore their hair short, girls just like boys, and that the girls were very strong, they ate three bowls of rice to every meal . . .

I got off the bus about Cheung Sha, to walk the cross-island road to Tung Chung. Two hours later I was on the beach.

8. On the Beach

I like to be where extremes meet, or maybe rather where complementaries come into play: land and water, male and female, East and West . . . where the lines break, sinuosities develop and intertwine, where physical experience attains to such a degree of density and intensity that we can almost call it 'metaphysical'.

The moon was up there in cloud, with a blue and bronze halo. There was a wind blowing, but it was warm. I spent three hours or so in love with that island: with the sand, the waves, the wind, the cloud, the moon, in one long, secret sequence.

When finally I fell asleep, with a great pond of silence in the pit of my belly, I did not dream.

And in the morning I woke to the white roar of waves. When I opened my eyes, I had the impression of being in Scotland. It was like a clear blue windy day on the Firth of Clyde. Then I saw a junk.

It was still very early morning, and there wasn't a soul in sight. Except that junk out there on the horizon. I thought of going for a swim, but put it off till later, and just sat still:

Another day
and the white sun shining
East and West.

THE TAIWAN ITINERARY

I shall lead you through the dark and mysterious gate to the source of the perfect Yin,
I shall guide you beyond the great light to the source of the perfect Yang.

Chuang Tzu

1. Formosa

'For the poet,' says Ralph Waldo Emerson somewhere, 'the world is always virgin territory.'

Virgin, Formosa?

Loud laughter, sneers and sniggers on all sides. Strains of the Generalissimo's last speech coming over the Nationalist megaphones. Thud of cannon at Quemoy . . .

Virgin, Formosa?

Like a snowball in hell. Lost once and for all in the nightmare of history. Plunged good and proper in the political pot-pourri.

And yet.

Even if it's only to refresh our vision, without necessarily 'changing the world', let's first of all try to see Formosa simply, nakedly, as it exists in pure cosmic space, out there in the Great Ocean, part of that chain of volcanic islands that extends from Kamchatka in the North to the Sunda Isles in the South.

In the long ago time, says the myth, there was a rain of fire, and all animals vanished from the face of the earth. Only a brother and a sister escaped the fiery flood, by hiding in a rock. When they emerged, they thought of making love, but found they didn't know how, till a fly landed on the girl's sex and that gave them an idea. So they made love, the girl became pregnant and gave birth to a serpent, which they cast into a bush. They made love again — this time they gave birth to a frog. They were beginning to feel desperate, when the sun goddess, smelling some strange smell on earth, sent down her son to find out the reason. He listened to the story of the couple and reported it to his mother, who thereupon despatched two guardian-gods with a section of bamboo. Once on earth, they split the bamboo and thereby released a very pink pig. This pig they cut into three pieces, offering them as sacrifice to the sky, the gods and the couple. Then the gods, the girl and the boy, all danced and sang together, and the couple made love again. This time the girl gave birth to a girl, then to a boy, then a girl. And it was the beginning of a new people: the aboriginal tribes of Formosa (Ami, Yami, Atayal, Kanabu, Paiwan, Puyuma . . .).

Theirs was the ancient Indonesian-Polynesian culture. They lived on rice, fish (with crabs, shrimps and oysters), wild pig and deer, with fruit that grew in abundance. They had no word for 'master' or 'servant' in their language. They practised a ritual nudity, because they knew the gods loved nudity: the sun is naked, and so is the moon, and the cloudless sky. Before undertaking anything of importance, they listened to the singing of birds. Their mode of greeting was to approach the stranger with the right palm extended — this right palm they would then place against the stranger's stomach, while patting him on the back with the left . . . But they had 'wilder' habits too — headhunting was a favourite game with them, and they collected skulls with great assiduity, preserving them with devotion. Another habit that may seem barbarous was the interdiction for women to bear children before the age of thirty-five; before that age, they had recourse to abortion. But wasn't there good sense in it too? The knowledge that if the good life is to be lived the population must be kept down?

And with them the island remained beautiful.

Ilha Formosa . . . the beautiful island — that's how it appeared on the sea-charts of the Portugals in the 16th century.

Although it was so close to China — only 90 miles or so from the coast of Fukien — the Chinese weren't interested. An imperial eunuch was driven on to it by a tempest in the 15th century, but he did no more than collect a few plants. In the 16th, it was visited by a more vicious character, the pirate Lin-tao-kien, who made a quick razzia and a massacre, using the blood of his victims to caulk his ships before sailing off again. A few Chinese of course probably trickled and dribbled across at various times, fleeing from troubles, nosing out a market, nothing like a mass immigration. Not yet.

But there was a fever and fermentation in Europe, a fever compounded of religious fervour and commercial zeal. Pretty soon godly and greedy Europeans would be setting foot on Formosan land, ready to plough the spiritual field in the name of the Lord, and exploit the commercial possibilities in the name of Profit.

The first detailed account of the island was drawn up by a Scotsman, William Campbell, in the early 17th century. He makes no bombastic talk about religion or glorious expansion — and we're grateful to him for that — but sticks cannily to the facts and the commercial possibilities. With the idea of opening up a China Trade on a big scale, he presented his Report to the Honourable English East India Company in London, proposing himself as future executor of the plan. He suggested that the ships for the trade be small, but well manned, and with guns placed high above the water line. Money should also be provided for a Chinese junk, that would cost 140 reals, for trading up the rivers — it would carry four guns, be manned by twelve Englishmen and four Chinese (the latter to be paid six shillings a month). A pilot would be needed too, well acquainted with the coast of China and Formosa. In time too a fort could be built. And a very profitable commerce would result from it all. One example: it would be possible to barter cheap calico for deerskins with the 'wild people' of the island — the calico would cost about four pence, and the skins could be sold in Japan for three shillings. John Company read Willie Campbell's report with interest, and paid him five pounds for his pains, but estimated they could not afford to start up a new trading post at that point.

So the English stayed out. But there were others.

The Spaniards were there, quite timidly and ineffectually however, according to the criteria of big business, and they were soon to be outdone and ousted by the more pushing Dutch. A Japanese squadron had landed in 1620 and established a little garrison. It was to them that the Dutch, having looked on the island and found it fair, applied for permission to build a house: just a small house, covering the territory enclosed by an ox-hide. The Japanese gave the permission, at which the Dutch, using an old trick, cut their ox-hide up into very thin strips, laid them end to end, and proceeded to build a fort. The Japanese were rankled at first, then amused, and pretty soon, losing interest, they abandoned their position entirely, quietly leaving the island to the Hollanders.

The 'beautiful island' (the Japanese called it Takasago) was a Dutch East Indian Colony for about forty years. The first Governor, de Heer Marten Sonk, and the first missionary, the Reverend George Candidius, arrived in 1624, and they set about zealously reforming Formosa, rooting out the noxious weeds of idolatry, fornication, abortion, polygamy, nudism, intoxication (in short, the nature of the First Adam) and doing a roaring trade in hemp, raw silk, ginger, sugar, rice, deerskins and buffalo hides.

The Hollanders had it made. But the best laid schemes . . . They were about to catch a Tartar. Or rather a Chinese who'd had enough himself of the Tartars, and was looking for a quiet place to stay.

Troublesome times in China. The Manchus were on the move. To the fore in the resistance movement, in the wake of his father, was the Chinese chieftain Cheng Cheng-kung, known to the Europeans as Koxinga. Eventually he found that things were becoming too hot for him in China, and he looked to Formosa as a place of refuge. The Dutchmen, however, were not willing to relinquish it without resistance, so in 1661 Koxinga unfurled the blood-flag and advanced on Formosa with a thousand war-junks. After a siege of nine months, he expelled the Dutch from Formosa and proclaimed himself sovereign of the island.

Neither he nor his son was to enjoy it long. The Tartars took over, and Formosa became a Chinese province, which it was to remain for two hundred years, till the Sino-Japanese War, when it was ceded to Japan, in 1895, after the treaty of Shimonoseki. Japan kept it for a half a century, largely as an anthropological reserve, but had to hand it over again, in 1945, to the Republic of China.

The rest is common knowledge. By 1949, China was divided in two: Nationalists and Communists, and the Nationalist government, under General Chiang Kai-shek — who had come there with a million sympathisers — was set up in Taipei.

Formosa took on the old Chinese name of Taiwan, and became a political problem.

2. *Hello Taiwan*

Cathay Pacific flight 410 for Taipei and Seoul. Will all passengers please proceed to Gate 21 and have their boarding passes ready.

I'd been in the Hong Kong waiting hall about a quarter hour, drinking a coffee, noting the time all over the world on the international clocks, observing the girls of the ground staff as they moved about: cute little slightly vaudevillesque dolls in floral blouses and little black bowler hats tilted over one eye.

At Gate 21, another wait and an Australian voice:

'Oy boy moy woife expensif joolery ere. Y'see y'save 27½ per cent soyles tax.'

There was a typhoon hovering about the South China Sea, not a big one, but enough for the radar to show quite a lot of turbulence ahead at one point, so we went off the normal course to avoid it. That meant some delay, but I was in no rush, and no one was waiting for me in Taipei.

At Taipei Airport I went to the Information Desk to enquire about hotels. They showed me a list, and I got them to phone up one for me. There was a room free, yes. I cashed a cheque at the airport bank, and took a taxi to the hotel.

Drab, hot, fuming Taipei. Hordes of taxis and shoals of motorcycles. The taxi I'm in is a battered red Yue Loong that has seen very hard service.

I don't like the room when I see it. A wall rises slap up against the window, so there's hardly any light. On the other hand, there's a lot of noise: you've practically got the traffic in bed with you. I ask for something quieter. After phoning down to the desk, the luggage boy conducts me to another floor. Here I meet Bob. He's in charge of this floor, and he's got everything taped:

'You a sailor?'

'No, why?'

'You look like a sailor.'

He shows me a room. I look around. Maybe a little better than the other one, but not much: ugly, little light, and noise again.

'Best room in my hotel,' says Bob complacently. Then, seeing that I'm not convinced and that even the best can leave something to be desired, he plays his trump card:

'I have girls. Good girls. Fifty dollars US. I send up one. If you don't like, I send up another.'

I express appreciation of his services, but say I think I'd rather look for another room. OK he says, just as I like, but if ever I come back, I'm to come straight to him:

'Just ask for Bob.'

So I'm back with Yue Loong in the streets, making for another hotel. On the kerb I'd asked the porter if he knew of one. He'd talked with the taxi-driver. I hadn't a clue where I was going.

I found myself at the luxurious Taipei Hilton. Well, why not, even if just to give me time to look around elsewhere.

But there was big business going on at the Hilton. Stacks of luggage. And talk of someone arriving for whom they were preparing 'VIP treatment': red carpet and flowers. I was asked at the desk if I had a reservation and when I confessed I hadn't they said they couldn't do anything for me. Whole parties had descended on them, flights having been cancelled because of the typhoon. All in all, it was just as well there was no room there. I still had the sound of that phrase 'VIP treatment' in my ears. Maybe third time lucky. I explained what I was looking for to a girl at the desk, and she made a few phone-calls for me.

A half-hour later I was settled in a good place: clean, quiet, plenty of light, and no VIPs. I was glad, very, especially as the typhoon was whooping it up outside. With the idea of celebrating, I opened the fridge, finding beer, coca-cola, and a 'vitamin drink' called Guronsan containing Glinoronolactone, Vitamin C, Vitamin B6, Nicotinamide, Sodium Panthothenate, Caffeine, Citric Acid and Ethanol. I shut the fridge quick in case any of it escaped. But there was hot water and tea bags ready laid out on the table. So I made myself some green tea, turned on the radio for Chinese music, and lay out on the bed.

'Hello Taiwan.'

3. In the Taipei Night

With the paraphernalia of plane and hotel behind me, I was eager to get down into some denser reality — meet the dragon. I knew, from having done some reading on Taiwan even before I left France, where I could expect to find it: down in the old port quarter, on the East bank of the Tamsui River, where the Lungshan (Dragon Mountain) temple is situated.

A word as to the dragon. In the old Chinese science of *feng shui*, or geomancy, geographical features — in particular the relationship of mountain, earth and water — are seen in terms of a concentration of power, and the dragon represents that power. For the *feng shui* man, the original world-dragon lies in the great Kun Lun range, between Tibet and Sinkiang. But this mountain range, and hence the dragon, branches off in all directions. Three branches stretch towards the East, branching off into smaller branches which again branch off into hundreds and thousands of smaller branches still — so that not only does every province have its dragon range, but every county, every town, every village. The Dragon Range in Taiwan corresponds to the South Range of the original three based in the Kun Lun. It crosses over the sea from Mount Wu Hu and arrives in North Taiwan from where it runs South right down the island.

If the Lungshan Temple is situated where it is, it's because that's where the *feng shui* man who was called in at its conception judged the dragon to be most present. But there's another story concerning the origins of the temple. It tells of a seaman who took a rest and had a shit on that spot three centuries or so ago. For some reason or other he took off his talisman and hung it on a bamboo branch, forgetting it there when he left. Later that night, people saw a phosphorescent glow in the bamboo grove, and when they came up close, with great precaution, they found the talisman, on which was written 'Lung Shan Temple, Goddess Kwan Yin'. It was all very strange, strange enough for the talisman to become an object of worship and sacralise the place where it was found. Which was what happened, till the residents of Wanhwa got round to collecting contributions and actually built the temple in 1737, dedicating it to Kwan Yin, that is the Avalokitesivara Bodhisattva, the goddess of all-embracing sympathy, who obtained nirvana by meditating on sound, and who in the process so refined her hearing that she can perceive, anywhere in the world, the slightest whimper of distress.

All this is going through my head as I walk through the Taipei streets on this late September evening, warm now after the fast passage of the typhoon, and with a big red sun on the horizon. Girls pass with tight-fitting T-shirts on which you can read: 'Love', 'Lovely pigeon', 'What have you done for me lately?' — little sexy bodhisattvas. Here's one now in soft washed out blue denim shorts, the lippy portals of her sex clearly visible under the cloth . . .

At the temple store, people are buying things to present as offerings: an old woman purchases three pears, a young girl a packet of biscuits. They also buy packets of golden paper and incense sticks. The offering table stands just inside the main door, and there's a brazier burning near it where people go to light their incense sticks, then hold the bunch of lit sticks up to their forehead, praying before depositing them on the table. *Kwan Yin! Kwan Yin!* — can you hear all this hum, can you distinguish what each is saying in all this crowd? *Pai pai, pai pai* — worship, worship. Blaze of the brazier, blue clouds of incense, yellow faces, flame-tipped sticks, the table of offerings, the general murmur and in the background, in the temple proper, the sound of chanting, with bells and drums. I watch a girl using the lucky sticks, two little crescent-shaped pieces of wood with front and back sides. She holds the sticks with both palms, makes three bows while saying her prayer, then casts the sticks on the ground. If both turn up back side, it's *Ying Kao* (bad luck); if they both turn up front side, it's *Shiao Kao* (half good, half bad); for it to be good luck (*Sheng Kao*) they have to fall differently. I didn't see how the sticks fell for the girl, but I presume not too well, because she's trying again. In fact she'll probably keep on trying — maybe adding a packet of biscuits to her offering — till she gets *Sheng Kao*.

Well, I wish you good luck, little girl, you certainly look as though you deserved it.

Back out into the Taipei night. Dragon range, dragon range. Just across the road I find myself in a maze of booths, a labyrinth of stalls. Food, food, food — spluttering, frying, sizzling, frittering. A man with great wooden tongs turning dough balls in bubbling fat. Further on, a strong man — look at the muscles on him! — sitting behind a table laden with a pharmaceutical product which was no doubt the origin of his strength. And over there, an old *kung fu* man with photos of his prowess — he's selling a powder. Dice games in many a corner, the flutter of ten-dollar bills. An apothecary store, and a man making a long spiel in front of a very tired looking alligator in a glass case — maybe he'll pep it up later with his stuff. Another apothecary man has a baboon that looks very bored till it suddenly bares its teeth and gives a loud hee-haw, must have thought of a jungle joke. Two old men, oblivious to the world and its harrassments, poring over Chinese chess. A palmist over there studies a woman's hands, left hand for the past, right hand for the future (she's got a nice fleshy rounded moon-mound). Here we are now at a snake shop: a bunch of multi-coloured serpents wriggling and writhing on a pole. The vendor selects one, slits it round the neck, strips the skin down a bit, and when he has a good piece folded back, blows into it, then in one fast gesture rips the whole skin right off, at which he slips his fingers into the body, pulls out the entrails, and squeezes the bile duct into a glass. Then into the glass he pours herbal wine, and states his price. It ranges from 30 to 100 NT dollars, depending on the quality of the snake.

Now we hit the red lights. A hundred little brothels, lit up by lurid red-mauve-purple strip lighting. Girls mostly silent, waiting, watching — those twelve little adolescents lined up there in singlets and knickers! — but some make calls: 'Hello-o,' 'Hello, I love you okay,' and one, slowly stroking the fly of her slacks as she leans in the doorway, says:

'Hei, hei; hei, hei.'

Walk on, walk on — how many streets, how many streets . . . Alone with the dragon in the Taipei night.

A massage place ('massagi', as you say in Taiwan, like 'tak-i-see'). Narrow hallway. Woman appears, shows me into a room: bed, mirror along the wall, shower place adjacent. The girls pass in the corridor. One little beauty, how'd she get in this place? In she comes. 'Come' is the main word in her vocabulary. 'Come, come.' When we're under the shower, she holds up her hands for me to admire — each nail painted a different colour. Funny I hadn't noticed that before. But I was too busy reading the *Prajnaparamita Sutra* in the wrinkles of her tits . . .

4. *Bronx*

The mini-bus was waiting outside the hotel. There were only two of us taking a trip that afternoon, me and the man, from another hotel, who was already seated in the bus: burly, gray-haired, chewing gum — Sam Hollis, from the Bronx, New York, USA, captain in the US army, stationed in Korea.

Yes, he was up there 'keepin' Korea clean', but he was down in Taipei for a rest. Used to come here a lot. But that was before inflation hit the island — 'You could live high for under 400 bucks for five days, 'd take 600 now.' He an' another guy used to hit Taipei together, get themselves a couple of broads, and have one hell of a time. That was when he was in Vietnam. Funny place, Vietnam. Those 'fuck you' lizards. Yeah, that's what they called them: fuck you lizards. Maybe Vietnamese for lizard, he didn't know. But they certainly fucked, dammit, they fucked like jackrabbits, on the wall, on the bed, everywhere — jackin' off there. Old times, yeah.

And Saigon. Those trees — jacarandas — in the main streets, you know, when they flowered, that was really something . . . And those Vietnamese broads, walking there, slim as rabbits, straight as trees, in their white shirts (*ao dais*, they call them) and black pyjamas. He used to meet 'em down in the bars on Tu Do street. They say it isn't the same now. Used to get a broad there and go swimming out at Vung Tau Beach . . .

Well, he'd done his twenty years. Going back soon to the States. Had a deal cookin' with a Japanese in Fresno. Yeah, would probably live in Fresno. Had enough of the Bronx — 'full a Irishmen, IRA men'. Wanting a rest. Go to Fresno.

We're on the Taipei–Keelung highway, which is still in its infancy, so we're bumping and jolting, jarring along. 'Jesus, this is wors'n a jungle jeep.' We'd left Taipei by McArthur Road. The young man who was doing the guide on the tour had pointed this out:

'We think he is a friend to Taiwan'

— Bronx had grunted:

'He wanted to take on China. Could a kicked the ass off them then.'

When we passed the statue of 'Mr Hu, philosopher', the guide had said:

'In Taiwan we keep the past'

— and Bronx had said nothing. But after a little while he turned round and whispered in my ear:

'Who's Mr Hu?'

— pleased as punch at his little joke.

When we get to Keelung, it isn't raining. That's extraordinary, it seems, for Keelung. It reminds me of Glasgow. Bronx had known a Glasgow man. A tailor. He had some way of delivering suits without buttons — got round the taxes that way. Smart. Boy, could he drink.

At Keelung there's a big statue of Kwan Yin, with portholes in her body you can look out of. Beside her sits a fat sugar-daddy Buddha. And you can get your photo taken. You get your photo taken, then you walk around up there looking at the Kwan Yin and down over at the harbour (can't take photos there — security), and when you come back your photo's right in the middle of a dinner plate: 'Souvenir of Taiwan'. Bronx buys it. He buys everything he's offered, anything and everything.

'I got three sisters. I send them stuff. They like it.'

We pass a group of school-children. 'Some discipline, these kids,' says Bronx, 'make swell baseball players. They won the World Series, goddam. Work like clockwork. Kinda frightenin'! Too much like the army.'

At Wild Pine Beach, Bronx buys up some more stuff — 'My sisters like it,' he says again, almost apologetically — and we go to see the aquarium. The most marvellous tropical fish: angel fish, rainbow fish, god-fairy fish, bridled beauty fish, white needle fish. Bronx stays a long time before one case, chewing his gum:

'Nature's nuts'

he says at length.

The trip lasted three hours. When we get back to my hotel, and I'm leaving the bus, Bronx says:

'Take care'

and then he adds:

'Be good.'

5. Silent World Beauty

'Concerning the style of Chinese painting, it is rather impressionistic than illustrative. The sense of the power of the brush of the artist is equally important. Basically, the Chinese painting more or less conceals the poetical sentiment of the artist's individuality . . . A good Chinese painting not only can show the concentrate form and colour of the scene but can also draw the deep recollection and meditation. To appreciate the Chinese painting is really an art. First, you must have a clean, spatial and quiet room. Second, you should hang the scroll on the monocolour wall of nothing but the painting itself. Third, you should sit at about ten feet from the painting and, do not let the outside noise come into the room. Fourth, you should look at the painting easily and remember not to concentrate your thinking on the painting by force. You should think only a little bit of the room in which you are. Suddenly, the true sentiment from your consciousness strikes out to your visual nerve with a super natural feeling of the beauty of the silent world.' So speaks Mr J. D. Jo in a little booklet called *The Fabulous Chinese Arts* (Hong Kong, 1970).

The beauty of the silent world.

There was a conspicuous lack of silence when I first entered the National Palace Museum that morning. A Japanese guide with a flag was barking at the head of a troop of Tokyo tourists, and two or three groups of uniformed high school pupils were being initiated into the 'national heritage' by their teachers. What had all this to do with Wang Hsi-chih, or Mi-Fu, or Wang-Wei, or Ku K'ai-chih, or Wu Tao-tzu, or Kuo Hsi, or Ma Yuan, or Liang K'ai, or any of the other masters of Chinese art? Nothing. Just the continuation of the social noise. In one of the upper galleries I came across a grey-robed monk who had a better idea. He wasn't rushing around from one object to another, he was sitting before a painting by Wang Chien (17th century): *Temple in a Lush Forest*, with his head bowed and his eyes closed — and he wasn't sleeping, that was evident from the way he held his body. He was really cut off from the world and into the mindscape.

For Chu Hsi, who founded Confucian scholastics in the 12th century, learning to know the world meant positive study and the tracing out of a rational process in nature. For Wang Yang-ming, who had more than an inkling of Buddhist and Taoist thought, to know the world meant, not the study of the exterior world, but a deep penetration into the mind itself. For him, all the knowledge in the world would never permit him to understand a grain of rice or a stalk of bamboo. In order to understand the nature of bamboo, he would have to understand his own self-nature, and to do that he went away into the mountains for a while. It was there he realised that there was no distinction to be made between his own original self-nature, before it was obscured by personal notions inherited from society, and great nature herself, and that, therefore, the way to live, the only radical and sincere way, was according to nature, not according to moral law. When it was pointed out to him, as it will always be pointed out to men of this mentality, that nature contains snakes as well as philosophers, evil as well as good, he replied that 'evil' and 'good' were preconceived all-too-human notions that did not exist either in nature or in the original nature of the mind. In short, real life is not 'human' . . .

It's an old, old quarrel, and a lot of ink has been spilled in its name, a lot of wrangling done. These paintings spill ink too, but in their own way, and they don't wrangle. What is striking about them is their cold distance. They have no immediate human preoccupations. You might even say they're 'inhuman'. But there's a strength comes from them, a virtue, in the old sense of the word, they seem to radiate with energy, and there's a great peace in them:

Whispering Pines on a Mountain Path

Looking for Plum Blossoms

Travellers among Snowy Mountains

Relaxing to the Sound of Pines

Old Trees by a Cold Waterfall

Fishing on a Snowy Day

Through Snowy Mountains at Dawn . . .

6. *Little Jane*

Taipei isn't just full of apple-arsed little whores with five-colour-painted fingernails. Oh no, don't think that for a minute, there are also *bona fide* Christian maidens to be found in that Gomorrah. Let me tell you of one.

I met her in a bookshop near Taipei station. I'd been hanging around the station because I'd heard there was a Chinese poet called Dream-the-Butterfly who sold newspapers in the quarter, and I thought I might make his acquaintance. But Dream-the-Butterfly must have been dreaming the butterfly somewhere else that night, for I came across no one like the description I'd been given.

Moving away from the station area, I passed this bookshop, and, having nothing particular in mind to do, thinking I might buy myself some books, went in.

I ended up at the dictionary shelves. Years ago I borrowed a

Mathews' Chinese–English Dictionary from a Belgian sinologist friend (it stands, black, on my shelves beside Couvreur's ox-blood *Dictionnaire classique de la langue chinoise*), and I thought now that if I could get a cheap reprint of the Mathews' here in Taipei (famed for its pirate editions), I might be able to return the copy borrowed from my friend. It was a praiseworthy thought and, if my Belgian friend ever reads this, I hope he'll appreciate it. But there was no Mathews' on the shelves. I enquired if they ever had one in stock, and the vendor I asked, asked another vendor, who talked about it to another vendor — and it was then that little Jane turned up. She wanted to sell me the *Encyclopedia Americana*. I didn't see the connection. 'You look for America book?' she said. I said, yes, I was looking for an American book, but not *any* American book: Mathews' Chinese–English Dictionary. 'You look for America book?' she said again. And I said, yes, I was looking for an American book, but . . . 'I show you,' she said. And leaving me wondering exactly what she meant by that, she went to get her coat. 'I show you,' she repeated, when she came back. Well, OK, I was ready to be showed. So out we went into the Taipei night. She was quite a good-looking girl, except when she smiled — but it wasn't a smile, she just had a way of opening her mouth now and then showing her big teeth. She was kind of prim and proper too, what with those glasses. But she really wasn't bad-looking. Maybe a bit scraggy and dressed dowdily to boot. But not too bad-looking, really not too bad-looking (was I trying to convince myself?)

When it turned out there was no Mathews' at the other shop either, I invited Jane to dinner. She took that as if she'd been expecting it, and asked me how I'd like to eat, naming a few places. There was a Korean restaurant not far. OK, Korean.

'Korean' meant a stove set in the middle of the table, with beef, cabbage and octopus floating in its moat, and the possibility of grilling strips of beef and mutton on its dome. On the side: lettuce, mushrooms and dumplings, and a sauce of egg and herbs for dipping the pieces of meat in before you cook them on the stove. After the waitress had done her work, the hostess came over to see if everything was OK. Indicating Jane to me, she said: 'Nice girl, beauty girl,' and I had the unpleasant impression of being sold Taiwan. Jane just showed her teeth and continued nibbling at a piece of octopus.

While the organ continued playing in a corner of the restaurant, and the twelve-guest table next to us continued its enthusiastic eating and celebration of something, I tried to talk a little with my companion. She told me her Chinese name, which she had roughly Englished phonetically as 'Jane', meant 'graduate', and she had majored at college in Chinese history, but she was interested in America. It turned out that what interested her chiefly in America (I think she thought I was American) was Billy Graham (my heart, which was already in my boots, sank definitively into the floor). She had recently been converted to Christianity, and was waiting for the Billy Graham Crusade that was going to take place in Taiwan in about a month's time. As preparation for it, she was reading a book called *The Jesus Generation*. I asked her what had attracted her to Christianity, and she said: 'A God who loves me.' She had found the answer to her life, and it was all kind of pathetic, and what could I say — that I felt it something of a pity that so many centuries of Chinese civilisation should end up with Billy Graham?

I think it was to get back to old China after this sad slough of cheap Christianity that I suggested we finish off the evening (I'd started it, I'd see it through, by God) at the Chinese opera. We were going to be late at the opera, and I think Jane would rather have gone to see a weepy-happy love-movie such as I'd seen many advertised on the huge hoardings of Taipei, but I wanted to save something of the evening, so we hurried through lanes and over bridges in downtown Taipei — one godawful labyrinth — till we came to the opera house, and got tickets, and, passing by the portrait of the T'ang Emperor Shian Tsung, also known as Ming Huang (the Brilliant Emperor), the god of music and opera (because he protected song and dance, before and after his abdication from the throne, he who loved the great beauty Yang Kuei Huei for whom he got Li Po to write a poem), entered the huge hall. What a welter of colour on the stage! The background, royal blue with a huge dragon motif. Crimson furniture. Actors in sumptuous dresses. And the noise: great clashes of music, high-pitched dialogue and tremulous falsetto monologue. Then, at the very height apparently of the action, amid all the noise and colour, at the highest peak of the crescendoing performance, on strolls a stage attendant and indifferently shifts a couple of chairs about in preparation for the next historic scene. Who's that character with the crimson mask? And that one with the white-painted nose? Or that one with the black flag? And that one with the long feathers on his hat? I'm bewildered, bamboozled and bedazzled, I don't understand a single damned thing. At one point, a character comes on stage shaking out bits of white paper from a red umbrella. A snowstorm? Another moves her hands slowly in front of her eyes. Yet another stamps on to the stage lifting his feet as high as they can go. Suddenly there's a crackle of fireworks . . . !!? It's total, it's colourful, it's high-flying, goes with a blare and a bang — every now and then the audience applauds some particularly fine moment. It's Brecht plus Victor Hugo plus pantomime plus Beethoven plus the Gothic Novel plus Rumplestiltskin plus the Fairy Queen . . .

Out on the midnight pavement, the crimson noise still in my head, I look for a taxi. Goodnight to Chinese opera. Goodnight to little Jane. Goodnight to Billy Graham. Goodnight, goodnight, goodnight.

7. *Autumn Stillness at Yangmingshan*

After an accumulation of detail, event, encounter, it's good to get back out into the emptiness again, which is why that afternoon I went ten miles or so out of Taipei to Yangmingshan (Grass Mountain), the national park. Yangmingshan is especially frequented in the Springtime, when the cherry trees are in blossom and when Taipei citizens will come to view them. It also has its crowds at weekends. But on this afternoon of an Autumn weekday there was hardly anyone at all.

There are miles and miles to Yangmingshan, so that a walker can walk to his heart's content, which is what I did, along paths that carried the perfume of September flowers, or the blue acrid smell of smoke from the bonfires of burning leaves in the garden allotments.

It was warm, very warm — I'd been glad to find a fountain playing just inside the entrance to the park, a rainbow flickering through its waters. I stood at the fountain's edge, watching the rainbow, and enjoying a very thin spray of water on my skin.

I was in no hurry to leave it, but finally I did, feeling there would be other delights along the way.

Now and then I'd pass a group, mostly young people, out for a jaunt, and was the object of many curious glances. It occurred to me how much the Chinese love groups, and how much the lone figure is something 'unnatural'. Even when a 'lofty scholar' of the classical literature goes to meditate in a mountain kiosk, he will have a friend with him, or at least an attendant. The only lone figure is the wandering Buddhist monk, and he is after all more Indian than Chinese. Convivial and gregarious, on the whole, the Chinese, rare with them the philosophy of solitude . . .

There's a long waterfall at Yangmingshan, of the kind that Chinese painting is full of. A steep, winding path runs alongside it, with niches and kiosks arranged among the boulders. It's good to sit in one of those niches at the side of the waterfall, listening to the sound of the water. Till you become the waterfall? Well, till there's a waterfall running through you, till you realise that you're part of a waterfall, and that what lies behind your personal being is a rush of pure power.

After walking for about five hours in Yangmingshan, stopping here and there, I went up to the red-pillared hillside teahouse. There I drank some very hot tea with sugar and lemon. It was late afternoon, a fountain was playing outside the window where I was sitting, a red sun was approaching the horizon, and my whole being was flooded with the sensation of Autumn stillness.

The evening sky was green and gold when I took the bus back to Taipei.

8. *'I want to speak with you many'*

In order to extend my knowledge of the aboriginal tribes of Taiwan, I'd gone that morning to the Provincial Museum of Anthropology in Longevity Park which is known for its life-sized models of Aborigines as well as its display of tribal artifacts. The Museum groups the Aborigines into ten tribes: the Atayal, Saisiat, Bunun, Shao, Tsou, Rukai, Paiwan, Puyuma, Ami and Yami. If most of the Aborigines, especially the Plains Tribes (Pingpu) who lived on the western plains of the island, have been assimilated by the Chinese, there are still extant tribal groups in the Central Mountain Range, the East Coast Region, and on Botel Tobago Island. It is in these areas that tribal customs, dances and rituals have survived, or are being revived (if only as tourist attractions). While ready for the worst, I knew I'd be trying, once out of Taipei, to get a look at some of these groups, but I wanted, in order to be able to interpret any sign that might intrigue me, to have as solid a knowledge of the background as possible.

Before coming to Taiwan I'd read Toichi Mabuchi's *Ethnology of the Southwestern Pacific*:

'Isolated in their island mountains, and virtually uninfluenced by the main currents of diffusion from such higher civilisations as the Indian, Arabic, European, and the adjacent Chinese, the Formosan Aborigines until recent times had presented a relatively higher proportion of aboriginal characteristics than their Indonesian cousins in other areas.'

I'd also read a more picturesque little booklet (*Customs and Traditions in Plain and Highlands of Taiwan* by Yunghai Peng) containing passages like this one, on 'wine habit and drunkenness' among the Aborigines:

'Generally the aborigines are fond of wine. Especially the old aborigines are drunkards. They would rather want the pleasant sensation after drinking wine than taste the deliciousness of wine. Owing to express the intimate emotion, they used to drink wine together. They who get drunk and lost reason dared to commit murder or used to behave themselves disgracefully. According to the observation of an eyewitness, one day he seemed to see a picture scroll of pandemonium . . . In the course of changing the cups each other, men and women got dead-drunk at last. Some dropped like a log at a corner or bed, and both sexes mixed together. One woman exposed her private parts, and then she showed the apparances as weep, appeal and rejoice in front of men, flaunting her sexual parts. Their dancing seems to be developed from the poses of sexual intercourse of men and women as women exposes her secrets and shake her waists skilfully in front of men during dancing.'

So I'd read a couple of books and a few articles and it was in order to complete this reading that, after looking at the exhibits in the Museum, I went to its Research Library in search of books. It was there I met the art students. There were a half-dozen of them, three boys, three girls, making a group (with one of the boys as 'group-leader'), and they had got this vacation job together, working among the catalogues of the library.

I don't remember exactly what we talked about, probably started with the Aborigines and moved on from there, but there was immediate warm sympathy and good feeling that strengthened as we went along — so that when it came to knocking-off time at noon they ask me to come and lunch with them.

As we made our way to the restaurant, one of them, who hadn't spoken so much before because his English was not so good, but was obviously bursting with enthusiasm, his eyes lit up and dancing behind his glasses, walked along beside me, saying in spurts: 'This is happy day . . . foreigners sexy . . . I want to speak to you many . . . very interesting person.' This student was the first of the group to write me later when I got back to France, and his letter, that is all the more interesting for being grammatically crazy, went like this: 'Remember me? A Chinese friend in Taiwan. I miss you very much since you left from Taiwan. You give me the glad and pleasure in that days. I can't forget that in my life. My English is very bad. I can't talk you what I think. I think you can understand me. I hope you come soon back to Taiwan. You will see many many things that you like. At last I hope you wealth, health, and handsome. Oh, wait minute, the last words is: my friend best regards to you from my friends. Now I say good buy.'

We sat at a big round table in the restaurant, and after consultation among themselves, they ordered a multitude of dishes (afterwards, they would not let me pay my share — 'it is Chinese custom'), which were accompanied by two kinds of rice, there in big dishes at the side of the table for you to help yourself: dry rice and Taiwanese glutinous rice. It was good. And the talk continued.

The boy with the glasses was much concerned with sex, and he wanted to know what I thought of Chinese girls, his own opinion being 'Taiwan girls beautiful, not sexual'. When I asked the other two boys what they thought, they said that was his problem, and when I asked the girls one of them got lost in the glutinous rice, another started giggling (she later whispered in my ear that the Chinese word for sex is *hsiang*), and the third — who had 'love' emblazoned on her T-shirt — just gave me a long, slow smile that spoke worlds. The conversation got more general after that. I remember one of the boys saying of the Chinese: 'We are an old people, gentle'; while the group-leader came up with: 'The Chinese have the German wisdom', meaning by that 'Nie tsa' (Nietzsche) and 'Scho-pen-hwa' (Schopenhauer) . . .

It was after we'd left the restaurant and were back out in the hot afternoon sun that I discovered sweet-and-sour-juice. This is *suan mei tang* (sour plum juice), made from stewed plums, liquorice root and *shan cha*, a mountain haw, producing a dark amber-coloured juice that, cooled (*ping chen*), is served in little plastic bags with a straw on street corners. It is delicious. I was thirsty after the meal, and drank a vast quantity of *suan mei tang*, much to the amusement of my new friends.

9. *At Wulai*

At Wulai, about seventeen miles south of Taipei, you can see what remains of the Atayal tribe. As the guide book says:

'Wulai is the most accessible area from Taipei to view the aboriginal tribesmen who once were the head hunters of Taiwan. Descendants of the proud tribe of Atayals, the present-day Wulai Aborigines for the most part dress and perform for the benefit (and tips) of tourists. On some of the old-timers you may see both a tribal tattoo on the forehead, and a chin mark that once meant the wearer had taken a head. If two upper front teeth are missing, the Atayal has come of age. And you can identify a married woman by the 'wedding band' tattooed across her face from ears to mouth. Since few of these tribal customs are perpetuated, the marks you see today are usually paint or an oily lampblack substance used instead of tattoo. A head hasn't been taken in Taiwan for more than forty years . . .'

Going up into the hills is always a pleasure, and that morning it meant following a green turbulent river that awakened in the mind a sensation of light and freshness. The bus climbed and turned and turned and climbed, up into the 'original' country, past Pitan (Green Lake), till it came to its terminus at the village of Wulai.

What you see first of all is a street of souvenir shops. You make your way along its clattered and garish insipidity till you come to a mountain gorge at the end of the street, with a rushing river and a suspension bridge. The mountain country up there is Atayal country.

There's a trolley track up the mountain side, and there are pushcars waiting there with their pushers ready to offer you 'an exciting ride'.

You may, however, if you have a certain amount of mountain pride, prefer to walk. That's what I did.

I found another village up there, but it seemed less trashy, and there were girls in tribal costume standing in front of the shops: they wore red jackets and short black skirts showing their thighs, and decorated calf-leggings. It was all a stunt, OK (most of these girls were probably no longer pure Atayal, and it's pretty sure that some of them were no more Atayal than I am) — but Atayal or no they looked good, and one was downright beautiful.

This second village had an upper level, and up there I went into a huge store selling mainly costumes and statues.

A little alcove just off the main shopfloor contained, not newly turned aboriginal 'souvenirs', but real remnants of the old culture. One little wooden statuette particularly appealed to me: a dark figure with Polynesian features and big ears squatting on his hunkers in a typical Pacific posture. It felt good in the palm of my hand, and suddenly I realised I was going to steal it. There was a price on its head to be sure, but I knew I wasn't going to pay it — that little fellow for me had no price, and I was sure, and still am, he preferred to be stolen than to be sold. So I palmed it, but didn't go out with it directly. What I did was to divert attention from my past presence in the alcove by going out into the main shop and there bargaining for a wall tapestry priced at 380 NT dollars. I offered 300, the vendor consulted with an adviser, and they said 350, and I said too bad, goodbye. The same tapestries, I found, were selling in a little shop on the lower level for 250. It was in that little shop I bought a painting done with bamboo brush and bark-juice on paper made from mountain grass: black, white and red against the brown of the paper, depicting a naked, braceleted and ear-ringed woman offering a bowl of fruit. The woman is black, her jewels are white, and there are four red touches: the fruit, her lips, a red flower stuck behind one of her ears, and the central link, full on her Venus mound, of a chain slung round her hips. She, and the squatting man, were the nearest I got to the ancient Atayal culture.

But there was a nice little thing at the end. A shop in that same village, and two young girls in it. They weren't in costume. One wore a shirt and a skirt; the other wore a shirt that was meant to be tied in front but she'd left it open, showing her midriff — and the little denim shorts she had on were sexy as hell, and she knew it. I think I'd gone in to buy a postcard, and we talked:

'Where come from?'

'*Su-gu-lan* . . . Why no costume?'

Smiles.

'Well, you look good anyway!'

— at least me and the girl in the skirt talked. Denim wasn't saying anything, but she knew I felt her presence, she knew her presence was all the stronger for her not saying anything. So, she didn't say anything, but as I was leaving she did a little dance, just a little dance, out of thin air, wagging her hips, for her own pleasure, but also, she knew it, for mine.

So I came away from Wulai with a nude painting, a squatting figurine, and the dancing vision of a little blue demon. There are worse ways of spending an Autumn afternoon.

10. Down the Coast

All set for my trip round the island, I'm taking the morning train down to Suao where I'll change to a bus for Hualien. It's another perfect day. That sense of absolute freshness.

Taipei station in the morning. High school kids clustered to incoming trains like bees: boys with cropped hair, girls bobbed. A crowd gradually gathers on the platform for the Suao train — two vendors go up and down, one with tea, the other with eggs, newspaper, cigarettes and fudge. A monk in a grey robe with yellow leggings and black shoes — for all the world like a heron (*ardea cinerea cinerea*) — points his nose at the sun.

I love those Taiwan trains. Plenty of room for one's legs, and a footrest into the bargain. A metal holder on my left with glasses for tea — bags of tea to hand, and a boy comes round to fill the glasses with hot water according to need. I settle back for the three-hour trip to Suao, taking out my notebook, learning a little Chinese. I'd got the art students to write down certain useful phrases for me, so now I'm learning them up: 'Where is the nearest highway bus station?' (roughly: *chin oon tsue djin de kong doo djü tse tsan tsai na li*?); 'Is there a temple near where I can stay?' (roughly: *chin oon who djin seu ho jo miao seu keu zung wo dzu su*?). And so on.

We're going right through the mountains, in the bowels of the dragon. The *feng shi* men must have had nightmares when they saw those tunnels being gouged out. Gorges, canyons, boulderstrewn torrents followed by cool rice paddies.

The sun's getting stronger — noise of window curtains being pulled along their rails.

Light and shade. Fast changes of scenery.

Clayey streams full of duck.

Suao.

I go into the huddle of shops and stalls that constitute the market. Buy a tin of guava juice and a couple of freshly-baked crevassed dumplings . . . mmm. Then I buy a bigger cake with a red top. Further on I buy a root of Korean ginseng — I'll be chewing at it now and then along the road. A little girl has a pee in the gutter. Two young girls go by hand in hand. Here at the corner is a little shop producing gold paper, and beside it a hole-in-the-wall temple where the gold paper gets burnt . . .

Then it's the bus for Hualien: little conductress in fawn blouse and skirt with a forage cap; blue whir of the driver's fan.

Only one-way traffic down the coast road.

Every bend in the road is equipped with mirrors. There have been rockslides. Maybe the work of the recent typhoon. It had done worse, but I was to find that out later.

The girl's voice announces the stops: Pu Ta, Sun tiao ling . . .

Blue heat haze.

Waterbuffalo.

Suddenly, as we emerge from a long long tunnel — the sea! A little island half-rising from the warm white mist. And fishing smacks, about fifty of them, dotted over the waters.

Flop! — a cold yellow towel falls on my knees. It's the conductress distributing them as refreshment.

A smell of pineapple, smack-smack of lips behind me.

The coastline.

So utterly beautiful.

First glimpses of the Pacific.

The Ryukyu archipelago out there, and a little further on, Japan . . .
A long time, Lafcadio.
But it's an anonymous archipelago I have in mind.
White mist, blue sea.
Ahhh.
That island half-risen . . .
Nets lying out on the rocks. Along the road, shacks of wood and bamboo hut. We must be coming close.
Mustard Seed Aborigine Bible School.
Hualien.
Toot-toot-toot of the whistle as the conductress guides her bus into the station.

11. A Rainy Night in Hualien

Everything was dandy. I'd found myself a very nice little hotel, at a very reasonable price, and was lying on my nice bed in my nice room, drinking green tea, when the phone rang and the bad news came. It was the manager, whom I'd asked to get me a ticket on the bus to Taitung, saying the road was blocked owing to typhoon damage and that there would be no bus running for a week at least. Problem . . . but OK, change of plan, what I'd do was cross the island by the east-west highway to Taichung, come back round by Taitung later. No, he was sorry, not possible, the east-west highway had been struck by the typhoon also, and there was no through road. Dammit! . . . stuck in Hualien for a week (at least)? What the hell would I do in Hualien for a week? Go back to Taipei, and start again round the western coast? Didn't fancy that at all . . . It looked as if all my plans were up in the air. Hey — up in the air! Were there any planes running? Yes, plane, yes. Well, could he get me a seat in the plane for Taitung, or, better, for Kaohsiung? He would try. A half-hour elapsed and he phoned back: all fixed. It would be a big hole in my budget, but things would be moving again, that was the main thing. I lay back on my bed, relieved. I thought later on I'd go up to the Ami Culture Village, but I was in no hurry . . .

Another phone call from the manager. Would I like to visit a marble factory (Hualien is famous for its marble):

'Arrange special for you. Say my friend. Good service'
— and although I'm sure it's exactly the kind of ploy I want to avoid, I feel the manager has given himself so much trouble over the plane reservation that I agree.

So off we go together, me and the manager, in a taxi, to the marble factory, which is not a marble factory, at least I don't see any factory, but a marble shop, a show case, a display, a whole accumulation of marble stuff just waiting for the tourist to pick it up, pay for it, and then get himself bundled elsewhere.

The typhoon must have kept the tourists in Taipei, because when we get to the marble shop, I, the sole prospective buyer in the place, am immediately surrounded by six pretty girls, obviously meant to cater for larger parties, trying to sell me marble. If I hadn't a will of iron, I'd have left that place with something a whole lot heavier than the white man's burden. As it was, I left with a paperweight — a *little* paperweight. And a lot of smiles and handwaves from the girls, to whom I'd explained the situation, and who saw the joke.

The manager probably wasn't too pleased at my lack of interest in Hualien marble, I certainly wasn't too pleased at his trying to get me into that tourist trap, so that when he tried again to find some tourist prey in me, offering to arrange for me a special show at the Ami Culture Village, I told him there was nothing doing.

Ten minutes later, I was lying flat out on my bed again. Hualien looked like a washout. It had even begun to rain. Ah, the ups and downs of travelling. For the moment things were down. But something might still turn up.

What turned up first was the floor boy:

'Twit-twee, twit-twee,'
— that was the doorbell. I hadn't noticed it was in the form of a Swiss bird-nest. And on my call to come in, in comes James Cagney — I mean the Chinese floor boy who talks out of the corner of his mouth like James Cagney:

'Lie Miss?'
he says, which is the formula for asking if a guest wants a girl. When I don't look too interested, he figures it's maybe because I don't want to pay for a whole night, so he says:

'Short time?'

— it sounds like 'shoot time'. I say maybe later:

'Hoe-kay'

he says.

I lie back on my bed. Maybe ten, maybe twenty minutes. Then there it goes again:

'Twit-twee, twit-twee'

— surely not James Cagney again already? No, this time it's the luggage boy, the one who'd brought my rucksack up to the room. A handsome fellow, but with something like St Vitus' dance, for every now and then he gives the most frantic jerks. I'd noticed that before, but as he talked to me there in the room, it was worse. I could hardly make out what he was saying, what with his rudimentary (but better than my Chinese) English and those spasmodic jerks, but I gathered he wanted us to go out 'one, one'.

OK, Why not?

So out we went, the two of us, to paint the town red, or chase the dragon, or whatever, I didn't know what he had in mind. I was just curious to see what might happen.

The first thing for him was to find a taxi, that is, a friend who drove a taxi, and we went from drinking booth to drinking booth enquiring for him. We found him at last with four cronies around a conglomeration of empty beer-bottles.

A short talk between the taxi-man and my friend and we were careering through the rainy night, amid crazy laughter from Zak (he was half-Japanese and I wondered if he wasn't also half-mad), and wild gestures from Lou the taxi-man whose specialty was holding the wheel with his pinkie — making for the Tribal Village.

We got there too late — too late, that is, for the dances. They were at the finale, but when I saw what that finale was, a big circle with Ami girls alternating with German and Australian tourists, all singing *Auld Lang Syne*, I didn't regret what I had missed. In fact I felt I had had a narrow escape.

Back in town — tyres sizzling in the rainy darkness, pinky on the wheel — we take leave of the taxi-man, on the understanding that we meet again early the following morning for a trip into the Taroko Gorges. But the night's still, relatively, young, and I can see Zak wondering what yet to make of it, his head's jerking like billy-o.

First stop is a pavement food stall, where we consume a bowl of hot octopus and a couple of bottles of beer. The rain is steaming off the asphalt.

Then Zak goes to make a phone call. To a girl — his girl? — I think. But I gather she's not home yet, or not free yet. So he suggests we go to the cinema. All right, let's go to the cinema.

A *kung-fu* film: Flying Knife, Whirling Hands and Magic Whip trying to get the better of one another, prancing and leaping all over the landscape, while the old expert, Kang Yen, the man whose skill these younger men would like to match, sits slumped in the corner of an inn, inconspicuous, inactive, pulling at a jug of wine and reading a book of poems . . .

Great stuff!

We were *kung fu*ing like mad, Zak and I, in the street outside the cinema, in the rainy Hualien night, when a friend of his came passing by on a scooter. Stop and conversation in Chinese, but if I don't participate in it linguistically, I'm partly what it's all about. It appears that this friend has a girl:

'Beautiful — oh my Gawd!'

says Zak, and that he would be willing to lend her to me, for a consideration. We discussed the consideration, and it seemed reasonable. But I also required to see, and when I had seen, it still seemed reasonable. That's how I came to spend an hour, in Hualien, in the rainy night, with the Candid Girl of White River, she of the ancient sex-manuals, as reincarnated here in the form of a little lady half-Ami and half-Chinese.

Back at the hotel, I was getting my things ready for the early departure in the morning when there came a 'twit-twee, twit-twee' at the door again. It was James Cagney, with a girl in tow — at two o'clock in the morning! — he obviously never missed a trick, that fellow.

12. Taroko in the Morning

At the appointed time, I was standing in front of the hotel, all serene, rucksack at my feet, ready to go, but there was no one else in sight. The air was chill — the rain had ceased during the night and the morning sky was blue — so I did a little dance round the rucksack to heat up. After about ten minutes, Zak turned up, bleary-eyed, and pulling on his jacket. Still no taxi-man. We went to look for him. He lived in a block of flats built in a square around what was still a waste-ground. We stood in the waste-ground and Zak threw gravel up against a second-floor window. A face appeared, dis-appeared, re-appeared, dis-appeared — till Lou made a full-bodied appearance, fastening his belt and trying to get his feet into his shoes. Greetings and apologies, then he went to the car — his old faithful Yue Loong — took a pair of pliers from the glove-box, and began to fix some wires. Thereupon he put the pliers back in the box, took out a metal comb, dragged it through his hair, and we were off.

We bumped out of the waste-ground, got on to the road and were already making good headway when Zak started shouting:

'Girl! Girl!'

— I said I didn't want any girl. What I meant was that if I didn't mind making my nights Taoist, I liked having my mornings Buddhist. But I couldn't say anything so complicated.

'You no fuck off?'

— said Zak. I told him to fuck off himself. But he didn't get that either.

'You no fuck off?'

— he really looked disappointed, as if I were refusing an important part of his hospitality. To make it simple, I said I had no money. He gave me to understand that didn't matter: 'for friend'; it was all part of the show. I shook my head, so it was obvious I wasn't interested.

'Taiwanese girl!'

— I said no. But Lou had already quit the main road and was lurching up a track to a cluster of huts and shacks.

'Taiwanese beauty girl!'

shouts Zak, jerking like hell.

They went into one of the shacks — the hamlet was still asleep — and eventually came out with a girl about eighteen years old wearing a sweater on which was written 'beautiful'. But she wasn't. So I wasn't even tempted. They bundled her into the car beside me, I said 'hello' to her politely, and we were off again.

'Taiwanee girl'
shouted Zak, pleased as hell, feeling he'd done his utmost to make the outing successful. Lou now added his own little touch by stopping at a roadside booth for a packet of Prosperity Island cigarettes, and then getting out his cassettes: *Killing on 10th Street*, *Rhapsody in White*, *Downtown*.

The entrance to the Taroko Gorge is about twenty miles north of Hualien, where the Li Yu creek pours its mountain waters into the Pacific Ocean. Called by many one of the seven wonders of the Orient, it consists of steep walls of blue-green marble, creating a canyon so narrow in places that the rays of the sun hit the stream at the bottom of the gorge only at noon. Where the walls are less steep, there is a high timberland, but in the narrow places you have only the polished, multi-coloured strata of marble and hard rock that are the heart of the Central Mountain Range.

It is very, very beautiful.

A blue paradise.

The road winds through this marvellous mineral world, making about fifty tunnels in twelve miles. Some of these tunnels have openings in the rock, so many windows full of blue-green light, affording quick glimpses of the canyon's beauty, then all is darkness again to prepare the eyes for another glimpse. To go along that road is in fact to have wet darkness alternating with flashes of blue-green brilliance in such rapid succession that the mind reels.

We made it in that old Yue Loong, with a fast and reckless driver, a young girl singing, Zak crazily pointing out the sights with cries of 'Many good!' and 'Oh my Gawd!', and the cassette-player going full blast with *Killing on 10th Street*.

As we'd entered the gorge by the red gateway, both sun and moon were visible in the sky — and there were waterfalls gushing everywhere.

Taroko!

Zak had got his fortune told at the Eternal Spring Shrine, and it was good, so he was feeling on top of the world:

'Many good!'

I was feeling on top of the world myself, though nobody had told me my fortune. Or maybe I was feeling not so much *on top of* the world as *at the heart* of it. Outside myself, at the heart of the world.

Taroko!

'In the three worlds there is no Dharma. In what place shall we seek for the Mind?'

Gone in the blue light.

The Great Truth, being present with what shall we identify it?

Taroko!

'He who is in touch with the road is not stagnant' . . .

Further up in the gorge we came to an inn where we drank beer and I bought a little bead necklace for the girl.

Then it was time for the return trip. I had my plane to catch.

Zak's last gesture was to give me the address of his sister in Kaohsiung, telling me she was 'many beautiful'.

13. Pacific Flight

Flying down Taiwan, hugging the coast. I'm on the port side — five thousand miles of blueness, all the way to Honolulu.

I hadn't expected to be up in the air again so soon. On Taiwan, I'd intended to keep my feet on Formosan earth. But here I was. That set me to reviewing the flight out from Europe: the Alps like a writhing of white dragons; old grey Athens; sunset over the Greek islands; a rainy dawn in New Delhi; steaming Bangkok; Hong Kong's blue bay and skyscrapers; drab, labyrinthine, crowded Taipei.

So, in the air again. Because of the damned typhoon.

I'd read an article about it in the newspaper:

'Twelve deaths were reported and three persons missing after typhoon Betty swept across the island and churned away through southern Taiwan before proceeding toward the Pescadores island group and the Chinese mainland.

According to the police, twenty-four persons were seriously injured and eighty-four others suffered minor wounds during the attack of the tropical storm.

More than 210 houses were levelled and around 500 others damaged throughout the island. About 800 people were said to be homeless and waiting for help.

The medium-strength typhoon, the second to hit Taiwan this year, struck at Taitung on the east coast Monday night with winds gusting up to a 100 miles per hour.

It went across the central mountain range and headed west into the Taiwan straits in the early hours of Tuesday.'

But now everything was calm again, the Pacific re-pacified.

The Great Morning.

A cool wind blowing over the ocean.

I thought again of Lafcadio Hearn, that passage of his in 'By the Japanese Sea':

'The blanched road winds along a coast of low cliffs — the coast of the Japanese sea. Always on the left, over a narrow strip of stony land, or a heaping of dunes, its vast expanse appears, bluewrinkling to that pale horizon beyond which Korea lies, under the same white sun. Sometimes, through sudden gaps in the cliff's verge, there flashes to us the running of the surf . . .'

Sudden gaps . . . flashes. That was Lafcadio at his best. That was Japan. That was what I had felt in the Taroko Gorge.

Sudden gaps, flashes.

The Pacific Ocean was a great open gap, and flashes everywhere. A gap between civilisations, like the other gaps between thought.

Thought and civilisation. And then the gaps where *something else* happens. Not just the opposite of thought and civilisation. No, the *opposite* of thought and civilisation is still bound in with the same logic.

Something else.

Another mind-space.

Prolegomena to Pacific culture . . .

Getting into the flow, penetrating through to the white.

Sunyata.

Sunyata and the sun.

Solar solitude . . .

At Taitung, there was a stop of about twenty minutes. In the tropical silence, only the sound of newspapers being used as fans. Then we made the hop across the southern tip of the island to Kaohsiung.

Kaohsiung, on the banks of the Love River, wide streets, the smell of fish.

14. The Country that does not Exist

Travelling, exposed to the elements, the unexpected and the unknown, stopping over in the temples of ancestors (the first hotels), you have to be careful, you have to take precautions. In the hotels, corpses of women may try to lie with you and suck all the juice out of your body. If you're up in the mountain, a good way to keep off the mountain-monsters, of which there are multitudes, is to stick a piece of bamboo in the fire — they don't like the racket it will make. It's as well, wherever you are, to have a solid hunk of jade in your baggage, it offers good protection; if possible too, wear a necklet of shells. And always carry with you the book called *Shan-hai t'ou* (*Images of the Mountains and Seas*) that gives detailed accounts of the regions you will be passing through and indicates even where you may be likely to meet — oh, marvel! — the Unicorn (*ch'i lin*) or the Phoenix (*fong-hwang*). Watch out for the river where there's an animal that looks like a falcon but with horns and whose call is like the sobbing of a little child. Beware of the mountain that has oxen full of bristles like a porcupine, and of the other where there are beasts with the body of a sheep, the face of a man, the teeth of a tiger, and whose eyes are set under its shoulders. There's an animal too that looks like an ox, but its head is white, with one single eye, and it has a tail like a serpent. A little further to the north you may encounter an animal with a dog's body, a man's face, and that laughs when it sees a human being: *hee haw! hee haw!* And at the source of the Blue River you may see the two daughters of the Great Sky Sovereign concocting storms . . . Don't forget to make sacrifices: a white cock, and some rice, when you're up in the area between Mount Yin and Mount Yen-tse. Do a little dance or two as well, you can never be too sure. With luck, you may find, in the River Kwan, some of the red clay that saves cattle from sickness if you smear it over the hides. And there's a bird on the Yu-ts'e Mountain, if you can get hold of its feathers, wear them in your cap, the lightning won't strike you. Look out for a tree with red berries on Mount Kun-lun, they'll protect you from fire, and if you eat them you'll never drown. Watch and be careful, avoid what is evil and gather in what is good. Keep your eyes open, there are many weird countries in the world, with strange inhabitants. To the East lies the country of men-with-a-hole-in-their-breast, to the North live the men-with-crossed-legs, and in the South, the men-with-no-arse. Keep your distance, watch where you put your feet. There are places where chaos reigns, where everything floats in unfathomable immensity. And at one point or another you may find yourself *lodging in a country that does not exist!*

It's at this point I stop my reading. For if I've been amused by the accounts of uncanny beasties and bogies and demonic spirits, this phrase sends a shiver up my back. This is *real.* This is where the fantastic gives way to the . . . what shall we call it: metaphysical?

Lodging in a country that does not exist . . .

The book I've been reading and from which I've taken the above information I picked up in a second-hand bookstore in Taipei. It's called *Le Voyage dans la Chine Ancienne* (*Travels in Ancient China*), translated into French by Fan Jen from the Chinese of Kiang Chao-yuan, and published in Shanghai in 1937. I put it in my rucksack when I left Taipei, intending to read it somewhere along the way.

Now I'm in Tainan, and I'm reading it in bed in my hotel. Having made up my mind for an early night, I was feeling good lying there in bed with the book and a little bottle of Chinese wine . . .

After wandering round Kaohsiung for a while, I went to the bus-station and took a bus for Tainan, making in it the acquaintance of Liu, who worked, he told me, in a factory of Kaohsiung and was going up to Tainan to say hallo to his brother, an engineer in a motorcycle factory. We talked about Europe, about Taiwan, about his plans to set up an import-export business, and began to strike up a friendship. When we get to Tainan, Liu suggested that I come with him to meet his brother, and that we spend the evening together. His brother, however, turned out that day to be a very busy man, so that he'd hardly said 'hallo' when he disappeared again among his blueprints. But he'd hitched us on to a young man working in the trade division who showed us round the factory.

I find it hard to work up an enthusiasm for machines and motorcycles (2 cycle, 5 speed, piston port, oil injected engine), even ones ridden by bare-thighed girls, ones with which 'you will find a personality, the craving to lead all the way', motorcycles which have gone through 'a series of violent competitions' and come out with the

International Perpetual Trophy — 'just as genuine gold dreads no burning, Phoenix enjoys the thrills of competition and loves the joy of conquest'.

This factory had won production diplomas; they were displayed on the walls, along with moral sentences to keep the workers thinking right: 'Work hard for the company and bring home happiness to the family'.

It was agreed that the young man from the trade division would join us later in town for dinner. In the meantime I had to find lodgings. So Liu and I left in search of a hotel, which we found with no great difficulty, phoned back to the factory to say where we were, and waited for our friend. While we were waiting, Liu gave me demonstrations of slow motion *t'ai chi ch'uan* and the tougher *t'ai chi tao*, which he had learned during his military service. He knew these as gymnastics and fighting technique, but he was aware of a further dimension — he'd heard that someone really into *t'ai chi* could make people recoil off him, feeling his energy radiation . . .

Our friend in the trade division turned up eventually and we went to have dinner. We had a good dinner (the man from the trade division had picked the restaurant, an inconspicuous place, away at the end of an alley, but with a reputation), then walked around the streets together tasting some more little delicacies from street foodstalls, till it was time for Liu to go and get his bus back to Kaohsiung. We said farewell, the three of us, and I came back up to my room. I thought I might go out later and wander some more night streets, but all I did was go round the corner and buy a bottle of wine, and settled in for the night with *Travels in Ancient China*.

The one person who didn't want me, who didn't want me at all, to settle in for the night on my owny-o, was the floor-boy of the hotel. I'd hardly fixed my pillow and opened my book when a head popped round the door (I hadn't locked it, and the bastard hadn't even knocked):

'Goo girl?'

— it was a variation on the 'Lie Miss?', but it came to the same. I said no thanks, I was tired, good night. He suggested I have a little sleep, then he'd wake me up and supply me with a girl — all night: 2400 NT or 60 American dollars; short time, 25. A little irritated by his insistence, I pointed to the door, and said, very distinctly: 'No — goodnight.' He went, and I went back to my book (after getting up to lock the door).

I must have dozed off a little, for I woke to the sound of a key rattling in my lock. For Christ's sake, I thought, what's this? It was our friend again (locked doors were nothing to him — he had his master key), this time with a girl in tow:

'Goo girl!'

he said, pointing to the dumpy, pimpled damsel he had with him, then, seeing I didn't register immediate acquiescence, he added, almost in the same breath:

'20 dollar goo'

— offering me a 5 dollar reduction. I looked at him cold, so my refusal would sink into his hustling skull, then told him in deliberate, well enunciated terms, to take the girl and scram. Which he did. Reluctantly, incredulously.

We can now, after this existential interlude, get back to 'the country that does not exist'. The phrase, I said, had sent a shiver up my spine.

I was thinking of that chapter in the *Chuang tzu* called 'Heaven and Earth':

'Having continued his journey north of the Red River and climbed Mount Kun-lun in order to examine the regions of the south, the Emperor Hwang-ti lost his black pearl. He sent Investigation to look for it, but Investigation could not find it. He sent Discussion, but Discussion met with no more success than Investigation. Finally he sent Abstraction, and Abstraction found it. Is it not strange, said Hwang-ti to himself, that Abstraction should have found it?'

Now what this little allegory is saying is that, if you've lost your essence, or the core of your being, or your principial reality, it is not science (research, investigation of things) that's going to help you to recover it, nor dialectics (philosophy, argumentation), but 'abstraction'. What exactly is abstraction?

The Chinese word in the *Chuang tzu* text is *wang-hiang*, meaning 'that which is without perceptible form'. But in another version of the same allegory (in the *Hwai-nan tzu*) the word used is *hu-huang*, meaning 'vague, impalpable, or a floating state of mind'. It can be used of a forgetful, 'abstracted' person, but it is also the term used in the *Tao-te Ching* to refer to the Tao: 'This is the nature of Tao — it is inconceivable (*huang*) and undetermined (*hu*). Indistinctness (*hu*)! Confusion (*huang*)! In its midst there are forms. Confusion (*huang*)! Indistinctness (*hu*)! In its midst there are beings. Mystery! Obscurity! Within it, there is an essence.'

This essence is the black pearl, and 'abstraction' is the Taoist state of mind (or working of the mind) through which one can 'recover the essence'.

We come back to our *Travels in Ancient China*. We'd interrupted our reading at the point where we'd come to 'places where chaos reigns and everything floats in unfathomable immensity' and to 'a country that does not exist'. The fantastic errancy of the *Travels* leads to the area in which there lies the 'country that does not exist'. This country is the equivalent of the 'black pearl' in the allegory.

It's what I call the 'white world'.

Many names.

One reality.

Beyond the names and forms.

My innermost being lives in a country that does not exist, but is more alive than all the nations, all the institutions, all the constituted forms.

And this 'country' can turn up everywhere and anywhere. So that I am, potentially, everywhere and always 'at home'.

When I was a child I wanted to become 'a foreign correspondent'. I've just taken that ambition about 10,000 miles further out. I'm the correspondent of a country that does not exist, but which is best approached, I think, by a fully explored existence.

You see what I'm getting at?

OK, so I can go to sleep now in peace.

15. Professor Confucius

There are five temples consecrated to Confucius on the island, and the oldest of them is in Tainan. Under the Ching dynasty it was referred to as Taiwan Prefectural College and Institute of Highest Learning.

The morning I went to visit it was a particularly appropriate time to do so, in that the date was September 27th, and September 28th is a national holiday known as the Birthday of Confucius, and also Teachers' Day, Confucius being 'the greatest teacher', 'the master of the ten thousand generations'. On September 28th, ceremonies are held at the Confucian temples: feather dances are performed, archaic musical instruments played to provide ritual music, and the altars are laden with ancient bronze vessels. All this was in preparation. The courtyards were being swept and the ritual vessels washed; the feather dance was being rehearsed; and the musical instruments were being set in place: the stone chimes (*pien-ch'ing*); the bell chimes (*pien-chung*); the great single bell (*po-chung*); the great single chiming stone (*t'e-ch'ing*).

These activities were going on in the central courtyard, the original temple grounds, and in the 'Great Success Hall' where Confucius is enthroned, flanked on either side by his four most distinguished disciples and the twelve sages. But the temple is not restricted to this original centre, there is a whole compound, with walls the colour of dried blood, consisting of pathways, gateways and shrines. The topography is ponderously moral: The Righteous Road; Shrine of Filial Sons; Ethics Hall; Great Achievement Gateway; Shrine of Chaste Women; Gate to Virtue. When one comes to the Shrine of the God of Literature, one can be in little doubt as to what kind of literature is intended.

K'ung Fu Tzu's father having died when he was three years old, he was brought up by his mother. At fifteen, he decided to become a scholar and a cultural reformer. What obsessed him was *li* (ritual, sense of propriety, right behaviour, the order of things, the harmony of the universe) — Confucianism has always been known in China as *li chiao* (training in *li*). And he was concerned with setting up, or preserving, institutions that looked to this *li* as their principle and reflected it in their practice. He was always looking for a state in which he could apply his doctrine, and instaurate a kind of moral politics, with aesthetics to back it up. After obtaining little success in this line, he packed up at sixty-eight and went into retirement. It was then he edited or wrote, according to tradition, the Six Classics: *The Book of Odes (Shih Ching), The Book of Rites (Li Chi), The Book of*

History (Shu Ching), The Annals of Spring and Autumn (Chun Chiu), The Book of Changes (I Ching), The Book of Music (Yueh Ching). The latter text having been lost, the Six Classics became Five. Later two chapters were taken from *The Book of Rites* and became two independent books: *Ta Hsueh (The Great Learning)*, and *Chung Yung (The Golden Mean)*. Then there was the collection of the master's sayings recorded by his disciples: *Lun Yu (The Analects)*. And, finally the *Book of Mencius* (fourth-century spokesman for Confucianism). All these volumes together form the 'Four Books and Five Classics', the Confucian canon — which 'every schoolboy' knows, or used to know.

Like every other doctrine, Confucianism is open to interpretation. The Taiwanese interpretation is heavily ideological. While I was on the island, there was a big meeting of the Confucius-Mencius Society at the Town Hall in Taipei, bringing together 600 members. In the course of the proceedings, a message from President Yen Kia-Kan was read out, exhorting the Society to carry out the instructions of the late President Chiang Kai-Shek concerning the renaissance of Chinese culture, meaning orthodox Confucian culture, and twenty school-teachers were given awards for their essays on Confucius and Mencius.

As to the Communists, the least that can be said is that they don't take Confucius to their hearts. I've got a little collection of anti-Confucius pamphlets published in Peking: 'Confucius, Sage of the Reactionary Classes'; 'Ghost of Confucius, Fond Dream of the New Tsars'; 'Critique of Lin Piao and Confucius' . . . The 'Sage' pamphlet is an attack on Confucianist humanism as the bulwark of a slave-owning State; the 'Ghost' one is a comment on the 'farce of Confucius-worship and opposition to the Legalist School by the Soviet revisionist renegade clique'; while the Critique slams the 'bourgeois careerist, conspirator, double-dealer and traitor, Lin Piao, who was an out-and-out devotee of Confucius'.

The polemics are amusing for a while, but only for a while. Right, left; right, left — it goes on and on. Couldn't we get out of it all, at last? Begin to think in a space with other co-ordinates? It's just possible that, beyond the right-left ping pong, there might be room for a less orthodox Confucius, a Confucius beyond the caricatures, a Confucius no one has ever really used:

K'ung walked
by the dynastic temple
and into the cedar grove
and then out by the lower river
and with him Khieu Tchi
and Tian the low speaking
*and 'we are unknown' said K'ung . . .**

16. The Laughing Buddha

Confucius was trying to set the world right, make it give forth a goodly sound (like a stone chime), instead of the usual cacophony; the Laughing Buddha just laughs outright. For Confucius, or the Confucian pedagogue, life was like a *pensum*, something to be worked at and composed; for the Laughing Buddha, it's an *absurdum*, and it's best to laugh at it, because if you take it too seriously, it's all going to end up in sweat, blood and tears. When things get fouled up, and, Christ knows, they do, everybody thinks now and then of suicide as a solution. Even Confucius must have thought of suicide now and then (a quiet little ceremonious suicide, I mean, let's do things *right*). But Buddhism, as I see it, is a technique of suiciding yourself *while remaining alive*. Confucius stands on ceremony — the Buddha stands on nothing, he not only stands on nothing, he *is* nothing, and being nothing, he is — hah! — something else. Buddha is those leaves swirling in the wind.

I'm in the courtyard of the Laughing Buddha temple in Tainan. The Laughing Buddha is Maitraya (*Mi-Li* in Chinese), 'the Magnanimous One'. He was a Bodhisattva in Sakyamuni's retinue, but is not counted among the ordinary disciples. Sakyamuni came across him in the Tushita heaven and appointed him as his successor, to appear after the lapse of 5000 years. So he is the Buddha-to-come.

You meet him in the first hall of the Buddhist monastaries: fat, hilarious, with breast and belly naked.

* Ezra Pound, *Cantos*.

There he is this morning, with two packets of biscuits laid before him as offering. If I were a one to make offerings, I'd present him with a tin of green peas. Why? Private joke. But I know he'd accept them, laughing. Big belly Buddha, good morning.

It's still early. I'll visit the monastery, and be away on my road before the first cameras arrive.

In the inner courtyard, there's a monk sweeping leaves. He greets me with a monosyllable or two. I bow my head and give a grunt. He gives me another monosyllable, a different one. I give another grunt. I think we both got the message.

Over all, a great silence. Only occasional sounds: chirping of birds, a few monosyllables, the swish of a brush or mop (nuns and monks are at work), water pouring into closed space — it's a nun I'd seen carrying flowers preparing vases at a tap.

Sounds of a drum now, and cymbals. There's a service going on in one of the shrines. Before the altar, the man with the drum, then, slightly in front of him, a line of four nuns (dressed in yellow and black) and a monk (dressed in yellow and red), with cymbals, bells and various percussion instruments. Before them, kneeling, two young men dressed in white shirts and black pants. While the service is being entoned and chanted, there's something else going on at either side: to the left, a nun seated at a table, talking with a client — she also sells trinkets and prayer-books; to the right, also at a table, and totally disinterested in what's going on, a scribe, barefooted, smoking a cigarette, wielding his brush.

I watch the scribe, then I go over to the other table (the woman client's gone — confessed? advised?), and buy a scripture book: *'hen hao'* says the nun, recommending it to me, then she points to the roof and indicates a staircase, suggesting I go see the shrine above. There's a statue of Kwan Yin up there, golden, sitting on lotus flowers, with thirty-six arms and hands holding axe, shell, lotus, beads, ring, mirror, bell, bow, sword etc. On the altar before her are two vases of flowers and two pears.

In the *Surangama Sutra* you read an account of how Kwan Yin, alias Avalokitesvara Bodhisattva (she was male before she was female), achieved Buddhahood:

'In the remotest antiquity, back beyond aeons countless as the grains of sand in the Ganges, I, Avalokitesvara, came into existence in the world. I developed in myself the Bodhi mind and for my entrance into Samadhi I was instructed by the Buddha to practice meditation by means of the sense of hearing. At first I detached my sense organ of hearing from the object of hearing. The aim of this practice is to make the organ of hearing reflect upon itself and hence trace the sensation of sound through abstract meditation. Then all external sounds were inaudible to me, and I cut myself off from the disturbances of the experienced world. However, the sensation of stillness is itself a barrier to the achievement of perfect peace of mind, because both disturbance and stillness are mental experiences relative to each other. I therefore kept on practising meditation until both disturbance and stillness ceased to exist. But the awareness of void is also a barrier, so I continued my meditation until the awareness of the experiencer and the experienced was eliminated. Beyond subject and object, beyond creation and annihilation, I took a sudden leap into the great brightness.'

That is the real meaning of Kwan Yin. But of those who worship her, few actually try to practise the meditation through which she achieved Buddhahood. They are content to worship her, and ask her compassion.

Suddenly a bird came in the open window, flew about the room for a while, then made out again into the sunlight.

I did the same.

There's a meditation hall in the temple compound. Outside it, a series of little paintings daubed in blue and white: a snowy mountain in cloud, a lake with boats, a road with pine trees, a waterfall. No Kwan Yin there, no Laughing Buddha either (Buddha isn't coming, he's already there, everything's already there), just natural phenomena. That's more like it.

My last visit (with a look at the cells in passing: a shelf for books, raised dais for sleeping and meditation and study) was to the temple shop. The nun in charge there, wearing a washed out fawn suit with black bands under the knees, shaven headed, with a lovely smile, was sitting over by the window with a tape-recorder, going through a language lesson. When I appeared, she came over to me, said 'English', and made a negative gesture. I pointed to a tin of guava juice. She drew out a seat for me at the table in the middle of the room and said 'stand please'.

After drinking, I went back to the outer yard again, where I sat under a banyan tree (I was really in no hurry, and the morning was beautiful), accompanied by the smell of burning leaves. A little meditation on smell?

'When our mind clings to neither good nor evil,' said Hui Neng, 'we should take care not to let it dwell upon vacuity or remain in a state of inertia. Rather should we enlarge our study and broaden our knowledge, so that we can know our own mind, be congenial to others in our dealings with them, get rid of the idea of "self" and "being". In this way we shall come to "true nature" and enlightenment, breathing the incense of knowledge that fumigates from within.'

It's all in the smell of burning leaves.

17. Tainan to Chiayi

On the road again.

Leavetaking first of all from my Tainan hotel. There was another floor-boy, younger, quieter, less of a hustler. Not that he was forgetting business either, but he operated in a less unobtrusive way. The conversation went like this:

'You leave?

— Yes.

— Where?

— Chiayi.

— You speak Chinese?

— No.

— How you say Chiayi so?

— I pick up things here and there.

— Leave now?

— Yes.

— Girl?

— No time.'

After the hotel, I made for a bank to cash a traveller's cheque. It was in there I saw the pearl of Tainan. Aī, aī, aī! Small breasts and broad hips (but not too broad), in jeans. Parents on hand, father banking fistfuls of notes. Out they go, and are gone, and I'm still there with my traveller's cheque. Oh, the hardships of travel, oh, the inaccessibilities, oh, the distances!

There were no seats on the 12.23 for Chiayi. I took a ticket for the train at 13.00, and went into the station restaurant to drink some tea.

I think I said it before, I love those Taiwan trains. Darkblue seats in this one, darkblue seats that recline. I give the price, for financial experts and sociologists of the 23rd century: 68 dollars (NT) and 50 cents.

I hit Chiayi about two o'clock.

Wander the streets, till I come across a Travel Service, and go in to enquire about possibilities in the region. I'm interested in Alishan and Kwantzuling.

I spend about an hour in there, covering (owing to linguistic difficulties) innumerable sheets of notepaper with drawings and diagrams. We have a good time, the four of us, me, a girl, and two young men.

At the end, once it's decided I'm going to spend the night up at Kwantzuling, one of the young men offers to show me around Chiayi on his scooter.

So we do a quick tour of Chiayi, ending up at the Sun Yat Sen Park. Up there we meet another chap, from Taipei, in Chiayi to visit his brother's tomb. He suggests we spend the evening together. When he learns I'm going up to Kwantzuling he says I'm crazy (he speaks good English, with an American accent), I should stay in town. But although I like my two new friends, I know I'm going to Kwantzuling. So we go and have a drink together, and exchange addresses. The man from Taipei says to look him up there when I get back. I say I will, and I did. In the meantime, I scoot down to the bus-station with my Chiayi friend, and get on the bus for Kwantzuling.

Kwantzuling is a village in the mountains . . .

18. At Kwantzuling

The bus is climbing up through the green bamboo, past rice

plantations and lotus ponds, in the light of late afternoon. A college boy beside me is reading a book on engineering. Two phrases in English stand out from the Chinese text: 'common magnetic core' and 'mutual flux'. They seem to be speaking for me. They leap out of the pages of that engineering textbook into my own thought.

Thoughts in an omnibus . . . But the eye rests lovingly all the while on green bamboo, rice paddies and lotus ponds — and the profile of the schoolgirl (sixteen, seventeen years old?) a few seats away.

Kwantzuling is indubitably Japanese. A huddle of houses and inns gathered together around hot springs, it's pure Japan: the situation, the style of the houses, the whole atmosphere. It's the kind of place described in the novels, say, of Kawabata. The mountain spa. This Japanese feeling was strong in me as soon as I saw Kwantzuling — I didn't know then I'd be sleeping that night in a Japanese-style inn, on a tatami. I thought I was going to be sleeping in a temple up in the hills.

But before we go further on the erratic road, here's a little presentation of Kwantzuling from the back of a postcard:

'Kwang-tze-ling hot spring locates at 21 kylometer east of Hsin-lug. It is on 270 meter of sea level and surrounded by Mt Pillow, Mt Tiger Head and Mt Eagle. Because the Hot Spring is rich in healthy essense and beautiful surroundings, it is usually called the first hot-spring in Taiwan.'

I wanted to get up to Da-sien Buddhist temple before nightfall. I knew there was a temple up there in the hills, but I didn't know exactly how far away, nor the condition of the road. Anyway, the first thing was to find a car for hire. That was easy enough, I mean to find the car. To discuss the terms of the hire, with my infinitesimal fraction of Chinese and a man who spoke not a word, not a syllable of English, but spoke fluent and voluble Taiwanese while crimsonly chewing betel, wasn't so easy. Pretty soon we had a crowd around us, the whole street was participating in the discussion, but we still weren't getting anywhere — until a little lisping schoolgirl-interpreter turned up and bashfully, encouraged by the crowd, helped us to get things straightened out.

We were off.

Now if I thought the Taroko drive was wild, it was gilt-edged security compared to this. And Lou of Hualien in his Yue Loong was a Rolls Royce chauffeur from Kensington compared with the betel-chewing, bullet-headed maniac that was on the job this night. The road could never have been good at the best of times, but now that the typhoon had passed that way it was bloody murder. It was mud, mud, mud, with ruts in it like trenches, so that the car swished and swivelled and skidded, then got stuck and had to snort with all its engine power, spurting arches of mud, till it got out again, which it would do lurchingly, drunkenly, and suicidally, because there was a sheer precipice gaping there at the right-hand side. But that maniac at the wheel was laughing his head off, his mouth getting crimsoner and crimsoner, chewing on his betel as if his life depended on it, and maybe it did — and mine with it.

I had a phrase of Confucius in my head: 'Even by-ways are worth exploring, but if we go too far we may get bogged down.' I was beginning to think that this time I'd really gone too far.

But we made it.

There was the temple.

Before going to walk around it, I arranged with the driver to go back with him that very evening. I'd given up my original idea to sleep at the temple, I couldn't ask him to come back up that road at five o'clock the next morning, which is the time I would need to be leaving, for I had a date with another mountain on the following day (had already booked on the train) — I couldn't ask him, both for moral and linguistic reasons, and even if I had been able to ask him, maybe he wouldn't have accepted anyway. There was a whole lot of reasoning and explanation going on in my head, but it was translated, as you can imagine, in the most succinct terms. Seven gestures, and we were all agreed.

Maybe the motion and emotion of the journey had something to do with it, by contrast, but the whole setting up there at Da-sien temple seemed extraordinarily beautiful and peaceful. Evening mist, green bamboo, a big red sun . . .

In the temple, my eyes met those of an old man, and they stayed met a long time. There was also a young nun — I felt her looking at me, but when I turned round, she turned away. And there was a young monk, alone in a room, lost to the world.

With a last long look at the hill peak rising behind the temple, I got back into the car.

Darkness had fallen and at one point on the road back we saw a pillar of fire rising into the air. The driver, eager for me to see it from closer at hand, stopped the car and we got out. It was a hot sulphur spring — 'the hole of fire and water' — a strange phenomenon and therefore to be worshipped: before it stood vases of flowers and a holder for incense sticks. We admired it for a while, then, noticing that one of the shacks at the spot sold drinks, I suggested a beer. We sat down on a bench, and a young girl took the order. When she came back with the beers, she started up a little conversation:

'I no English,' she said, 'No China?'

I shrugged apologetically.

There were two or three kids dancing about the yard. She pointed to them, laughing.

'Beautiful,' I said.

'No,' she said, 'China no beautiful. You beautiful.'

Back down in Kwantzuling, things had changed. On the way up, apart from the little crowd round the car, I'd had the impression of a sleepy little village steeped in sulphur. It was still steeped in sulphur — seemed maybe even more so, in the darkness, and in the smir of a warm rain that had started — but it was no longer sleepy. The narrow streets were crowded, and buses seemed to be arriving all the time. The spa has a reputation, and this was a national holiday.

The result, so far as I was concerned, was that there was no room at the inn. I went from one hotel to the other, and got no's, sometimes not too amiable, all the time. I'd practically given up and had resigned myself to spending the night under a porch or something (I'd stay as long as I could in a restaurant, then find myself a shelter), when a young man invited me to share his room. He was one of a party of 200 from Kaohsiung — a trip organised by a co-operative society, or a bank, or maybe a cooperative society bank, it wasn't too clear to me when we talked about it later. Part of the group, mainly younger people, were living at a Japanese-style inn: bare room, with tatami on the floor, and pillows and quilts in a cupboard.

After enjoying a sulphur bath, 'Mr Ken' squatted down on the tatami with six or seven of these young people from Kaohsuing and we had a talkfest.

One little fellow, in junior high school at Kaohsuing — he spoke very little, but would intersperse the conversation every now and then with a delighted '1, 2, 3 — *hao*!' — wanted to know (he made gestures to indicate that I was 'strong') if I was a boxer. A waiter, I remembered, in Hong Kong had been convinced I was a football player . . .

One chap wanted to know if I was 'a boss'. I tried to explain that to be 'a boss', to be at the top, you've got to accept a system and work in it, work up it, whereas I didn't, I didn't accept any system, so I couldn't be 'a boss', I didn't want to be 'a boss'.

The one who did the most talking, because he had the most fluent English, was an engineering student. Like the art student in Taipei, what was uppermost in his mind when he thought of the West was the sex-question: 'Sex free in Europe — I admire;' 'Mr Ken, Chinese girl virgin before marriage.' But, unlike the art student, who wasn't that much concerned with 'politics', Shu, the engineering student of Kaohsiung, was full of ideology. Maybe all the more so because he was about to leave on military service: 'Mr Ken, must do military service, it is our duty.' Shu was a convinced Chiang Kai-Shekist: 'Mr Ken, when Chiang Kai-Shek dead, all Taiwan sad,' and he was equally convinced that, not only was it the mission of the Nationalist Republic to reconquer mainland China, but that it could be done: 'In Red China, 70 billion people, 70 billion hearts. In Taiwan, all one heart.' Listening to him talk this way, I had the same sensation as I had when talking with little Jane of Taipei.

It was time to sleep.

I set my travelling timepiece for 5 o'clock.

At 5.15 the next morning, I moved out of the inn, having folded up my quilt and left a 'thank you' note on top. It was still dark as I stood at the end of the bridge waiting for the bus to Chiayi. An old man, who maybe couldn't sleep, was standing there too, just listening maybe to the river. He offered me a cigarette, and began to speak to me in Chinese. Out of necessity, my Chinese was improving, so I was able to tell him I was from Scotland, did not speak Chinese, and thanked him very much. He seemed pleased, and let go another flood of Chinese at me. But I'd exhausted my stock. All I could do was shake him by the hand. Normally I don't smoke, but I was glad I had accepted his cigarette.

19. In the Misty Forest

Alishan!

Alishan is part of the great North-South Central Mountain Range, forty-five miles due East of Chiayi. To get up there you have to take a narrow-gauge mountain train operated by the Forestry Commission.

I'm standing on the station platform at Chiayi, waiting for the little red single-track train to pull in, when two good-looking stalwart young men appear. One is wearing a bright-coloured headband, the other a skullcap with two long feathers. Fellows out on a fancy-dress spree, or native Taiwanese asserting their ethnic differences? I think the latter, because they don't look exactly Chinese. I give them a smile of recognition and appreciation, they give me a reciprocal sign back. But I don't want to get into conversation. I want to make this trip alone.

We move out. The engine doesn't pull, it shoves. It pushes its way redly through the lush green tropical forest, a forest that, as we climb, is going to move in type from tropical to sub-tropical, and from sub-tropical to temperate. We go slow — so slow at times that you can put your hand out the window and touch leaves as you pass. The plant-life is beautiful. One plant particularly catches my attention, with the sun shining through its beetroot-red heavy-veined leaves.

At one time you'd have the forest on your left and, on the right, hills floating in mist, at another time it'd be the reverse.

Little stations all along the way: Jang Lao Niao, Dwu Lih Shan, Li Yuan Liau, Jiau Lih Pyng, Fenn Chii Hwu, Duo Lin, Shyr Tyzh Luh, Dih I Fen Daw, Ell Wann Pyng . . .

Now we're really high. The world — the 'red dust' as the Tao-Buddhist phrase puts it — lost away down there in the mist. All that remains is the mountain.

At Alishan, I wandered down the village street: a lot of furs for sale, and walking sticks with handles in the shape of a bird. At the end of the street, there was the forest. I'd thought of visiting the Forestry Museum in order to learn more about the trees, their names, types and pedigrees, but now I decided just to stay with them in the mist.

You can learn from a museum. What can you learn from the mist? *Koan*.

I'd hardly taken a few paces into the forest when a cock crew from the village:

Cold mountain village —
the cry of a cock
among the cryptomeria

I spent three hours in there:

In the forest darkness
the sound of a mountain stream
deepens my loneliness . . .

20. *Alone with the Sun and the Moon*

Back to Chiayi. Late afternoon. And I make for another station. A bus-station this time. Waiting for the bus to Taichung. Here it comes, and we're rolling . . .

I must have dozed off. When I woke, it was to the intense green of rice paddies and a huge cherry-red sun.

Then night came down — greengold, dark orange, dark.

Rolling through the night toward Taichung. Passing through small towns. All the industrious work-booths open to the street. Lights, hoardings, noises. Then only the dark rolling road again.

Till Taichung, where I took a room in the first hotel I saw.

Next morning it was south-east out of Taichung and up into the mountains: sugarloaf hills; tobacco; pineapple; lemon trees; banana palms; a green-flowing river. Then the fir belt.

Sun Moon lake is about two bus hours from Taichung and lies at 2500 feet above sea-level. Rocks rise high all around it. Along its shore are scattered temples and aboriginal settlements.

It gets its name from an old legend according to which a dragon held the sun and the moon captive in its waters.

Hiring a rowing boat, I rowed out to a little island in the middle of the lake. An old woman was selling food there: cakes and sweets and boiled eggs. I bought some cakes in case I was hungry later on, then rowed away to an open expanse of water, shipped the oars, and let the boat drift.

That was the beginning of a mytho-cosmological afternoon.

According to the sun-myth current in these parts — by 'these parts' I mean Indonesia, South-East Asia — in the beginning there were several suns, too many in too low a sky, for with so many suns in a sky that was too low there was eternal daylight, and with their heat they scorched the earth. Someone had to go and eliminate the superfluous suns, raise the sky. The Atayal tell the story of how it was done:

A young boy and a young girl, about sixteen years old, decided to undertake the task. So they started out on their journey to the sun, scattering orange seeds as they went so as to be able to find their way back. The journey was long. Before they reached the suns, they had time to have two children, and the children had time to grow, and the original couple had time to grow old. But they did come at last to the suns, and the man shot at them with arrows, killing some, wounding one (it paled and became the moon, its blood falling in drops being the stars), leaving one intact. The archer was burned to death himself in the process. The three survivors, with the cosmic task accomplished (the arrow shooting had also raised the sky), retraced their steps, following the orange seed trail, but the old woman died on the way, and the young children had time to grow old. When the second couple got down to earth at last, they explained how the sky-changes had come about, and after initial incredulity the people worshipped them, considering them as gods.

OK, it's just a story.

But Sun Moon Lake is the very heart and nombril of Taiwan.

Which is why I plunged into the water, as a kind of baptism.

And swam around there.

Alone with the Sun and the Moon . . .

Back down in Taichung, I learned that all the trains to Taipei were fully booked. So I went to the bus-station. There was a seat available in the 3.30, but it was a bus without air-conditioning. At 4.10 there was an air-conditioned bus, but the only seat available was at the back. Finally, at 6.10, I would have a good seat in an air-conditioned bus. If I'd been in a hurry, I'd have taken the 3.30 and no questions. But not only was I not in a hurry, I was loathe to leave — glad to find excuses to hang about a bit.

Browsing in a bookshop, I came across a *Selection of English Prose* published by the Students' English Digest Association of Taipei and with it made for a coffee-shop where, ensconced at a corner table (rain was falling at the window), I read Hazlitt, Thoreau, Fitzgerald, quietly absorbed, my eyes maybe resting now and then on the rainy window.

When it came time to leave, there was a song on the record-player: 'He's got a ticket to ride an' he don't care.'

21. Taipei City Revisited

On my return to Taipei, with finances very low, my first job was to find a cheap hotel. But since I knew the city better by now, this was not too difficult. The one I finally picked on was a poky little place downtown.

Directly after breakfast I phoned the man I'd met in Chiayi. Or at least I tried to phone him, but what I got on the other end of the line was the Taiwan Navy. When I asked them if they knew a man by the name of — and here I read the name on the slip of paper I had — they said to hold on and they'd check. They did. Yes, they knew a man by that name, a retired admiral of the fleet. I said that wasn't my man.

Now, in addition to his phone number, Jason (that was the English name he chose to be known by) had given me his address. It only remained for me to go straight to the address. That should have been easy. It wasn't.

Jason lived in Panchow, away out all to hell in the suburbs of Taipei, and once we got out there the taxi-man was every bit as lost as I was. The car weaved its way from street into lane into alley, among fish, bananas, papayas, babies, *pomelas*, mangos, eggs, and the rest, with the taxi-man asking his way, in a kind of humourous despair, at every turn. There are God knows how many million people in Taipei, from all over China — Honan, Szechuan, Hupei, Fukien — and the town has grown cancerously, labyrinth within labyrinth, so that finding a needle in a haystack sounds like a problem of classical simplicity compared with the baroque task of finding one single separate person amid all these daedalian dens.

All glory to the Taipei taxi-man, he made it. Still not quite believing it himself, he rang the door bell for me, intending to check. It was a young woman came to the door — she turned out to be Jason's wife.

We still had a little linguistic problem, but that was nothing, and she asked me up to the apartment while she phoned her husband. Up there, I found a child and a grandmother. I paid my respects to the grandmother, and, like any male introduced into a Chinese family, immediately became the kid's 'uncle' (*ssu-ssu*).

Now it turned out that the phone number I had on the slip was good: Jason was a navy lieutenant. Where things went wrong must have been my pronunciation of the Chinese name, although, aware of the danger, I'd got him to pronounce it in Chiayi and had thought I remembered it. But apparently I hadn't. Anyway I had him on the phone now.

He suggested we meet at the Grand Hotel and have lunch together. Thinking of my finances, I said I hoped he didn't intend we lunch at the Grand Hotel, but he reassured me we wouldn't stay at the Grand, it was just a convenient place to meet.

It's true that in Taipei, you just can't miss the Grand Hotel. It's a great splendiferous palatial crimson-and-golden turd crawling with fat-arsed moneyed maggots from all corners of the globe. It is No. 1 on the Oriental Revelation Tour organised by the Meet-the-World Club of Sydney, Australia. It's a grandiose eyesore, a colossal dollar-catcher, and an ornate cavern of yawning you-asked-for-it boredom.

We met there, and beat it. To the naval base, where we had lunch in the canteen.

Lieutenant in the Taiwan Navy though he was, Jason was a quiet, intelligent, sensitive fellow who took ideology for what it was (he'd spent four hours that morning — it was 'political day' — discussing the texts of Chiang and Sun Yat Sen), and wasn't too happy about his situation. Sure, he had his ideas. He didn't want to live under

Communism — his people had come over from Szechuan in 1945 — but he wasn't an all-out military and militant Nationalist either. In fact he was going to retire from the navy in about three years' time and go into business. Not that he thought that Red China was invincible on the military plane, or even homogeneous on the social plane: 'Can have many arms, much money, if the people do not love you, you can do nothing', he just wanted to try and live a different life. He wanted to know how I lived. He was curious about life, felt he didn't know enough. Was it true that hippies ate insects? He'd seen that in a film.

After the meal, he said he wouldn't be off duty for a few hours yet, but he proposed that we get together later that evening and take a look at Taipei City. For the moment he'd try to get a jeep to drive me to wherever I wanted to go.

That's how I made my second visit to the National Museum in a jeep belonging to the Taiwan Navy . . .

We met that evening in the hall of one of the main downtown hotels, and made straight for Wanhwa, the old riverside district I've talked about already. Jason's first consideration was food. He was anxious that I should not be hungry and took some convincing that I wasn't hungry at all — even then he insisted that I have something to eat (he'd eaten an afternoon snack himself), and lead the way to a food-shop where we ate two bowls of black sesame paste (*tsze mahu*). In fact it was just a beginning. We were to go from snack to snack and from drink to drink the whole evening through. In addition to satisfying hunger and thirst, Jason was eager for me to feel that I had well and truly absorbed and imbibed Taipei.

Over the sesame paste, which was delicious, he told me that once he'd been to Hawaii for a week, but (ruefully, laughingly), he'd never got any further than Waikiki beach. He was afraid of getting lost, because he didn't have a map like mine. He was alluding to my much-marked vade-mecum which he'd already admired in Chiayi. I brought it out, even more marked than when he'd seen it last — covered with circles, squares, triangles, arrows, remarks and notes, itineraries, orientations. He said he'd been trained in navigation and liked it, but that map of mine bamboozled him. Had I had a good time at Kwantzuling?

We had a good time in Wanhwa, eating and drinking, going from booth to booth, enjoying the sights.

When we finally parted company, he said he'd try to come and see me off at the airport next day. And he was there, on time, with a little present wrapped in red paper. He said he hoped that the plane wouldn't come, that he would miss me, that if I ever came back to Taiwan I could live at his home . . .

The plane was announced.

BANGKOK METROPOLIS

'This is my estate,' said Mara. 'These are my pleasure-groves, my jungles of lust, my pond of indulgence and my rivers of passion. — 'Evil One' said Maracarya-visaya-vimala, 'you should offer this residence of yours to the Tathagata for his use.'

Surangama sutra

1. City of Angels

It's a long time since Bangkok was 'hog plum district' and a fishing village on the left bank of the Chao Phya. Owing to its convenience as a stopping-place and storage-place between Ayudhya and the sea, and the digging of a new channel in the 16th century, it had increased in importance and grown into a flourishing trade centre. When Rama I, feeling cramped and ill-at-ease in Thon Buri, just across the river, and wishing to make a fresh start for the nation, decided to transfer his capital to Bangkok, it was ripe for metropolitan status. The Grand Palace was built on what had been Bangkok's Chinatown (which re-assembled three kilometres south, at Sampeng) and around the Grand Palace and the Temple of the Emerald Buddha that stands within its compound, Bangkok entered on a new phase of its existence as Krung-tep, the City of Angels, its full name being Krungtep Maha Nakor Amorn Ratanakosindra Mahindrayudhya Mahadilokpop Noparatana Rajdhani Burinom Udour Rajnivet Mahastan Amorn Pimarn Avatarn Satit Sakkututtiya Vishnukarm Prasit — i.e. (roughly) City of Angels — Great City — Emerald Buddha Residence — Strong City of Indra — Grand World Capital with Nine Precious Gems — City of Bliss — City of Royal Palaces like the Heavenly Realm of the Reincarnated God — City given by Indra, built by Vishnukarm . . . That was in the year 1785.

One hundred and ninety years later (Buddhist Era 2519), it comes across as an exotic wasteland, a polluted paradise, a putrifying swamp (with lotuses growing here and there). I think of it in terms of the Chinese-Buddhist underworld, say that Taoist-inspired Sixth Court that 'welcomes', for torture in its hell (the hell where you're soaked in a dung pit; the hell where you're gnawed by rats; the hell where fire is shoved into your mouth, etc.), those who have offended against the Tao by miscalling and mistreating the elements, shitting in the face of the Great Bear or emptying their slop-water in the rays of the Sun or Moon . . .

Every place, every situation, is a kind of test, a kind of challenge. Every locality contains the four realms of existence as seen by Buddhism: the realm of punishment, the realm of sensual bliss, the realm of form and the realm of formlessness. The thing is to go through them all, till you maybe definitively reach the cool space, the no-place. That is my approach to Bangkok.

Bangkok:

Shuddering, fuming, traffic blocks; on the pavements, women and girls making garlands of flowers; monks walking about like two-legged sunsets; just beyond the traffic noise, in a temple compound, bodhi-bells tinkling in the wind; ten million coconuts being unloaded at a jetty; the sizzling sound of cooking; film posters — explosions, tortures, spasms; 'Can I help you, Sir — massage?'; a betel-chewer showing her crimson gub; market place — cocks fighting, kites flying, and fish in jars like little dreams; girls like flowers; taxi-drivers hunched in the corner of their seat, raising their hands to their forehead when they pass a temple; the *morbido* taste of *lamud*, the sweet milk of a coconut, cool slices of papaya and salted pineapple; five junks in a string down from the North with teak; waterbuses skimming up and down the river, wasting no time at the piers; scented star jasmine, the yellow flower *champa* . . .

First impressions, first emotions.

First encounter:

It was in Suriwongse Road. I was standing at the kerb, waiting to cross, when I saw her (or maybe it was a transvestite) out of the corner of my eye: a hideous zombie of the streets, painted like hell, a mask of paste thick and lurid on her face. I let her come up to me and make her spiel:

'Hello, you come with me? My name is Angela. I am from Lao. Vietnamese. I been to Sikako and Flankfoo. I have apartment and sister. You come with me? You come to massage, fuck, make looove. Bangkok No. 1. You No. 1.'

A daughter of Mara.

2. *Dawn*

Do you know Shankara's morning meditation? It goes like this:

'At dawn I evoke the essence of the Shining Self, eternal, felicitous conscience, the aim of the Supreme Swans, the *paramahamsa*. I am that being, the *brahman*, which looks from afar on the states of dream and waking. I am indivisible, I am no mere ego-function. I am far from family concerns and wordly considerations. I am the Eternal Witness, the Inner Self, the Happy and Radiant One — *Shivo'ham*!'

This was composed about the year 800 in India, by the man who, having learned a few things from Buddhism, was out to renew the Hindu-Vedic tradition. I'm reciting it this morning in Thailand, with a certain amount of fellow-feeling, but at the same time a sceptical smile at its grandiloquence and all-too-transcendental tone. He doth protest too much, one might almost suspect that he is trying to convince himself.

It's 5.30. Although I stayed up late last night, engaged in learning some Thai, I'm up this morning with the monks, intending to get into Bangkok life right from the start.

'Monks, there are trees, there are solitudes, go and meditate' — so spoke the Buddha, as we read in the *Majjhima Vikaya*. Without making it a *sine qua non*, for in some ways his was an accommodating mind, recognising that some people would get on better with roof, walls, and a few rules to follow (eventually two hundred odd, if I remember rightly), Buddha favoured the homeless life, and for early Buddhism there were nine recommended places for meditation: a forest, the roots of a tree, a mountain, a hillside, a cave, a cemetery, the depths of the jungle, the open air, a heap of straw. Buddha himself achieved illumination in the roots of a tree, which is why in most temple grounds you will see, ensconced in a banyan, the wooden figure of a bodhisattva, worn by the elements, with a scrap of yellow cloth across his naked body.

The nine far out places were the best, but they were also the most dangerous, for, if they were free of the hindrances and the impediments to meditation which go with crowded social residence, they might have their own nuisances, in the shape, for example, of mosquitos, snakes, and inclement weather. Which is another reason why monasteries came into being. But even if he felt the need of a monastery, the judicious meditator would be careful in his choice. He would avoid too new ones, where there was work to be done; too old ones, needing repairs; ones with too big a reputation, too much in the public eye. A good place would be quiet, offer a kind of collective solitude, and a minimum of hindrances in the shape of things-to-be-done-for-mere-upkeep; and also, important point, be near a convenient alms-place.

There's a convenient alms-place close to where I'm staying: the market. That's where I'm making for, this chilly morning.

It's still dark, but there's a big golden-hazy moon in the sky, and somewhere a cock is crowing. A man in shorts and singlet, with a balaclava over his head, out for exercise before the air's become too polluted, jogs by on the opposite pavement, peching clouds of breath.

Things are already well underway at the market. There aren't many customers yet, but the vendors are all in place with their produce: a woman piling up pineapples, another slicing coconuts; a man sifting soya shoots, another cleaning a hog's head; at the meat section, the stone floor is running with blood, and at the fish stall I see a restless little fish wriggle off its slab and flip-flap its way along a drier and drier path . . . It occurs to me that's how we all started. I mean Ancestor Fish, the fishy creature that one day, some time back, found itself stranded on the sands when the tide went out or, who knows, simply took it into its head one fine morning to try dry land for a change. And found the going tough, and decided it had to develop limbs, and then to specialise its limbs, and, and, and (that's short for progress — drier and drier all the time). He probably regretted it more than once and in fact, at the basis of his developing psychology, there was probably that one big regret: of having left his fishy element in the first place. Which is why we've all been looking for our element ever since . . . It's this conscience that the real problem of man is that of being a fish-out-of-water that you find in the East. The West tends to have a shorter memory, and to get worked up about secondary and absurd issues, like how a lot of half-dead fish are going to be able to live together and get to heaven. The East, the old East, is concerned about how to get back to the ocean, or at least to find some substitute for it: cosmic consciousness, nirvana.

The sky is breaking with dawn, and suddenly it's sun-up. It's at this moment that the alms-seeking monks begin to appear, coming along the pavement singly, in a long scattered line, out from the nearby monastery. In his *Pilgrimage* ('printed by William Stansby for Henry Fetherstone and sold at his shop at Paul's church-yard at the sign of the rose', London, 1617), Samuel Purchas describes the scene as follows:

'They have amongst them many Religious Men, which leade an austere life, and therefore had in great reputation of Holinesse. These live in common: they may not marrie, nor speake to a Woman, they goe alway bare-foot, in poore array, eating nothing but Rice and greene herbes, which they begge from dore to dore. They crave it not, nor take it with their hands, but goe with a wallet at their backes alwayes, with their eyes modestly fixed on the ground, and calling or knocking, stand still, till they receive answere, or some thing be put in their wallets.'

Little or nothing has changed since his day. The same figures with the same shaven pates, wearing the same yellow-dyed cloth, passed by in 1610, in 1240, in 963 . . . The monk is timeless, outside history, representing the will to transcend change and the suffering that change entails. As such he is holy, sacred (*phra*) — respected as such by those householders, those market-vendors whose life, they know themselves, is incompatible with the Way, and for whom nirvana is out of the question. All they can hope for, apart from very rare exceptions (see the *Questions of King Milinda* where there is a grudging acceptance that a layman *may* obtain nirvana, but, even then, only if he has lived the monastic-meditative life in a previous existence), is to acquire merit by helping those for whom *nirvana* is the be-all and end-all.

If the householder's life is incompatible with the Way, what is conducive to it is an austere existence, unencumbered by possessions, family or institutional concerns, wordly considerations.

The monk has three robes, an upper robe, a lower robe, and one for ceremonial purposes. Of other possessions, he will have a begging bowl, a bed covering, a towel, a cloth shoulder bag, a cloth for straining water, and bandages — with, in addition, if he finds them useful as an aid to meditation (for there is no accent on austerity, asceticism *per se*), a pillow, a mosquito-net, an umbrella, a teapot. Among the austerity practices recommended, but not enforced (that of wearing clothes made of rags for example, is not compulsory, and is generally avoided, as indicating perhaps a tendency to morbid asceticism), the two which concern us here this morning are that food shall be obtained by begging (*pindapatikanga*), and that eating shall be done out of one bowl (*pattapindikanga*).

So the monks, those 'so-called selves' (*atmabhava*), as they refer to themselves, pass along the pavement, receiving offerings of food, lifting the lid of their bowl for the householder to pour in the rice, and the vegetables, and the fruit fresh and dried, with a flower, a stick of incense, and a candle, for later Buddha worship (the flower for fragrance, the candle for light, the incense for purification). Most women bow before them, even kneel; most of the men are content with a salutation of the head. The attitude of the monks themselves is one of stolid indifference. They must show no interest in what is offered, accepting the food as a patient might accept medicine, considering it only as a means of ending discomfort, a factor of bodily strength and mental serenity. Later they will eat it with restraint and moderation ('when he has eaten enough, and could still eat four or five morsels, let him drink water'), once, just after returning from the alms-seeking, twice (and last), about half past eleven. If by any chance any one of them receives no alm, he will not eat that day. It is, apparently, an excellent diet and regimen, as most of the monks look remarkably fit and healthy.

What is going on in the minds of these 'so-called selves'? Who knows, but according to the prescriptions, they should be using this 'divine moment' (*brahma-muhurta*) of dawn, particularly (along with high noon and evening) auspicious and appropriate (it was at dawn that the Buddha reached enlightenment), to further their meditation-practice. 'Monks, you should train yourselves to be vigilant, purify your mind from hindrances, either sitting or walking.' This is *jagariyanuyoga*.

At this place and time, the *bhikshu* may be meditating on the loathsomeness of food, repeating to himself the word *patikulam*, *patikulam* (loathsome), reflecting on the inconvenience of having to look for food, the repulsive sights you must pass in doing so, and on the transformation food undergoes in the body: mixed with saliva, chewed into a colourless mess, being worked over by other secretions, giving rise to gases, turning into piss and shit. This meditation will give him not only mastery over food, but over the senses, and the passions, help him to realise the transient nature of phenomenal existence. Or else he may meditate on the notion of element, saying to himself that his robes, his bowl are only made up of elements, mere aggregates, devoid of form, ultimately empty, like all they contain. Or else he may reflect on the body: I must grow old, I must suffer pain, I must die, I am transitory, I have no self, nothing is mine, nothing is I. Or else he may do a breathing exercise, thinking as he breathes out (into the emptiness): 'I meditate the Dharma', and as he breathes in (receiving existence): 'that is without lust'.

I was moving away from the market when a young monk stopped beside me as I waited at the kerb:

'Excuse me, sir. How are you? Very cold this morning. Excuse me, sir, where is your home?'
— but before I had a chance to reply, the traffic had cleared and he was off across the street, saying 'OK, OK', and maybe feeling that he had run the risk of jeopardising his prescribed attitude of aloof indifference.

3. Patriarchs and Prostitutes

There was a flurry, and in ancient blackness came up out of the ooze: the antediluvian head of a turtle . . .

I was in the temple compound of Wat Benchamabopit, standing on one of the little bridges over the canal that runs through it. Wat Bencha is not the oldest temple in Bangkok, but it is where the patriarch of all Thailand lives, and it boasts a whole line of Buddhas — Buddha in all his postures: calming the ocean, telling people not to fight, teaching, walking, meditating, blessing, subduing Mara. I'd gone along the line, but the Buddha that attracted me most was not in that line, it was elsewhere, on its own, stuck all over with tabs of gold foil, and those bits of gold foil flickering in the breeze, so that the Buddha looked there like a bird with ruffled feathers, a golden bird-thing with feathers atremble, and all the more fascinating because of his departure from the human.

The golden Buddha, and now the black turtle . . . The waters had closed up again, I had no idea how often the old black monsters broke that polluted silence, waited for a while in expectation of a reappearance, then, having seen none, walked a little further up the canal to a bench at the foot of a tree.

I sat there, watching the sun shimmering through the tree branches, then closing my eyes and just enjoying the feel of the sun on my skin.

'Plenitude is this, plenitude is that. From plenitude comes plenitude. When you take plenitude from plenitude, what remains is plenitude.'

I probably hadn't been sitting there long when I felt a touch on my shoulder. It was a young boy — no, a young girl, selling peanuts. Her hair was cut short, and she was wearing bermuda pants and a shirt, which explains my first impression, but she had little tin rings in her ears and there was a suggestion of small breasts under the shirt. She was none too clean, and she was barefoot.

I bought a packet of peanuts, not because I wanted peanuts, but to help on her commerce and encourage her to move on so I could get back to my solar meditation, but her immediate commercial success had maybe made her feel she might be able to sell something else, so instead of moving on she sat down beside me on the bench. I pointed to the sun, and closed my eyes again.

She was quiet and still for a while, then I felt her stroking the hairs on my arm. When I opened my eyes at that, she gave me a big smile and then, putting a questioning look into her eyes, made an international gesture with the index and the thumb of her left hand and the index of her right. I smiled back, but shook my head, and closed my eyes again. All I wanted was to be alone there with the sun.

This time she snuggled up to me and began stroking my cheek, then, finding I made no response to this, but remained motionless with my eyes closed, she put her hand on my prick. Despite my preoccupation with the sun, my prick hardened and rose (Shiva, you know how it is), and I opened my eyes. The girl put her hand over her mouth, with an 'oh!' expression on her face, pointing to the mound under my pants. Then she made another sign, nodding her head. I shook my head in reply, and made a negative gesture. She took my hand and placed it inside her shirt over a breast. Small, that breast, but very firm, and not unpleasant to the touch. I caressed it a little, then withdrew my hand. At that, she raised her shirt, showing me the breast quick as a flash — hardly bigger than half a lemon, with a dark-brown teat. I gave her to understand that there was nothing doing, and pointed to a monk about twenty yards away on the other side of the canal, suggesting she try her luck with him. She made a grimace and shook her finger in protest, then pulled out her necklet and pointed to the Buddha image. I also pointed to the Buddha image, then pointed to myself. She looked as if she didn't believe me. I nodded my head to convince her. Then, taking from my shirt-pocket some *champa* flowers which I'd bought on my way there, I gave them to her. She put one in her hair. I showed that I thought it very beautiful, then made a sign of farewell. I was walking away when she called something. I turned round, and there she was smiling, returning me my sign of farewell. No hard feelings. Good.

I made for another temple.

4. Skoshi Heaven

Wat Arun.

Here there was a phenomenon like the golden Buddha at Wat Bencha. If what transformed the Buddha there was the flickering of gold-foil, what transformed the temple here was the tinkling of the thousands of copper bodhi-bells with which its walls are hung, turning it into a sonorous, gleaming mass, a myriad-tongued and shining tintinnabulation in the wind.

I was listening to this illuminated sound when a little man with a face as brown and wrinkled as a nutmeg came up to me:

'You like the temple?' he said.

I said I did.

'Wat Arun,' he said, 'Dawn Temple.'

There was something forlorn about this little man. He told me his people were farmers 'up country', but he was an officer in the Thai Navy. This was his day off. He often spent his day off going around the temples, he knew them all. Now he was going to visit a friend of his, a retired navy commander, in Thonburi, would I like to come?

As we strolled over to Thonburi, I was thinking how very little my companion filled the normal image of the 'officer'. He seemed doubly out of place: a peasant at sea, and a profoundly peaceful man whose trade was martial. I'd read that when the Americans were here, they had trouble understanding the psychology of the Thai fighting man. Philosophers, theologians and chaplains have so worked at the Christian precept 'Thou shalt not kill' that the Christian soldier can march onward into combat operations without qualms, but the Buddhist tends to take Buddha's 'Refrain from taking life' more seriously. He'll do his army job if he has to, but he'll do it differently. The American report I've read (written by a US chaplain with a degree in sociology) put it this way: 'The Thai is not emasculated by his religious beliefs to the degree that he will not fight, but due to pressures of belief and societal forces, he goes about his combat in a manner quite different than do the Americans. He avoids conflict situations as much as possible and tends to engage in battle only when other alternatives are denied. In theory, only defensive military operations can be tolerated.' The Americans engaged in 'counterinsurgency military operations' with Thai personnel would tear their virile hair out when Thai cannon went off with little or no effect, aimed at innocuous parcels of ground . . .

Innocuous. Forlorn and innocuous, that's how my little companion came across to me. He might have been more at home ploughing behind a buffalo, or doing his *bhikshu* at some up-country temple, but here he was lost. He no doubt performed his duties scrupulously, taking orders and giving them, but 'without initiative', as US brass would say, not believing in it all, and filled his leisure time going around temples and probably getting drunk. He told me his name was Mr Hoonprachoom.

Mr Hoonprachoom guided me to a little drink-shop in Thonburi, just a shack at the side of the road, with a rotten klong flowing sluggishly in the background, and left me at a table while he went to look for his friend. In the meantime, I ordered a bottle of Mekong, the local whisky. This was enthroned in the middle of the table when they showed up, and Mr Hoonprachoom had introduced Mr Bhukanchana.

'If you buy this, very hospitable,' said Mr Bhukanchana, indicating the bottle. I said I thought it was called for in the circumstances, and hoped he liked it:

'I begin drink at twenty-seven years old,' he said, 'in navy. At sea six months. I go mad. I drink. All good.'

'What brand?' asked Mr Hoonprachoom.

'All kinds,' said Mr Bhukanchana, 'but Mekong the standard.'

Unlike Mr Hoonprachoom, whose drinking made him lapse more and more into a heavy-headed silence, Mr Bhukanchana was talkative in his drink, telling me of his life and his philosophy.

He told me this little party reminded him of drinking with the Japanese during the war. He did not like the war ('War stupid. All fight. All trouble') but he had drunk a lot and he had learned some Japanese (when I filled the glasses, he would say *'skoshi, skoshi'*, a little, just a little). He had retired from the navy with a pension just two years before: 'I born sixty-two years ago. Everything splendid. Now everything hell. But this is heaven. Skoshi heaven.' He now spent his time just walking about, and cooking ('I like cook. Old men like cooking. Hobby'). He did not like Bangkok ('Bad men in Bangkok, be careful'), and would prefer to live in the North, in Chieng Mai, but the climate up there was too cold for him, he'd never be able even to wash himself up there unless he drank a lot of Mekong for heat ('I drink Mekong, I take a bath — no Mekong, no bath'). He liked Chieng Mai ('very beautiful' — *'kirei, kirei'*), the people had 'white skin' up there ('white skin people. Like you. I black'). But the world was hell, and he wanted to go to heaven ('I want to go to heaven. Not hell'). Meanwhile, he had to live. He knew the mind was very important (it's in fact the opening of the *Dhammapada*: 'Mind is the fore-runner of all conditions. Mind is their chief. They are mind-made'), and he tried to keep it as right as possible. When he was out walking, or when he was cooking, he liked to hum songs to himself, sweet songs ('I like sweet song'), like *Swanee River*, and he began to sing it now, and I joined in with him, and Mr Hoonprachoom (whose sole contribution to the conversation had consisted, when Mr Bhukanchana spoke about the war and how his friend had spent it up in Korea, in a shudder accompanied by the words 'very cold!'), beat the time slowly with his glass:

Way down upon the Swanee River
Far far away . . .

Skoshi heaven.

5. The Wheel of the Dharma

Hindu deities, Mahayana bodhisattvas; statues of Prajna Paramita and Vajrasattva; a big fat Javanese Ganesha; yakshas; the lingam and the vajra; howdahs; a five-tiered state umbrella; misshapen elephant trunks; Buddhist fans and bags — I was in the National Museum, looking at all the objects (religious, mythological, aesthetic) therein gathered. But the object at which I'd stopped longest, and to which I returned was the stone 'Wheel of the Dharma and Deer', symbol of Buddha's first talk, the talk on 'setting in motion the wheel of the law' (*Dhamma-Chakka-Pavattana-Sutta*), delivered in the Deer Park of Benares about 2500 years ago.

The first thing to be noticed about this Buddhist symbol is that Buddha is nowhere present, there is only the wheel, representing the ever turning and expanding Dharma, and the deer, representing the locality at which this notion of Dharma, at least in its Buddhist connotation, was originally made public.

Images of the Buddha in person were made only about 400 years after his death, in north-west India, probably under Greek influence. Before that time, the Buddha was conspicuous by his absence. As one who had overcome life-illusion in himself, free of *karma*, deconditioned, beyond personal limitations, outside birth and death, he has, as they say on passports, no 'special peculiarities', either as man or as god — he is beyond both humanity and divinity. The most characteristic sculptures of these person-less statues of Buddha are those which represent his temptation by Kama-Mara (Desire and Death) as he sat under the Bo-tree. The hordes of Mara throw rocks and uprooted trees at him, trying to interrupt his meditation, ruffle his calm, arouse fear in him. At the same time, all that is seductive in life appears before him in the form of divine women, trying to provoke desire in him. But to no avail. He is beyond the fear and the desire, the pleasure and the despair that constitute the web and woof of existence. It is this 'being beyond' that is suggested by the omission of any Buddha image. Among the whirling hordes of demons and the lascivious attitudes of the women, the seat under the Bo-tree is absolutely empty. Buddha is an *empty place*.

How he achieved that emptiness is the story of his life. He was born into a warrior family, the Gautama, in the little state of Shakya, north-west India. His mother died a few days after his birth and Siddhartha, as he had been named, was raised by his maternal aunt. Sages (according to the story) had predicted at his birth that he would become a holy man, but his father was determined to prevent this and keep him living the normal social life, which is why he tried to make sure that Siddartha would never see or hear of any of the less pleasant aspects of existence that might make him want to look beyond his confined illusion. This plan worked right up to the young man's marriage and the birth of a son, but it was just at that moment that the moral crisis came. On one single day, the prince met an old man, a sick man, and a corpse being carried to the funeral pyre, and realised that pain, grief and death were as much part of life as joy and pleasure. A little later, he met a wandering ascetic who seemed serene despite his poverty. That made Siddartha think that there was a solution to the problem of grief and death somewhere, and he went out to seek it, leaving home and family behind him, going south-east. For seven years he wandered in the region of Patna, listening to sages, studying yoga. But these studies did not satisfy him, and he decided to look further. Five disciples followed the one now known as Shakyamuni (the silent sage of the Shakya). First of all, he pushed asceticism to the limit, almost dying in the process, and realising at the same time that it brought the solution no nearer. Abandoning asceticism and fasting, he adopted a frugal diet, at which his disciples, considering that he had weakened, left him. He continued alone in the region of Gaya, till he came to meditate under the Bo-tree, his face turned towards the East, determined that he would not get up till he had solved his problem. It was after the attack by Kama-Mara, the magician of life-illusion, that the one who was about to become the Buddha felt the Great Awakening. Absorbed in the experience, he stayed under the Bo-tree seven days and seven nights, then, feeling that he was ready to go on his way, he got up, but found he could not yet leave. So he sat under a second tree, again for seven days and seven nights. Then a third tree. All in all, he sat under seven trees, spending seven times seven nights and days. And the awakening was complete. At the same time he felt that what he had experienced was impossible to express, and could never be the object of a teaching — so he decided not to try. But (according to the story), appalled at his silence, afraid that the secret, which was the solution to existence, would not be revealed, Brahma (also, though a god, a victim of passion) beseeched him out of charity to become a teacher, teaching deliverance, a proposition which he finally accepted — and went to Benares, where, in the Deer Park, he met up with his five ex-disciples who, once they had heard his first sermon, become the first members of the Buddhist community. During the next thirty or forty years, the Buddha continued his teaching and the community expanded under his influence. When he was about to die, he is supposed to have said that even if the original teacher, himself, who had set the 'wheel of the dharma' in motion, must die, that teaching would remain so long as there were men to understand it.

What of that teaching — the Dharma?

Let's look at it first from the orthodox point of view.

The first tenet, the first of the Four Noble Truths, is that existence means suffering: birth is suffering, ill health is suffering, old age, death, grief, regret, confronting things unloved, separation from things loved — sorrow, anxiety, frustration is the essential condition of life. Why? Because (and this is the Second Noble Truth) of ignorance, because of attachment to form, sensation, perception, impression and consciousness — none of these are real, the person itself aware of them is not real. None of these things is real, because everything is related to something else, conditioned by something else. To escape from suffering is to realise the whole co-productive process, to detach one's self from name-and-form. Is it possible, is it feasible? The Third Noble Truth states that it is indeed possible to escape from mundane existence, get rid of the burden of the self. How? By holding (and this is the Fourth and final Noble Truth) to the Eightfold Path, which means right understanding, right thought, right speech, right action, right livelihood, right effort, right mindfulness, and right concentration — a discipline of life comprising moral rules, exercises in meditation, having for result the penetration of wisdom. This is the way, by obeying the rules (to take no life, to avoid sex, to take no intoxicants and stimulants), by meditating on flux, change, no substance, no soul, no self, realising that nothing in the field of conditioned existence is permanent, to achieve *nibbana* (*nirvana*), which is detachment from that field, and the extinction of any desire for anything in it.

This, summarily stated, is Hinayana or Theravada Buddhism — the Buddhism that flourished in Ceylon after Asoka's mission to the island had planted a branch of the Bo-tree there, the Buddhism of the Pali Canon.

None of it is to be scoffed at. Who would deny that suffering, anxiety, frustration are essential ingredients of existence? Who, with a little reflection, would fail to realise that most of what we *do* in life consists in more or less lucid attempts to dull our consciousness of living, to 'forget ourselves', maintain a level of mediocre comfort? Buddhism simply pushes this state of affairs to a logical conclusion. It is not to be scoffed at, but at the same time, it will still seem to some — even those who are not attached to person, or a personal God, and accept the flux-and-change philosophy — not a satisfying solution. There is the excessive purity of the discipline, for one thing, the accent on renunciation, the hygienic atmosphere, a certain heaviness in the enunciation. One likes in orthodox Buddhism the absence of transcendental flummery, the absence, in a word, of *religion*, one shares its analyses, but something is wanting — a freshness, an aesthetic sense, a liberty.

These objections to Hinayana Buddhism were felt by Buddhists themselves, and it was men who felt such objections who evolved a different type of Buddhism, Mahayana Buddhism, the texts of which were condemned by the older school as 'not the Buddha word, but poetry made by poets'. Just to indicate the difference of climate in the two schools, when Sadaprarudita, in the Mahayana sutra known as the *Astasahasrika*, comes to the town of Gandhavati to seek wisdom at the house of the Bodhisattva Dharmodgata, he finds the house surrounded by lotus-ponds, full of beautiful women, with sense-pleasure on every hand . . .

The bodhisattva, who renounces *nirvana* in order to remain in the world and help others to 'get to the other shore', is at the centre of Mahayana Buddhism. If, for the Hinayanist, the world, mundane existence, is hell, to be escaped from, for the Mahayanist it's a fantasmagoria, to be laughed at — for it is full of emptiness. That is the great transformation of the Mahayana. If, in the Hinayana, emptiness is something to be *achieved*, in Mahayana the whole mindscape is *struck with emptiness*, and there is in reality nothing to be achieved, nothing at all. In one of the Mahayana texts, when the gods have gathered in great ceremony to celebrate the teaching of Buddha, proclaiming all over the firmament: 'This is the second glorious time the Wheel of the Dharma has been turned', Buddha turns to Subhuti and says in a low voice what the gods wouldn't understand: 'This is not the second time, Subhuti, for *there never was a first time.*' Another conversation between these two, Buddha and Subhuti, goes as follows:

Subhuti — 'Deep is ultimate wisdom.'
Buddha — 'Deep as a chasm, deep as space.'
Subhuti — 'Ultimate Wisdom is difficult to reach by Awakening.'
Buddha — 'That is why nobody ever reached it through Awakening.'

And elsewhere we read: 'The Enlightened One leaves on the Ferry (to the Other Shore). But there's nowhere to leave from. He leaves the world, but he really leaves nothing. His boat has all the perfections, in fact none at all. Nobody ever left. Nobody's going anywhere. Because there's nowhere to go.'

The Mahayana agrees with the Hinayana that the Buddha must be known by his 'law' (Dharma) but no sooner has it said that than it adds (in the *Diamond Sutra*) that 'the essence of the law cannot be known' — any claim to knowledge (scientific, religious or otherwise) is naïve, and any talk of the Dharma is beyond the point, mere conventional discourse, what in the West is called philosophy.

So, where do we go from here? Well, since there's no 'we' (separate from the going, it's all one continuum), and since 'where' is neither here nor there, there's really no problem, no question. The thing is just to keep going, living, sceptically-joyously, a dissolution.

This, anyway, is the result of my Dharma meditations in the National Museum. As I leave its precincts, a bird shrieks somewhere up in the white glare of the sun, and I take it as a sign of approval.

6. *Siam Square*

If my lodgings away up in the northern part of town constitute my 'empty place', Siam Square has become my headquarters. It's here I start my day, eating a breakfast of coffee and hot rolls and learning up some Thai before hitting the streets.

I pursued my coffee-drinking and language-learning somewhat longer than usual this morning, and it must have been after ten when I left the shade and cool of the coffee-house and came out into the burning sunlight. I was still in Siam Square, intending to make for the Chinese Market, when I saw a girl coming towards me: tall and very good-looking, in pale blue-jeans, with a blouse open at the neck, showing — as I saw when she stopped in front of me — a beautiful pair of firm and fullcurving breasts:

— 'Where you go!'
— 'Nowhere special.'
— 'You come with me?'
— 'Why not?'
— 'I do you happy.'

I asked her how much she was going to 'do' me. She said sixty baht for one hour. Now, sixty baht is not a lot of money, in fact it is damn little, so damn little that in this transaction you could smell a rat a mile away. I asked her where we were going. She said to her apartment, she shared it with a friend, but her friend was at the hairdresser's, so we'd have it all to ourselves. Well, I was curious, I decided to go all the way, but I'd be on my guard. It would be a little game of who catches who. In any case I didn't have a lot of money on me, so if the worst came to the worst and she did manage to rook me, the result wouldn't be disastrous.

We took a taxi. She paid. And came to the back court of a hotel, fitted out like many another in Bangkok with special rooms. The inside of this room was 'special' too: a round bed in the centre, a large mirror on the wall, and a set of switches for lighting and other effects, with a bathroom adjacent.

While we were in the taxi, Blue Jeans had been stroking and massaging me, making as if she just couldn't wait. Now we were in the room, she practically ripped the pants off me, fondling and sucking cock and thighs, putting on a really heavy act, trying to make me lose my head — but the harder she tried, the cooler I got.

There was a hump on the bed. I'd noticed it when I came in, and thought it must be a pillow. But it wasn't a pillow. When the initial stage was over, Blue Jeans indicated the bed and got me to lie with my buttocks on that hump. She then pressed a switch, and the hump started making crazy coitional movements. It was all I could do not to burst out laughing and spoil the show, but I went through that Reichian rumba there on the bed while Blue Jeans did a striptease in front of me, cupping and caressing her breasts, but keeping her pants on . . .

It was after she'd come over to the bed and was sucking again that her friend came in (I'd been expecting her). She was on the fat side, the friend, and if it had been her I'd met in the street, by this time I'd have been at the Chinese market. She came in quietly, maybe in fact I wasn't meant to see her, but with my eyes wide open, though appreciating the activity of Blue Jeans down between my thighs, I did. When she saw I'd seen her, she made out as if the very sight of me had struck her delirious with desire. Putting on the big sex act, hissing between her teeth, jerking, saying 'ohhh, ohhh, ohhh' with her eyes on my dick, she took off her blouse and shook her big blabbery boobs at me, then took off pants and knickers, bending back with legs spread and showing me her hairy hole. After that little display she came over to join in the fun. She was after my cock, Blue Jeans relinquished it to her and would have retired to the corner, where she no doubt thought my big wad was, had I not grabbed her by the neck and made her lie down beside me. So that the next few minutes were spent with me sucking and licking Blue Jeans' tits, while Lady Boob sucked and licked my cock and balls.

I then made signs to Blue Jeans to take off her pants. She wasn't very keen, suggested I fuck the other girl who was more than willing — she'd stopped sucking and was kneeling on the bed diddling herself. I said no, I wanted her. She said she couldn't, her hole was too small. The other said: 'No pussy, only dick.' So Blue Jeans was a hermaphrodite? I didn't really want to fuck Boob, that was obvious, so Blue Jeans said: 'I suck you off,' and I said OK, and Lady Boobs at that would have gone into the corner had I not grabbed *her* by the neck this time and handled her big boobs while Blue Jeans worked at my cock. The session over, I left my two lovely crooks and, going over to the corner to collect my things, went into the bathroom. Blue Jeans came in after me:

'I clean you wash,'

and she washed me, soaping cock and thighs and then indicating the shower behind the plastic curtain so she could have another go at finding the wad. I took my shower, but didn't pull the curtain, and when she went to pull it, I told her to leave it open. She looked desperate.

When we came back into the room, Lady Boobs had left, probably on the hunt for a better client. I took a hundred baht note from my pocket and put it on the table. Blue Jeans smiled:

'Smart boy,' she said.

Outside, there was a taxi waiting, with one girl already inside. As we rolled back towards Siam Square, this girl pulled up her dress and pulled down her panties showing me a very neat little cunt. Indicating my original companion, she said:

'I have pussy, she no pussy, only dick. You want my pussy? I give you much love'

— and indeed she had a very attractive little pussy, a little peach of a pussy, with black glistening hair, but I decided not to push my luck any further, so patting her on the pussy, I said not now, maybe some other time. Pulling up her panties with a laugh, she imprisoned my hand, and I diddled her till we got back to Siam Square.

7. *The Oriental Hotel*

'I met H. G. Wells for the first time at the flat which Reggie Turner had near Berkeley Square. I was living then in Mount Street and sometimes I would drop in to see him. Reggie Turner was on the whole the most amusing man I have known . . . He was one of the few of Oscar Wilde's friends who remained faithful to him after his disgrace. Reggie was in Paris when Wilde, living in a cheap, dingy hotel on the left bank of the Seine, was dying. Reggie went to see him every day. One morning he found him distraught. He asked him what was the matter? "I had a terrible dream last night," said Oscar, "I dreamt I was supping with the dead." "Well," said Reggie, "I'm sure you were the life and soul of the party, Oscar" . . . H. G. Wells was fat and homely. I once asked one of his mistresses what especially attracted her in him. I expected her to say his acute mind and his sense of fun; not at all; she said that his body smelt of honey.'

I'm on the terrace of The Oriental Hotel, reading a collection of essays on literature (picked up in a second-hand bookstore this afternoon) by Somerset Maugham, who frequented this hotel whenever he was in Bangkok. I believe it even has a 'Somerset Maugham Suite' which can be rented by those who get a thrill from sleeping in the beds of the famous and the dead.

The Oriental is an old world haven, all green and white cool inside, fronting the river with a terrace garden full of palm trees, orchids, irises and frangipani. It's about five o'clock. *The Oriental Queen* has just come down from Ayudhya, unloading a batch of tourists and tying up at the pier, blocking the view of the river. Before that, there was just the river flowing, carrying bits of jungle flotsam, a copper reflection from the sun, and an old woman paddling a sampan among the junks and barges.

The scene, since the arrival of the boat, has become more European — European and Australian. A Frenchwoman is talking a couple of tables away: *'C'est une ville délirante pour s'orienter, je suis encore paumée'*, and for her to be disoriented in a town, it really has to be a corker, for to her trade she is an organiser of tours: *'C'est mon métier de faire voyager les gens'*, although for the moment she is on holiday. She intends to go down to Malaya soon, to see something different. Oh yes, she likes the old Oriental: *'Ici, il y a un style'*, it has style, whereas elsewhere, from Bangkok to Paris, *'c'est toujours la même chose'*, it's always the same.

Back to Somerset Maugham.

'In his discovery of what is called the exotic story, Rudyard Kipling opened a new and fruitful field to writers. This is the story the scene of which is set in some country little known to the majority of readers. It deals with the reactions upon the white man of his sojourn in an alien land and the effect which contact with peoples of another race and colour had upon him . . . When one travelled in the East it was astonishing how often one came across men who had modelled themselves on the creatures of his invention.'

These gossipy little essays are just the thing for reading on this warm, lazy evening, with a *Singapore Sling* or a *Shangai* or a *White Lady* to accompany them . . .

Now I hear a Swiss voice, it's saying in an intense whisper that it doesn't trust the British, they're all left-handed . . . Later it's raised and stating categorically that if Stendhal in his time took as model the *Code Civil*, the equivalent for writers today would be *Pekin Information*.

By God, it's an education to be sitting on the terrace of the Oriental Hotel, Bangkok!

8. Dockland

Klong Toey is a long line of palm trees and shacks till you get right down to the dock area:

PORT AUTHORITY OF THAILAND

It begins with three single Eric Satie notes which are the names of three restaurants:

Sea Dragon
Golden Gate
Copenhagen

then becomes a polyphonic rush with money-changers, stores, restaurants and bars:

Rose Kitchen
Ship Inn Coffee Shop
Long Beach Store
OK Night Club
Venus Room
Shanghai Restaurant
Mosquito Bar

There's a crowd gathered at the docks today, for a political meeting, with big hand-written posters and effigies of public figures about to be hanged and burned. The meeting is animated by a band, but when I arrive among the crowd, the scene is held by a phoney monk in floppy sunhat and orange robe who ad-libs with the straight political man, causing a lot of laughs. The official religion is obviously taking a beating along with the official politics, the monk doing a mock-chant over the effigies before stringing them up or consigning them to the flames. All the musicians are doing for the moment is providing a little accompaniment, punctuating the speeches with cymbals and clappers. But when the comedian and the party man have gone, the band takes over, and the singer sings something like this (I found the translations later):

Do you remember the events of October 14 and 15
Do you remember the blood, the tears, the nightmares?
Our young men died among bullets and tear gas
Throwing up their bare hands they died crying for freedom
Now let us be silent and remember them
As encouragement to those who live to fight on . . .

It's called, this kind of song, *pleng pua cheevit* (music for life), and it had its origin away back in the 1932 revolution, when it was seen as the expression of popular revolt.

The tone is bitter-sweet, the rhythm slow and insistent, a lot of it in a minor key, the instruments being bamboo flute, guitar, mouth organ and drums:

With every mouthful of rice
Remember
The sweat you swallowed
Until you were born a man
That rice came of suffering
Suffering and bitterness
Look at the rice in the fields
See it growing
And think of the interest growing
In the capitalist's pocket . . .

When the show was over and the crowd had dispersed, I went into the Mosquito Bar and, making for a table in a corner, ordered a beer. While waiting for the beer, I let my eye roam over the place: all along the walls, life-buoys from Oslo, Hamburg, Köbenhavn, Gotesburg and other ports round the world; a staircase beside the 'lady room' and 'man room' with a notice pinned beside it saying WELCUM UP STAIRS; two or three prostitutes planted here and there.

I sat there in the shadow drinking my beer. Outside, the noon sun had turned the street into a desert of white heat. A big ship showed its nose through the window.

Docks . . .

I was trying to recall poems I'd written years before about the docklands of Glasgow. One about gulls drunk on the smell of whisky, one about a boat just in from Christiansand, one about 'men with red dreams in dark corners' . . . That was in the tearoom known as the White Tower, where I'd end up after my peregrinations through the city.

Peregrinations through the city, and from city to city, mainly harbour-cities.

Glasgow, Bangkok.

Antwerp, Amsterdam, Barcelona.

Hong Kong.

A bit of a Buddhist poem now turns up in my mind: 'we wander through them dreaming'.

On the good ship *Fantasmagoria* . . .

9. *Aquatic Reflections*

There are two ways of getting out of the steaming hurly-burly of Bangkok without actually leaving the city. One is to make for a quiet *wat* with a waterlily pond, the only other human presence being maybe a monk meditatively scratching his toes; the other is to hire a long-tailed boat and take a slow trip along the klongs. That's what I did this afternoon, spending a long siesta on the water.

The pre-history of Bangkok is a sweltering swamp and if you look down many an alley leading off the thoroughfares of the modern city, it's still there: the lush green silence of the jungle, criss-crossed by a labyrinth of waterways.

It's another world.

The boat noses its way through greengold shadow, the water rippling along its sides, sometimes through thick lotus-beds, overhead a slight breeze quivering the leaves — bird-cries, sudden and staccato; blue dragonflies; fish breaking surface; a golden flurry of butterflies; flowers . . .

'Just as, in great etheric space, the stars and the darkness, dew, foam, lightning and clouds, emerge, become visible and disappear, like the features of a dream, so must we consider things endowed with individual form.'

One can know by heart passages of the *Diamond Sutra*, accept its analyses, and still enjoy the dream.

Houses are scattered all along the canals, old Thai wooden houses, with fish nets jutting out over the water. Two young boys have just raised one, but the catch is poor: two tiddlers and a water snake — *mai pen lai* (it doesn't matter). They laugh and wave, and lower the net again. Better luck next time.

Now and again other boats pass: one loaded with bananas; another full of the mud of dredging work; another with an old woman in it picking her nose . . .

Stop at a little pier. A clearing with a huddle of shacks. Get the top sliced off a coconut at the drink-booth and enjoy the milk. Further on, there's a pit where, if you care to see it, a snake will fight a mongoose. Further on still, a booth with rows of jars containing fighting fish; again, if you care to see the show, a young girl will stir them into action.

On the water once more.

A string of orange robes hung out to dry.

'Just as the Ganges flows towards the East, so must the *bhikshu* flow into *nibbana* . . .'

Beyond the temple, only the rippling of the water . . .

'Listen close, the sound gets better.'

Rippling.

Ripp-ling.

But there are blue dragonflies also, and orchids and fish.

Instead of trying to *reach* 'emptiness', realise you *are* empty, and let all those things ripple through your mind.

I see a frog hunched all alone on a banana leaf.

I wait for the plop.

Plop!

10. One Little Tattooed Thai

A medley of bars and girlie-joints, Patpong is, roughly, the equivalent of Pigalle. I took a trip down there the other night. Without much enthusiasm, I admit — in which I was wrong, for down there, in that banal and sordid precinct, I came up against a perfect little miracle of nature.

Why go out to pigallise or patpong one's self? Well, to the orthodox

Buddhists among us, I will say, by way of prolegomena, this: that the bodhisattva goes everywhere and anywhere, roaring the lion's roar; that (to quote the *Jnanasiddhi*) 'through actions identical with those through which mortals rot in hell for a million years, the yogi is liberated'; and that (to quote the *Kularnava Tantra*) 'When you fall, you fall on the ground; it's by making use of the ground that you rise again.'

'OK,' I can hear somebody say, 'you don't have to make all those excuses. Let's go to Patpong.'

OK, let's go.

Where stop first?

Lady Hill?

Mississippi Queen?

The Red Door?

Big Boy?

Sugar Daddy?

The Golden Bottle?

Playboy?

Let's try Playboy.

You go up a flight of stairs, and you see a long corridor with various doors (behind them 'special shows') opening on to it. Hustlers crowd around you, each vying with the other to get you to enter 'his' door. They'll shout '25 baht', '30 baht' — inside you'll invariably find that the first drink is double that. Well, a little lying is all in the game. Which door to choose? You can just take pot-luck, or you can pretend you're looking for friends and have a quick look in at several before making up your mind, or again of course you may have decided that you're going to do a glutinous grand duke's tour of the lot.

Let's try pot-luck.

Back of the door, after the glare and blare of the corridor, you have to get used to the obscurity. You're in a dark room, with a little dim-lit bar, and tables and chairs round the walls. In the centre, the only lit spot, a small circular stage, with four couches placed around it for those who want a close look. Let's take a seat a little further back. Distance lends enchantment to the view.

A glass of Mekong? OK. Now settle back, or lean forward, as you like, and enjoy the show.

There's a girl doing a bit of a dance on the stage. She's stark naked. A well-built solid golden little body that in its sheer physical presence makes notions of Eve in the garden of Eden look like the dream of an anaemic Sunday school teacher. Ah, yes, the gold of their bodies . . . But it all turns into cheap coinage when the girl picks up a pentel pen, licks it, winds it corkscrewly into her cunt, then, having placed a sheet of paper in a strategic position, leans back, supports herself on her hands, and writes on the paper: Welcome to Playboy.

Applause — and a gangly fair-headed character over there on one of the couches is drooling at the mouth. Two fat Frenchmen on the couch beside him snigger at each other.

Second act.

This time, in place of the pentel pen, it's a banana. The girl unpeels it — unpeels it slowly, slowly, writhing her hips all the time, then with legs spread slowly shoves it up her flim, opening her mouth and gasping to show the pleasure it's supposed to be giving her — the fair-haired character practically has his head in there alongside the damn banana — then closing her thighs and pressing them one against the other, now left on right, now right on left, absorbing herself in an imaginary coition, she works herself up into a semblance of orgasm, till, opening her legs again, she shits the banana out in bits, offering the first bit to the fair-haired character who takes it in his mouth like a holy wafer, the next to the Frenchmen who, slightly embarrassed, refuse (they prefer their bananas fried).

Applause.

Another glass of Mekong?

Act Three.

Same girl. This time it's three ping-pong balls that go up the way of all flesh, and then, after a little promenading and writhing, are dropped — one, two, three — like eggs, into a glass.

Act four.

Change of girl. A little fire-dakini. She does a slow dance first of all to reveal the attractions of her nudity, and let them sink in, then, standing in the centre, turning to her materials, breathes fire, adopting postures like Kali the destroyer in the Indian paintings.

Suddenly there's the sound of a buzzer, the girl grabs up her panties and jumps off the stage, another girl, dressed, takes her place and is dancing casually when the door opens and in comes a policeman, takes a perfunctory look around, then disappears again. Everything now is ready for —

Act five.

A girl who, after performing her striptease, takes a candle, lights it, then, doing a slow dance all the while, lets the wax drip down over her arms, her thighs, and her belly, as though drenching herself in hot sperm.

Act six.

More classical. A couple of girls fucking, one with a big rubber dildoe strapped to her waist. They go through half-a-dozen postures then transfer the prick and go through half-a-dozen more . . .

It looks at this point as if the series is just going to begin all over again, with some slight variations — this time the girl with the banana smokes a cigarette between the lips of her cunt — so let's bugger off and try another spot.

Same lay-out, but the organisation's different. This place has floating bar-girls whose job is to encourage the customer to drink while snuggling up to him and adding to the pleasure of the spectacle.

So I'm sitting there in the dark with a girl, drinking Mekong, when a VERY cute little number in a scanty two-piece, starts performing on the stage. Nothing but a dance, just a simple erotic little dance, no special effects, but what a body, what a fascinating little beauty of a body . . .

She must have noticed me watching her, although she'd seemed so anonymous and neutral up there, for when she had finished her performance she came down to me. After a moment or two, the other girl left.

It was the *skin* of the little dancer that was the miracle. I was amazed at the sheer perfection of it. Smooth as a peeled onion!

'You sleep with me?' she said.

'Sure.'

Of course I should have said: 'No, no my dear, I do not wish to encourage the prostitution trade in Thailand. Get thee to a factory and earn a living by the sweat of your brow. Become a *person*, not a *thing* . . .'

But hell, I hadn't come to Patpong to play the missionary, and as

Pascal might have said, the body has its reasons which the mind knows nothing of.

That skin!

'We go hotel.'

OK, the hotel rigmarole again. It was one of those back-court rooms only a couple of hundred yards along the street.

When the room-boy had come and gone, she took off her clothes and stood naked fingering the gold chain round her neck. It had, of all things, a little abacus fixed to it. She held the little abacus in front of her nose and made as if she was counting on it, saying aloud: 1 baht, 10 baht, 100 baht, 1000 baht . . . I stopped her at 10 million.

On her right arm was a blue tattoo mark. She said it was her name. Why not? But she had a nasty sore on her crotch. When I pointed to it, she gave me to understand it was the wax from the candle. Maybe it was.

'Fuck now?' she said.

'No fuck,' I said, 'only touch.'

11. White Beach Meditation

A time comes when you decide to get out of Bangkok for good. There are white beaches in the South . . .

I took the bus for Hua Hin, leaving the City of Angels in a dusty red sunset that soon became dark night. The bus was packed, both with people and with packages, and was thick with smoke, blaring with music.

Dark miles, villages, dark miles.

There's another European in the bus — two seats in front of me to the left: young (about thirty?), bald, tired-looking. When we reach Hua Hin, he also gets off. He says he knows a hotel. Says it in the *lingua franca* which is English, but with a French accent. Yes, he's French.

We take pedicabs (he speaks to the men in Thai), and make for the hotel. A long quiet street, boom of the sea in the background. Palm trees outlined against the moon. As we turn down a shore-road, the sound of crickets.

Hotel Division, State Railways, Thailand.

Old colonial, antiquated atmosphere. The smell of polish.

It seems tonight there's only one room available, we'll share it, change over tomorrow.

The dining-room's closed.

We leave our things and go to hunt up a restaurant in town.

While we are eating — fish, rice and tea — the Frenchman, in that extinguished voice he has, tells me about himself. He'd been living for four years in Laos. But, apart from the troubles up there now, by this time he had had enough: *'On tourne en rond'* (you just go round in a circle). He had got on to the opium habit up there too, he wondered if you could really understand Asia without smoking opium. But he was ill now, and he was trying to kick the habit. He'd come down to Bangkok, but Bangkok was infernal, and he didn't like or understand the Thais, he felt they were dangerous, he could never foresee their reactions. Especially in Bangkok. That was because they were uprooted. With the Laos it was different. Well, it *had* been different.

He went on and on, always in that extinguished voice. It was like listening to a zombie.

Later that night I saw his sharp features outlined against the window.

Early next morning I took a stroll along the beach. Wild palms, a warm wind, a gurly green sea — there had been storms. In the garden of the hotel, a notice: *'Beware of jelly fish on the rainy day'*. Full of jacaranda trees, palms, and flowering shrubs, this garden, with the carcass of a fishing barque to evoke bygone times.

When I got back to the room, my companion was up, and we went to have breakfast. When I'd got back from the beach, he'd asked me where I'd been, what I'd done, and when I told him he said *'c'était bien?'* in such a tone of voice, as if to walk along a shore in the morning could only inspire the most unmitigated boredom, that I decided I'd had enough of him and would sever our relation quietly the first opportunity came my way.

After breakfast, he suggested we play chess. I said I'd rather go for a stroll through the village. He told me, of course, that there was nothing to see.

It's true that there wasn't much. But then I don't need much. Just a few details, and the rest is up to me. Try and explain that to a zombie. Anyway you can't go around explaining all the time.

After going through the market I ended up in Mr Who's Love Coffee Shop whose closed shutters keep the sun out, leaving the interior dark and gropy. Erotic posters on the walls, showing Western girls. I ordered a coffee. There were a lot of waitresses around. More than it takes to serve coffee.

Outside in the sun again, a pedicab man cycling by put both hands to his mouth in a gesture signifying pipe and said:

'Want smoke watla?'

I went back to the hotel.

The zombie had found company, compatriots to boot. They were talking about Singapore, Penang and New Orleans and where they were going to have lunch. They invited me to accompany them, but I declined with thanks, saying I was going for a swim. The zombie said the water would be too cold.

As I left, I heard a woman saying that she didn't like Asiatics at all, she found them ugly:

'Je n'aime pas les Asiatiques, ce n'est pas une belle race.'

— thank God, I had escaped that lunch.

The ocean of pure reality exists externally . . .

I'd just come out of the water and was lying out on the sand when a gang of boys came up, with a bottle of Mekong well in evidence. They introduced themselves:

— 'I'm Clint Eastwood'

— 'I'm Yul Brynner'

— 'I'm Alain Delon'

— 'I'm Charles Bronson'

— 'I'm Charlie Chaplin'

They wander on their way after a few sallies but one hangs back. He is, I think more than a little drunk. He strokes the hair on my arm, touches the top of the belly hair too, thereafter lifts up his shirt and shows his own. He then picks up my denim jacket and puts it on. He wants me to give it to him. I tell him I need it. He insists, pulling it tight around him. When I say no a second time, wondering if he is not going to run off with it and I'll have to chase him, he says, pointing to himself, looking ugly and authoritarian the way he's seen it in the movies: 'Police, Bangkok!' — and pulls out a revolver. Well, I hadn't quite expected that, and was the thing loaded? He was drunk and might after all be stupid enough to use it. Careful, careful. I told him his friends would be waiting for him. He looked along the shore. I made to gather up my clothes and held out my hand for the jacket. He took it off, hesitated, handed it to me. I said thanks, but didn't turn away yet. He did, turning back after a couple of paces to shout: 'Police, Bangkok!', then running away along the shore.

Ouf.

I walked a few yards, then settled down again.

Quiet now.

The wind was combing the wild palms, the tide lipping against the white sand. I was thinking of the 'doors to concentration' listed in the *Astasahasrika Sutra*:

— Leaving behind the jungle of opinions and actions
— Following all substantial excellence
— Feeling no rigidity
— Within the body consummating all dharmas
— Penetrating essential nature . . .

THE NORTHERN ROUTE

As for the sun world, it is to be reached in
the north, through searching for the self.
Prashna Upanishad

1. *Night Train North*

My last vision of Bangkok was of a beggar dressed in scraps of plastic, hunched on the bank of a filthy klong — all kinds of flotsam and jetsam gliding slowly down its dingy waters — with his right arm dangling like a monkey's, waiting to plunge in and pick up whatever goody had caught his eye. The compleat angler . . . of the 21st century?

It was about one o'clock. I'd purposely taken a ticket for a slow train, the one that leaves Bangkok at 1.30 and gets into Chieng Mai at 5.05 the next morning, sixteen hours of a journey.

Wandering around the station concourse, in my head the phrase:

'The Tathagata neither comes nor goes . . .'

We pulled out.

Blue sky. Wind. Long grass with a silky flourish. Red waterlilies. Dark birds with very blue streaks on their wings. Water buffalo up to the neck in reedy water, a young girl riding him . . .

I'm on the east side of the train, with some shade from the afternoon sun that's blazing out there. Not exactly alone, there are five Japanese further up the carriage, and behind me someone is smacking his lips after eating out of a pungent-smelling paper bag. But there is a feeling of solitude nonetheless, solitude and long-distance.

Ruined *stupas*. Grassgrown Buddhas sitting staring in the wilderness. Birds skimming over the marshes. On a jetty a young woman has just bathed and she's wringing out her dress, showing her thighs.

Outside Tha Rua, I got a sight of the first hills, a blue thickening in the blue sky. Then closer red hills. Then a huge white Buddha head — like a nirvanic exclamation in that coloured landscape!

And evening came on. Children riding home on magnificent buffalos. The mauve-orange glow of the setting sun. Then the mauve-orange glow was gone, and the sun stood out firm red outlined in purple . . .

A bluegreen duskiness thereafter, and the attendant brings round blankets. The man behind me has gone, so, on the attendant's recommendation, I swivel round my seat, and with the seat facing that makes a kind of couch. I settle down. Rocking motion of the train. I take the *Surangama Sutra* from my rucksack, intending to spend a good part of the night in reading.

By Buddha, it's cold.

'He has sounded the unfathomable ocean of omniscience, and endlessly he turns the wheel of the Dharma, always preaching the identity of the mind with earth, water, fire and air. Having entered the realm of the Tathagata, he himself does not preach but perseveres with patience to gain more insight-knowledge.'

'One does not gain Enlightenment by way of becoming or ceasing, nor does one awaken to *Bodhi* by taking one's stand on any *dharma*. Where there is no becoming, no ceasing and no adherence to anything whatsoever — that is *paranirvana*.'

'You must get rid of twelve ingrained views. Which twelve? Attachment to the belief in "one's ego", holding fast to the idea of "a being", of "a life principle", the insistence upon a "personality", annihilation and eternity, "I" or mine-making, the postulate that there must be a beginning as well as an end, the clinging to the theory of a soul and of existential constituents.'

'At whichever place Enlightenment is gained, that place is like a diamond.'

I'd been so absorbed in my reading — looking also at times through the window at the starry night, at other times closing my eyes and dozing a little — that I didn't feel the cold too much, but I was frozen to the marrow when we got into Chieng Mai.

When you arrive at the small station of a strange town at five in the morning and it's cold, bitterly cold, where do you make for? Right, the market-place.

There were fires there.

I hung around them for a while, warming up, then decided to go for a stroll while waiting for the market to get livelier. As yet the stalls were barely under way, with vegetables being piled up, meat hacked, pineapples peeled, coconuts ground.

I went across a bridge over the river. There was a temple on the other side, and I walked around the grounds followed by a suspicious dog. It was only when it saw me lying out harmlessly with my back against a tree that it lost interest and left me alone.

When I came back across the bridge, it was dusky red dawn over the water. Travelling monks were emerging from their tents on the shore, and I saw two Meo tribeswomen, one very old, one young, with her bonnet set rakishly askew on her head — attractive — making for the market. I later saw the young one, excited, buzzing around the toothpaste and perfume stall, but always with an air of independence — like a bird of prey.

I was looking for some breakfast, and found it at a soya milk counter. It was an old happy-go-lucky looking woman with a wart between her eyes who was selling, her pot of soya milk boiling on the stove beside her. I pointed to a glass. She picked it up and picked up an egg at the same time, raising on eyelid enquiringly. I nodded yes. She then broke the egg into the tumbler, poured the hot milky soya in over it, and added a spoonful of syrup.

It was delicious. I had another one.

Thus fortified, I was ready to meet Chieng Mai.

2. *Chieng Mai from Dawn to Dusk*

I got myself a room at the Pathum Hotel.

There's a notice well to the fore at the reception desk:

'Avoid lonely places — try to avoid going about alone — if molested by gangsters try to remember car number'

and inside the door of the room there's another:

'Please keep your valuable belongings with the manager of the hotel *or else*.'

Well, we have been warned.

I'm glad to see that there are three gold marks on the outside of the door. At least the evil spirits will be kept away . . .

I have a shower, a second breakfast of coffee and rolls, then go back out into the streets.

Chieng Mai, the blue and the gold . . . Yes, it's a bright blue morning, still chilly, and floods of early golden light on every hand. In a *wat* just off the main street, a monk is wrapping himself in his robe, another is lighting a fire with a yellow blanket round his shoulders, while other blankets are airing on the base of a *stupa*.

A notice nailed to a tree in the temple yard carries the precepts:

'Try to avoid the suffering.
Stop in the right way.
See in the right way.
Escape in the right way.'

while at the street-corner the proposition is:

'You want to smell white powder? I have. You want girls? I have.'

Later, man, later.

For the moment let's just enjoy the freshness of the blue and the gold, and think about the 'right way'.

I go up into the old town and find myself in the grounds of another *wat.* I meet a student there, who lives in the monastery. It was his friend — 'retired from a monk' — who had got him the room: 'I pay not anythings.' I say it's a good place to stay — peaceful. He says: 'Much peace, no fun.' For fun he goes to the YMCA — he's going to sing Christmas carols that afternoon.

'Are you a Christian?' he asks.

'No, nothing at all.'

'Some people say Buddhism is not religion because it believes in no God. It is philosophy. I think better.'

'Me too' — thinking that there's something better still than philosophy.

'Are you interested in the opium? All the hill tribes grow opium and sell it to CIA. The father of my friend has opium farm. Next month I go see the opium flower. Very nice, very beautiful. Do you like Americans?'

'Some.'

'The Americans give us many things. I do not think they are honest. But my teacher says I must not talk about the politics so that tourists will not think it is bad. You like Chieng Mai?'

'I like it this morning.'

'In Chieng Mai we have only old things.'

Maybe, my friend, but there's also the blue and the gold — the sheer cool beauty of this bright December morning.

For my midday meal, I bought some mandarin oranges and a bunch of bananas.

Now I know my nostrils are turned towards the earth.

I spent the afternoon strolling about the streets, going in and out of shops, and ended up in the coffee-shop of a hotel where I wrote a little. Towards evening I was out in the streets again when a taxi stopped beside me.

'Doi Suthep?' said the driver.

I knew Doi Suthep was a mountain just outside Chieng Mai with a temple at its summit. OK, why not?

'How much?'

'Alone? — 100 baht.'

'Too much.'

'60 baht.'

'30.'

'50.'

'40.'

'45.'

'OK.'

'Very cheap one person.'

Maybe it is. But he needs to get up there, he tells me. Must see a friend about business.

At a petrol-station, he asks me to pay — 20 baht. The notices in the hotel have made me suspicious, maybe even unreasonable.

'No. You pay.'

'I can no pay,' he says. Then, to assert his good faith, he adds:

'I a good man, no a very bad man.'

I pay, feeling a bit ashamed at not trusting him.

When we're moving again, he takes out his Buddha necklet:

'No lie. Buddhist no lie.'

We take the road up the mountain. At the foot there's a monument to the old monk who begged at that spot till he'd got together enough cash to build that road up to the monastery. As we pass the monument, the driver raises clasped hands to his forehead in a gesture of piety.

The car parked on the esplanade, I climb up the dragon staircase to the temple. It's cool blue evening now, shadows lengthened. There's nobody up there but the sparrows, and a skinny yellow effigy of a bodhisattva lodged in a tree. Tinkling of a wind-bell. And I run my finger along a big bell slung on a rack that gives a feathery whisper like a lost wind wandering round the globe . . .

When I get back down to the car, the driver's nowhere to be seen, but he turns up eventually, mekong'd out of his mind. His pronunciation is all to hell:

'You like Thai whizky? Not stlong. Thilty-flife deglee. No make silick.'

It seems he still has his problem, he hadn't seen his friend, and their business remained to be settled:

'We gotm buym noo tyles.'

So we roll gaily back down the mountain road with a drunken driver and bad tyres.

'I have flen. Her father Chinese. She has lestolan. You like Thai food? Vely hot! Maybe she lie for you. You look baby, oh yes!'

I was savouring that last phrase, when he followed up with another, though related, suggestion — maybe he thought he'd rather keep his half-Chinese friend for himself:

'After lestolan, maybe you like shake Chieng Mai gil? Pootsie pootsie!'

No objections at all to 'shaking a Chieng Mai gil', but I didn't want this guy, especially in his present state, to play the intermediary. So I told him I had a dinner appointment with friends.

He proposed to pick me up next morning at my hotel to take me on a tour of caves, a waterfall, and a pottery factory. I told him I preferred to leave my day open, maybe I'd see him around.

His last words to me as I left the car were:

'Chieng Mai gil! Bootifool, vely bootifool! Pootsie pootsie!'

3. The Good Red Road

By a stroke of good luck that morning I'd come across a taxi-driver who'd offered to take me to a hill-tribe village off the normal circuit.

A clearing in the green jungle (the green shading off into blue on the heights), a scattering of about thirty huts on ground trodden bare, the smell of wood smoke; a Blue Meo village. Sewing machines have been set out in the open air and women are working at them, their feet on the tread mill, their hands guiding the cloth under the needle. Children run around naked.

We go to the grocery store kept by a Chinese family. Floor of beaten earth well swept. The woman offers tea and bananas. There's a Meo girl (black bodice, blue skirt, red sash, black leggings, thick silver ring round neck) at the table, feeding noodles to an infant. Her dark full breasts show clearly through the slit in her bodice. She's not overwashed, but looks healthy as hell.

We stand at the door to the grocery. Black hogs grunt and wallow in a mud-hole beside the raised granaries for rice and maize. We're at about 4000 feet. The Meo like to live along the mountain ranges, situating their villages just below the highest ridge. With their rice and Indian corn, their millet, sugar cane, melons, pumpkins, yams, flax, tobacco, chillies, hemp and the opium poppy, and for livestock their pigs and hens, they're practically independent.

This group came into North Thailand from Burma only a few years ago. They'll stay in a village for maybe twenty years or so, and then move on. The Meo (who sometimes resent this name, which is a pejorative Chinese designation, meaning 'sprouts' — they refer to themselves rather as *H'mong*) have moved a great deal in their time, from China into Burma and Laos, and from there, in the last hundred years or so, into Thailand. To what extent they will be able to continue to move, to what extent they are due to be integrated into more stable communities is now the question. But for the moment it's a blue day in eternity.

Looking out over the shacks with the grass or leaf-covered roofs . . . Water gurgling along bamboo troughs . . . The women hard at work stitching and embroidering cloth, feeding infants, tending gardens (the Meo men work as little as possible) . . . Is there evil lurking invisible in this blue air?

The Meo live with an awareness of the presence of good and evil spirits. They have no gods to worship, no temples, no sacred images — only that sense of good and evil forces. What religion means here is the handling of those forces, through the activities of the shaman, and the concern that the 'three souls' of a dead man be given a proper send-off: the soul that remains at the grave, the soul that goes to the abode of the dead, and the soul that will be re-embodied. It was Old Man Sho, the Ancestor, who taught them this, just as he taught them everything else, including opium-growing.

'Hao yeng' is Meo for 'smoke opium'. There's a famous old opium-smoker lives in his shack a little further down the the slope, on the edge of the village. We go to pay him a visit. 'No. 1 people grow opium flower,' says my guide, referring to the Meo, as we walk down the slope.

The old man's house: blue shafts of sunlight coming through chinks in the roof, and smoke from the fire curling its way up the shafts, blue in blue. The old man himself, crouched on a raised platform above the floor of beaten earth: long jacket, coloured sash, baggy blue pants, close-cropped grey-black hair. There's a green cockatoo on a bamboo perch in the corner. A crossbow with a quiver of arrows hangs on the wall.

Salutations, a toothless smile . . .

The old man brings out his tray of apparatus — a little burner with glass made of a bit of a coca-cola bottle, his pipe, and a blob of black tarry-like substance that is the raw opium. He wants to know if I like to smoke opium or would prefer hemp. I say I'd rather smoke hemp. He leans back and passes over a wooden box. I have a pipe with me, bought in Chieng Mai. The old man asks to see it and approves of it with a smile.

So the old opium-smoker lies on his side and puff-puff-puffs, sucking like an infant. I smoke my pipe of grass. The guide smokes a cigarette smeared with opium. Every man his pleasure . . .

No sound, except maybe an occasional cry from the jungle. The blue smoke curls up the shafts of sunlight, curls-up-the-shafts-of-sunlight, blue in blue. The green cockatoo, I really understand the life and the presence of the green cockatoo. In fact, I *am* the green cockatoo. But if I change my point of view, I'm also the fire. I am so many things, neither 'I', nor 'am' has any meaning any more. There's only a dense multiplicity of life, blue in blue.

When we leave the old man's house, my guide says he thinks I like hill-life a lot.

4. Back into the Hills

'We are going on the North of Chieng Mai by bus boat and on foot far from the city almost 200 kilometres near Burma border. See the hill tribes such as Akha, Karen, Lahu, Lisu, Meo and Yao. They are scatter living on the high mountains, who have attracted the interest of the scientist. But still keep in their original ways since their village has settlement can only be reached by walk. If so why don't you join one of our tour to see them, before the wood are spoilt and their original way of life are changed.'

Four people had seen this prospectus for a 'hill tour' or 'jungle tour' at about the same time as myself, and had signed on, so that on that appointed morning there were six of us leaving Chieng Mai: a German couple, a French couple, myself, and the guide — ready to spend three days and two nights together in the hills.

The first stage was by bus. The day was fine, and all might have been well, all manner of things might have been well, but we weren't the only party making for the hills that day. No, there was another party, and it was about three times as big as ours. Which made for a certain amount of congestion in the bus. But what's that among human beings? Not only was the other party bigger than ours, however, it was composed largely of sick Australians who'd drunk too much the previous night. Which meant that to the general congestion was added a certain amount of vomiting confusion. At a window, sitting beside a pale-as-death young man from down under, I had to change places with him quick so he could throw up. The result kind of spoiled the view. When he felt better, he fell asleep, and ended up slobbering on my shoulder. I wonder if Terence ('nothing human is foreign to me') ever travelled in a hot bus with a sick Aussie . . . Anyway, you take it as it comes. Who wants the ideal? I was glad nonetheless when we finally got to Ban Tha Ton on the river Mekok.

It was exactly how I imagine the American West in the early 19th century. Tribeswomen passing (old woman pipe in mouth, young woman suckling a child) — like in the paintings of George Catlin, Carl Bodmer, William Emory. Men playing at roll-the-coin: rolling coins down an inclined board to see who will get his coin closest to the wall — like a flatboat crew shooting dice on the banks of the Mississippi. The river Mekok flows brown under the blue sky. There's a blue haze on the forest hills . . .

Time to get back to the party.

The guide suggests we buy up sweets and cigarettes 'for the

tribespeople'. I don't much like the idea, but I comply. Then we go down and pile our rucksacks in the boat that's just come in. It's a long boat, and I think at first there's going to be plenty of room, amazing, but just at that moment the other party turns up, and my utopian vision of space is blasted. In fact, it's a degree or two worse than in the bus.

In place of the Aussie this time — he's folded over my rucksack up there at the brow of the boat — I have a couple of Dutchwomen, two extroverted and sprawling young ladies with appetites who spend their time smoking fags, munching peanuts and sucking mints, in quick succession or simultaneously, one of them, particularly liberated, getting her bare tootsies sunburned in the vicinity of my right ear . . . I can't help thinking of Terence again.

But it was morning river despite all, and a beautiful trip: burnt trees on the bank like totems; snags cropping up ideogrammatically out of the brown water; and a girl on the shore — darkblue skirt, lightblue skirt — washing her hair.

About an hour and a half later, we arrive at the Shan village of Ban Mai, where the parties split up. The walking starts here. We leave whatever we won't need for the next two days in the house in this village where we'll be sleeping on the last night, and start off.

Across the fields, then through the jungle, in single file. Bamboo, teak, orchids . . . Steaming greenery, and swift perspectives of distant shimmering blue. A steady pace, and nobody speaking, except the Bavarian girl saying now and then to her companion: *'guck mol'* (look!).

A couple of hours bring us to a Lahu village. Which means in the first place a horde of snot-nosed children with sore eyes touching the tip of their tongue with a finger. That's where the sweets come in. For the rest, the German takes photos of a young woman at 1 baht a time, two or three others get a cigarette. And that's about it. No, another photo of a woman carrying water, and an old woman crimson with betel . . . That's the Lahu, more particularly, the Lahu Nyi, known hereabouts as the Red Mussuh, or Red Hunters, a name which they resent, not because of the 'hunter' part, of which they're proud, but because of the 'red', which in this context signifies 'crude' or 'raw'. They do a lot of opium-smoking, and they also burn a lot of candles and joss-sticks — at the end of the last century a prophet told them to burn them continually till the Lahu received Enlightenment . . .

The jungle once more.

It's late afternoon when we get to the Karen village — hailed at the entrance from a house terrace by three drunks who insist we come and drink their corn liquor. The guide says they'll be vexed if we refuse. OK — but I regret my old Blue Meo man of a few days back.

After that interlude, we make for the place where we'll be spending the night, a house, which is the grocery, owned by a Chinese woman, down by the stream that runs beside the village. Blankets are distributed, and we spread out our kit on the sleeping platform. From now on it's just a matter of waiting till the guide gets the meal ready. I go for a stroll, the German and French couples do the same. Evening coming down blue and yellow. I'm lying out later on the platform, bored, when I hear the beat of a drum. Steady old monotonous beat.

I get up and follow the sound.

It brings me to what looks like a school playground. There's an old man dancing to the drum accompaniment within a circle of children. The children are laughing, giggling, squealing with delight, their eyes glued to the antics of the old man. He's a very old man, but agile as a goat, bent over double, tapping his hands from each other to thigh to heel, and waggling his arse like a fish — it's this arse-waggling that particularly provokes the children's mirth.

I'm standing at the fence watching the old man, as fascinated as the children, when a boy of about eighteen comes up to me:

'Hello, good evening.'

'Good evening.'

'You like dance?'

'Yes.'

'What religion?'

I'd seen a cross on one of the buildings in the yard, so I said:

'Christian.'

'Very good. I Catholic.'

He invited me into the compound:

'Please come.'

He rang a bell, and the crowd filed into the building with the cross on top. It was dark in there, only two small lamps on the floor giving light.

Then followed a very simple service of prayers and singing conducted by the young boy. I'd forgotten it was December 25th — and I hadn't known there were Christian Karen. A well-known hymn came out from Karen mouths as:

'Klo ria in ensailis dio o.'

After the service, the festival. Bonfires were lit in the quadrangle, and the crowd divided into groups: one group singing hymns and songs; one consisting of children dancing; and one round the old men who knew the old dances. I joined this latter group.

Those old men could dance! None of the younger men who tried came anywhere near them — they were clumsy and heavy in comparison. The old men danced: fighting dances, with bamboo sticks for swords; what looked like a cock-fight, with the defeated one lying on its back, legs twitching in the air; and a dance in which the two men circled round each other, as close together as they could come, weaving round each other, without ever actually touching.

I was with the old men, but pretty soon I felt a small hand slipping into mine. It was a lovely little boy, with a balaclava on his head, wanting me to come and join him and his pals. We had a good time, making crazy gestures and faces at one another, inventing dances, rolling about the grass.

Then everybody gathered together and there was a big farandole around the bonfires, a long line of dancers moving with the drummer in the van.

That was the grand finale.

The little boy said something like *'Pi ba, pi ba'*, which I took to mean that it was time to go home. I said good-bye all round and went back down to the house by the river.

There was a half-moon in the sky, and a thick mist rising off the stream. Inside, everybody (except the Chinese woman, who was snug in the inner chamber) was lying under blankets on the platform, but nobody was sleeping yet — because of the cold. The guide said there was some rice and meat for me on a plate beside the fire. I thanked him and ate, realising I was hungry. Then I also got under my blankets on the platform.

But it really was cold.

Damn cold.

Like everybody else I'd doze a while, then wake with the cold, try to get some heat by re-arranging the blankets, then doze fitfully again. The man beside me gave a horrible shudder about every half-hour.

Hellish.

It must have been about one or two in the morning when I decided I'd had enough and got up, intending to do some gymnastic exercises outside, maybe walk about for a while, anything would be better than lying there immobile freezing.

Hallelujah! Outside I found the remaining embers of a fire, a dull glow there under the frozen sky. I felt around for some twigs, strips of bamboo, grass, anything, and thus equipped came back to the embers. With the bamboo I wakened them, and by their light saw a woodpile. From that moment on, my troubles were over.

I settled down by the fire, with a pile of logs to hand, and a log for a pillow.

With the warmth of the fire caressing me, I could even appreciate the beauty of the moon and stars. I no longer *wanted* to sleep.

I just lay there, now and then replenishing the fire, watching the frosty moon and the infinite plurality of stars. Around me in the darkness, the snuffling of a dog, the grunt of a pig, the cry of a bird. All alone in the night with a sensation of very great joyance.

5. Blue Mountain

Dawn came white through the mist, the fire paled. In a way it was a let-down, because the night had been full of that primitive fire-joyance, accompanied by a sense of universal space. But at the same time, with the coming of morning, although I hadn't slept, I felt fully awakened and refreshed.

I took a stroll down by the river, listening to the sound of its gurgling in the mist, touching its rippling coldness, then retraced my steps, past the fire, into the village.

Here the sounds were of rice-pounding. As moisture dripped from the banana leaves, and as the water-buffalos, like great grey boulders with horns, raised their massive heads to sniff the morning air, the rice-pounder, actioned by a girl's sturdy leg, went *thud thud-thud:,*

thud thud-thud. It was the rhythm of the drum I'd heard the evening before.

When I got back to our lodgings, my companions were all up, stiff-boned, and the guide was making coffee, laying out bread. The Chinese woman took a long calculating look at her wood-pile, but made no comment.

After breakfast, we set out for an Akha village, about ten miles distant, further up in the mountains. The Akha like to live high, above 4000 feet — they distrust people who come from lower-lying land, considering them as bearers of evil spirits. They're very much concerned with spirits. They build altars in their houses to keep good spirits, and about a hundred yards out of the village on the trail leading to it they build gates to keep good spirits in and evil spirits out. They are particularly afraid of water spirits, which is why they seldom bathe, but prefer (at least up till recently) simply to *wipe* the dirt off their bodies. They're among the most primitive of the tribes, and live more directly off the jungle than the others, eating jungle vegetables along with maggots, grubs, larvae and animals that other tribespeople find unclean. They came into Thailand in recent years from Burma, and carry a strong Tibetan influence with them.

Moving up through the jungle silence — sun filtered gold and green across bamboo.

At one point, there's a sound of singing on the air, and three Akha women, an old one in front, followed by two young ones — all smoking pipes (no Akha, man or woman, is ever without a pipe) — come down the trail, with baskets on their backs, and machetes in the baskets, off to work. They are wearing the distinctive headdress of the Akha women, that conical hat of cloth stretched on a bamboo frame, decorated with silver coins (mostly Indian rupees), buttons, beads, embroidery, and tufts of monkey fur, held in place by a cord going under the chin. They are also wearing the short (about 14 inches) skirt, worn low round the hips, aprons of tassels and beadwork, fancy bags and decorated leggings. They look dirty and colourful, gay and independent. The old woman declares by gestures she wants cigarettes (puff! puff!), and soap to wash her face (rubbing cheeks with both hands), while the young girls giggle, feeling the foreign eyes on them. After some banter and barter, they go on down the trail, picking up their song again.

We move on towards the village.

Here's the gate, presenting bamboo strips in the shape of asterisks and garlands.

A sturdy old woman on bandy legs, pipe in gub, arrayed in dusty jacket and mini-skirt, wants a cigarette: *'Sigala? Sigala?'* Another old woman, her skirt hung so low round her hips her bum shows at the back and her pubic hair at the front, prefers soap. A man sitting cross-legged on a platform grinds maize . . .

About forty houses. They'll stay here ten to fifteen years, then move on. Pigs, chickens, and dogs (edible to the Akha) all over the place. Children with sores and a man shaking with malaria.

The men here wear their hair in a short queue — if they were to lose their queue they would go insane. They are proud of their tobacco boxes, and like corn whisky.

Akha people bury their dead, and let the grave be covered with thorns. The bodies are carried away to the West. Nobody knows how life began. But there are spirits everywhere.

Will soap wash away the spirits?

The next stop was at a village founded by remnants of the old Kuomintang armies, an hour or so for a meal and a siesta.

Little black pigs grunt in the yard, a turkey comes gobbling down the dusty street, while a little boy lays a yellow turd right in the middle of it. After rice and bananas, I'm sitting on a bench writing, and an old Chinaman comes up to my shoulder, watching me. I hand him the pencil and pad, he points to my writing and makes a smiling gesture: no. It's not that he can't write, I think, but that he thinks I want him to write *my* way. I draw the Chinese ideogram for sun. He smiles, nods his head, and points upward.

At a Lisu village later on that afternoon, we bought a goodly supply of grass. I smoked a pipe in honour of the 'spirits of the hills and valleys'. Then another one, to make sure none would be offended if I inadvertently did something against the universal harmony of things. A man who dislodges a rock for example, is running a big risk. It's as though these people consider that human establishments may be convenient, but are unnatural, so that the spirits of nature must be propitiated and wheedled into accepting them.

The smoke was well into my blood when we got on the trail again.

I felt as if I could walk to Peru. Every step was a delight, a muscular delight.

Down in the riverside house after our evening meal, I got into conversation with the French couple over a smoke. I remember answering to the man, who'd asked what I was 'looking for', that I wasn't really looking for any one thing, I'd found a lot of things separately, all I wanted, but now I was trying to get it all together, find the coherence. I remember also talking about 'shooting ideas', like 'shooting stars' . . .

After his meal with the people of the house, the guide came over to join us: 'Enough beer, try grass', telling us that 'Buddha stick costs 20 baht in Chieng Mai', whereas in the Lisu village it had been 2 baht for a handful. He took a draw on his stick and then said dreamily: 'No. 1.' The lamps burned in the house behind us, we puffed on the pipes, and in the background at one point there was the sound of monks chanting . . .

When it was time for the house lamps to go out, our host built us a bamboo fire in the yard. We sat around it for a long time, till there was no conversation left, and we just sat there with blankets round our shoulders, motionless, saying nothing — gazing at the burning bamboo.

6. Down River to Chieng Rai

I was up before dawn, walking in the village — only the mist and the dripping banana leaves. Then an old woman came out of a house to light a fire, and soon another followed suit, and another: bushels of yellow flame dotting the misty silence.

In our lodgings, a sooty black kettle is hissing on the fire and everybody's folding blankets. This is the end of the hill-trip. The guide is going back down to Chieng Mai with the two couples. I'm going on to Chieng Rai, will have to negotiate for the boat after breakfast.

The guide comes with me to consult the local Chinese boat-owner. Yes, OK, for a trip to Chieng Rai, in one hour's time. Meanwhile, down to the landing-stage to bid the others goodbye. The river still a vague mistiness with strokes of gold. The boat comes up, the travellers pile in, farewells, and the embarcation chug-chugs up through the mist in the direction of Tha Ton . . .

A half-hour later, my own boat leaves, with the prosperous-looking Chinese owner, and a less prosperous-looking Thai handling the tiller.

Morning waters.

The cold mist continues for a while, and we stay wrapped up for warmth, the Chinese in a padded blue anorak, the Thai with a balaclava, me in an old Breton *caban*.

The man at the bar has to keep his eyes skinned, because of the many boulders and snags. He weaves the boat from side to side of the river, sometimes scraping the bottom as we cross some shallow place.

We pass a couple of boats fishing, and floating stocks of green bamboo.

Now the sun's fixed in a blue sky.

Incredible freshness. High clarity.

I'm almost sorry when we arrive.

At Chieng Rai, after finding myself a hotel, I sally out into the streets.

Saturday afternoon.

Deserted.

I go into a restaurant, being hungry. Nobody at the tables, but at the cash counter a girl sleeping, with her head cradled on her arms. And a bluebottle buzzing . . .

The girl wakes startled, with big eyes. She is very good-looking. The girl who serves me later at the table points to her and says: 'She No. 1'. I say they are both No. 1. But in fact the first girl is the prettier of the two. The waitress tells me she is a Yao.

'No. 1' and personal names are the limits of our possibilities of verbal communication. To order my meal I point to the refrigerator, the door of which being opened I make my choice. What comes up later cooked is a big plate of rice, meat and vegetables, and another plate with fried rice and a frittered egg on top. It all goes down well with a bottle of beer, and thus fed I come back out into the streets.

Empty, or almost.

A man passes by with a megaphone advertising films.

'Where do you go?' — a young boy passing by.

No idea.

Saturday afternoon in Chieng Rai.

I settle for a coffee-shop, order some tea, and spend part of the time writing, then return to my hotel and spend an hour or so sleeping.

Around eight, I mosey out again, thinking I'll make for a restaurant, have a meal, and see what turns up.

Nothing does.

And yet it isn't unpleasant. Nirvana. Nirvana at the end of the world.

I follow my nose and it leads me to a night-club, the *Chieng Rai Moondance Night Club.*

Dark in there, very dark. To call a waiter you raise a match or a lighter in the air.

I drink Thai whisky and watch a moon-girl dancing.

7. *The Face of the East Wind*

The next day I went up to Mae Sai, on the Burmese frontier.

Mae Sai is a shop-bordered street with a river at the top, and a bridge. Burmese and Thais go to and fro on the bridge. I have to content myself watching the movement. Although I have a visa from the Socialist Republic of the Union of Burma, obtained for 100 baht from their embassy in Bangkok, I can't go into Burma on foot — the only legitimate way for me at the moment would be by plane from Bangkok to Rangoon. I could make that trip, go back down to Bangkok right away, travel the road to Mandalay, but I have other ideas. I'd like to find myself an individual kind of monastery in these parts, a quiet room where I intend to undertake some little experiments in mind-exploration, 'insight'.

Insight — I have a little booklet with me on Insight (*vipassana*), written by a Thai *bhikshu*, based on the methods of Thai and Burmese teachers of meditation. I've read I don't know how many books on Buddhism, often hefty tomes and ponderous studies, by historians of religion, philosophers, philologists, I've delved into Buddhist literature, sutras, commentaries, commentaries on commentaries, but here I am now, at this 'journey's end', with a little twenty-page booklet:

'What is Insight? The well-known answer is to see all conditioned things as impermanent, unsatisfactory and non-self. How do we achieve that? By developing Mindfulness (*sati*) and Full Attention (*sampajanna*). The Master once summarised his teaching in one sentence by saying: "O brothers, be mindful and fully attentive. That is all I have to teach you."

'Sensation and ordinary feeling are like water and waves respectively. Waves are water, forms of water. Developing Insight is like diving into the deep water of sensation.'

'There can be real peace only in movement and real stillness only in arising and ceasing.'

I go up into the hills, and come across a temple behind which a flight of steps leads up to a *chedi*.

A snake lies sunning itself on the eighty-first step. A hundred and twenty steps further bring me up to the hill-top, with its Buddha protected by four scorpions.

I turn my back on the Buddha.

Before me, blue woven into blue, is Burma: hills, a river, a village, a temple.

I take these elements, work through them: the temple, the village, the river, the hills, the curves, the blue, the blue energy, the pulsions . . . All pulsant blue: moving silence, mobile immobility.

'The unity of contemplation and action is illustrated in a Zen drawing of Bodhidharma with his face and body perfectly calm, while his robe is fluttering in the wind.'

THE WILD SWANS

The mindful exert themselves. Like wild swans that leave their pools, they abandon home after home . . .

Dhammapada

1. *Another Departure*

For some time, the idea had been taking shape in my mind of a Japan-trip that would be yet another geopoetic pilgrimage: a salutation to things Japanese (things precious and precarious) and a haiku-journey in the wake of Basho, a dreamlike documentary of roads and islands, a quick and elliptic plunge into Emptiness — all in all, a wild little Nipponese book full of images and mental zig-zagging, written in 'flying white style', as the painters say.

After that, I thought to myself, I shall hole up in my cosmological observatory on the Breton coast (to work at the next cycle) and walk the still unencumbered coastal paths, wrapped in wind, rain and silence . . .

By the Autumn of 1985, I felt ready for it, and had laid out roughly my itinerary.

I'd take Tokyo as point of departure, and thereafter travel up North, finally reaching Hokkaido . . .

Sitting in that Paris airport café a sunny morning in September (I'd left my beautiful Breton hermitage the day before), I listened attentively to the Japanese sounds I could hear in the air all around me, especially those of one long, moon-faced girl, and let Japan literary memories run scattered through my brain: Dazai's setting sun; Rugetsu the haiku-teacher in Nagai Kafû's east-of-the-river story; Kawabata's young student walking alone on the Izu peninsula and meeting up with a group of dancers ('to hear them speak of Oshima, my heart filled with poetry') . . .

Nipponese ground:

Sea-coast and mountains. Gulfs, bays, promontories. Volcanic earth, convulsed, ravaged, washed by wind and rain, by tides and fogs, by a vaporous play of water, mist and sun. Tumbling streams, waterfalls, red leaves . . .

I wanted to get into all that: the energy and the rhythm and the light of all that. And I wanted, if possible — it would be a kind of bonus — to see the wild swans coming in swooping and whooping from Siberia to winter on Japan's northern lakes.

Yes, I wanted that.

'Flight for Tokyo. Gate 17.'

2. *Que pasa, man?*

In the night above America, a little Japanese girl slumped down beside me and began smoking like a volcano. When she'd puffed herself into contentment, she snuggled up luxuriously in the seat and fell asleep. Pretty soon her head was lying against my left shoulder.

I must have dozed off myself. When I woke, the little Jap girl had gone, and a voice was announcing that we were moving down to Tokyo.

'*Hoteru Sundown, ku da sai!*'

Once I'd got that out to the white-gloved taxidriver and he'd answered smartly back: '*Hoteru Sundown — hai*', I settled back on the immaculate white-covered seat with my eyes at the window ready for all sorts of signs (though I know I'm after something a lot more immediate and substantial than signs), vaguely listening to the pep talk being delivered on the radio by an avant-garde American padre to his flock of Armed Forces: 'Learn to be yourself . . . your strength is in your Self . . . that's where God put it — God wants you to be your *self* . . .', saying to *my*self that the self is just a metaphor, which is to say a way of getting from one place to another . . .

Anyway, that's Tokyo out there.

At first glance, it's plug-ugly.

It isn't a city, Tokyo, it's a calamity.

No self-respecting city could indulge itself in such a pot-pourri of styles: neoclassical, neogothic, neobaroque, neomodern, neoneo, all in red brick and ferroconcrete, drab, dull, dismal.

And what's that over there: a pyramid?!

Those hordes and hordes and hordes of citizens, the biggest human agglomeration in the universe.

Those flashing advertisements — it looks as if the cosmopolitan culture-circus has gone berserk here, throwing up all its images in this sprawling no-place at the Far-Eastern frontier.

Yet I know that behind those screeching, blaring façades, there must be back-alleys, quiet gardens, bits of old canals.

The other Japan.

Surely . . .

There were two Americans checking in at the Sundown Hotel at the same time as myself. One was a nervous, New York Jew type, the other a long slow Texan who kept saying to his buddy who was always busy with cases or cheque-books or forms: '*Que pasa, man*?' The nervous one was still busying himself with this and that and the lanky-laconic one was still saying '*Que pasa, man*?' when I took the elevator up to the twelfth floor of the building that lodged the hotel and found myself before a metal door that opened on to a teeny-weeny room with all Tokyo blinking red, yellow, green, purple in the window. When I opened that window, a twelfth-floor wind ripped by on its way from the Aleutians to Kyushu, Manila and other points unknown. Maybe it was the effect of the long flight from Europe, or maybe it was the tininess of the room, the vision of all Tokyo spreading out down there, and the wind, but I had the highly unpleasant feeling that I was liable to fall out plumb into space. It was only when I'd drawn the curtain that I felt a little more secure, though later that night I took the precaution of sleeping with my head at the foot of the bed, instead of at the head, which was stuck right over the gaping, dizzy chasm.

Once I'd settled in a little, I went to the restaurant on the eleventh floor of the same building to get something to eat, but the restaurant had been requisitioned that night by some Business Company who were holding a banquet — they had a table set up in front of the restaurant door, and were distributing presents to the Company people as they arrived. As an un-Companied individual, I was told politely I could get a meal in the bar next door.

I was sitting in the bar, quite content to be alive, with a plate of salmon, a bowl of rice and a bottle of Sapporo beer before me, when *the earth trembled*. There were other people, all Japanese, in the smoky red light of the bar, but they didn't seem to notice what was going on, at least they didn't stop their conversation for one second. I was sitting on a couch that ran along the window, and I couldn't help edging myself a wee bit forward on it, asking myself why the bloody hell I'd ever abandoned brightblue Brittany and come to this Tokyo — just to be swallowed up in an earthquake? It was to take me some time to get used to such tremblings of the earth, and even to get some pleasure from them — but not from twelfth- or fourteenth-floor rooms in a big city, even though they tell me the buildings *are* anti-seismic.

After my meal, I went for a stroll through Saturday night Roppongi.

It was there that I met up again with the little Japanese I'd slept with in the Boeing. Except that there were hundreds of her, thousands of her. They came pouring up out of the Roppongi Subway station, all the little girls of Tokyo, dressed in silks and satins, with little purses and sequins, looking for fun — a few hours of screeching rock at the *Capri*, or lonely blues at the *Blue Lady*, or something funky at the *Banana Junky*.

When I got back to the hotel, a drunken Australian girl singing *Waltzing Matilda* was being dragged out of the bar by three little Japanese, and in the elevator a girl was sobbing on the shoulder of her boy-friend who stared ahead at nothing with an air of total indifference.

As I got into bed, I heard the Texan in the corridor saying once again: '*Que pasa, man*?'

3. Sunday in Ueno Park

Next morning, at breakfast, in the hotel's bird's-eye-view restaurant, I'm looking at a map of Tokyo wondering where to go first in order to get into the rhythm of the city, when I come across the name 'Ueno', and that rings a bell for me — because of that haiku by Basho where he's in his little house and hears the bells of time ring over the city and wonders if these are the bells of Asakusa or those of Ueno . . .

So I go to Ueno, Ueno Park.

And I'm not alone, far from it. The place is full of families, baseball players and bums. As I pass on the leafy path before a little bunch of those nit-picking Nipponese nihilists, one of them, sake-soaked and with a mop of hair that could house three crows, calls out raucously and roguishly:

'*Amerika, desuka — okay!*'

I give him a little from-here-to-eternity salute, and pass on.

There really are a lot of bums in Ueno Park, in fact there seems to be as many bums gathered there as there are Bretons in Montparnasse, and maybe for something of the same reason. Ueno station, as I learned later, is the North Country station, with trains coming in from Sendai, Morioka, Aomori, Iwate, Nagano, Niigata, trains bringing in people to the big city looking for work and who, maybe not finding it, and maybe finding that jobless life in Ueno Park is not after all so bad, just stick around. So they sit there on the benches, some talkative, some dumb, all rheumy-eyed, probably not illuminated.

I walk along the scuffling pathways, among trees (lots of cherry trees) and fountains, temples and shrines, till I come to the statue of Ernest Fenollosa, that American of Spanish origin from Salem, Massachussetts, who took up a chair of philosophy at the new university of Tokyo in 1878, who was to finish his Japanese career not only as Imperial Minister of Fine Arts, but as *daijin sensei*, the teacher of great men, and whose notebooks were destined to change the course of Western writing.

I salute him too.

And then come smack up against the National Museum where I spend a couple of hours in the Aïnu section, admiring the display of embroidered cotton robes (*chikatkarpe*), leggings (*hosh*), earrings (*ninkari*), necklets (*tama-sai*), tobacco boxes (*tampako-op*) and knives (*makir*).

There's something about this Aïnu culture that attracts me a lot.

Those flowing white patterns on the dark blue cloth.

That feeling for salmon, bear, whale, geese and swan.

For stone and bone.

I'll have to go on up there.

Get closer into all that area.

Meanwhile, I've added to my general stock of images and information, but I still have no clear idea of Tokyo city's present-day mental meteorology. For that I need to get in touch with a Japanese.

4. *A Little Fever*

People in Paris had said I should meet this young writer. I met him in a café in the Asakusa quarter — which, as he told me, used to be the cultural hub of the city, where the Kabuki theatres were located as well as all kinds of restaurants and the Kamiya Bar, where we now were, and where writers like Nagai Kafû and Tanizaki Junichirô would foregather, drinking that mixture of vermouth, curaçao, gin, wine and brandy known as *denki buran* ('electric brandy').

'This town is like a sponge,' said Kenji.

He himself wasn't born in Tokyo, but in a small town up near Sendai, in Miyagi prefecture. Came down to Tokyo city five years ago.

'What do you think about Japan in general?'

'I don't like it, this Japan today. I like what the French call *japonisme*. I like to live in a country of the mind. In that, very Japanese.'

'Who are the Japanese writers who mean anything to you, I mean at this moment?'

'No one.'

'And in the past, the recent past?'

'I have met Mister Kawabata. He was sick at the heart. Mishima also I have met. He had many complexes, and he was a snob. I prefer much Tanizaki. Tanizaki, for me, is Number 1. *Sasame yuki* — "a little snow". Myself I am very like Mister Dazai — a little inhuman.'

'And the writers of the past, Basho say?'

'Poetry is difficult. It needs a lot of mind, a lot of heart. Basho goes far. Into the cold land, the snow country. No one does that today. We live in a cage.'

'What do you think of Kenzaburo?'

'Mister Kenzaburo is very Westerned. We say his writing tastes of butter.'

'What should Japanese writing taste like today?'

'I don't know. Maybe *awamori*.'

'What's that?'

'Japanese vodka.'

'Are you writing something now?'

'I'm finishing one book.'

'What's it called?'

'*A little fever never leaves me*.'

5. Street to Street

During the next few days, Kenji and I walked feverishly through Tokyo.

Ever heard of *denki-gai*?

It's the main thoroughfare in the Akihabara quarter, and if it's called Electric Street, it's because it's an electronics paradise, or hell, depending how you look on it. There are multi-storey shops there selling everything from refrigerators and air-conditioners on the ground floor to micro-computers on the top, passing through blue-blinking video sets, shining steel record-players and big black amplifiers. But that is not all. Behind the mammoth shops, you have the huddled masses of 'junkshops' (*jankumono*), laden with every kind of electronic gadget you can think of, along with a few, if you're like me, you'd never imagine in a hundred years. The whole area blares with noise and glares with multicoloured, multispeed light.

'This is tomorrow's world,' said Kenji.

'Let's get out of it while we can.'

Being an archaic type of character, I got more to feed my sensorial and imaginative needs from Tsukiji, the fish market.

A welter of sea-life there.

Eels coiling.

Crabs groping.

All kinds of octopus writhing.

But especially the tuna: those sleek, curving bodies still covered with frost, marked with characters in red, steaming in the early morning sun. Life from *elsewhere*: the big ones fished in the South Pacific, the smaller ones off Capetown. All those fat, lithe, slithery, gleaming, once fast-swimming bodies lined up on the quay, their blind eye-sockets blocked with grey ice, and prospective buyers cutting a little nick in them, examining it closely with the poking light of a torch (ah, that glistening dark-red flesh!), while the auctioneer, sturdy little bloke in skip cap, is nearly bursting a blood vessel and stomping on his platform like a big baby in tantrums as he keeps the prices racing and rising. When the auctions are over, the fish is lugged over to the stalls, where the cutting-up begins: with huge axes, with long knives, with electric saws — ready for the restaurant people of Tokyo who will soon be doing their rounds. Only the heads of the fish are left on the quay, scattered among the piles of styrofoam cases:

Those tuna heads
they look as though they'd like to say
a final word . . .

A lot of the crab in Tsukiji must find its way to the famous crab-meat restaurant in Shinjuku that has a huge crab gesticulating mechanically and uncannily above its entrance door.

Every time I think of Shinjuku, I see that crab.

Cancer city.

Shinjuku, an October evening, big Autumn moon, the crab slowly moving, loudspeakers blaring out rock 'n' roll, steel-balls cascading in the *pachinko* parlours and a string of 'love-saloons' exhibiting their photos of 'nude students' (*joshi gakusei nudo*) — 'You look, you touch, you fix a date'.

Girls galore: *gyaru ippai*!

There's nothing of the charm of old Tokyo here, says the young poet — the tea-houses have gone, the old canals have given over to expressways, but even here, even in the most garish of modern ambiances, there are vestiges.

In some of these love-saloons, for instance, as soon as you've paid the entrance fee, you're ushered into a room where girls line up, maybe five or six of them, naked, stark naked, *except for a little silk apron*. Now, in old Tokyo, in Edo, there was a type of prostitute called the *kekoro* (used to be found around Ueno hill), and the mark of the *kekoro* was . . . her apron, which is why she was often referred to as *yamashita no maedare*, 'the apron from under the hill'.

So, there they stand, the 'naked students', in the university of the flesh, in the cancer city night.

One there, like a heron among chickens.

Small, silky breasts, she has ('straight', she says ruefully), but I tell her they're beautiful . . .

Back out in the street, let's move away from the lights and the noise, away from the love-saloons and the knickerless (*No Pants Kissa*) cafés, into quieter areas, the alleys full of dusky little dives:

Space Den
Cherry Island
Havanna Moon
Silk Road . . .

and drink-bars (*nomiya*). Quiet little holes. Where you drink beer, sake, whisky, and eat, say, octopus tentacles, crab paste, salmon eggs, grated wild potato, or the dish *tsukimi* ('see the moon'). And listen to songs: sad songs, nostalgic songs, suggestive songs. To get the imagination going, to float in a little deep life, to sink into the past, or maybe just oblivion.

There are streets here called specifically *omoide-dori*, 'memory lanes':

Big moon, yellow moon, seen through the smoke of frying fish . . .

'*Mamma, birru!*' shouts the middle-aged business man, his round face lathered in sweat. 'And another one for the *gaijin*, for the foreigner!' . . .

The foreigner, that's me.

And the night goes on.

We end up in the Octopus Bar, a little *nomiya* in the middle of nowhere (on the wall, an octopus and a monkey are making love) whose manager is a haiku-poet. His poet's name: 'He who gets walked on all the time, but who's still around'. He recites one of his haiku, about shadows on a wall in Kyoto, and another about fish frying in a pan and the wrinkles on his mother's face.

Dawn comes with the taste of cold sake.

6. *The World of Books*

Jimbochô must be one of the most prodigious book-places in the world: streets and streets lined with book-shops, all of them crammed with books and books about books from floor to ceiling.

Kenji tells me one of the first Western books to be translated into Japanese was *Robinson Crusoe*, under the title: 'A Tale of Wanderings, written by an Englishman'.

I didn't find any Japanese first edition *Crusoe* in the course of my Jimbochô rambles, but I did find many another of equal, if not greater, interest to me: Sakakura Genjro's *Essay on the Northern Seas*, de Vries's *Reize naar Japan*, Wenceslas de Moraes' *Cartas do Japaõ*, the *Narrative of a Voyage to Japan, Kamschatka, Siberia, Tartary and various parts of China* by navy lieutenant Tronson, and Lapérouse's *Voyage*:

'Their head was bare, though two or three wore bearskin bandannas . . . They all had sealskin boots on their feet, very skilfully and

beautifully made, Chinese-style . . . Their manners were grave, noble and very affectionate . . . As to their cabins, they are built with intelligence, every precaution having been taken against the cold. Made of wood, they are covered with birchbark . . .'
— that's Lapérouse talking about the Ainu folk he met up with on Hokkaido.

There were those travel-books, and maps — scores of maps, original and reproduced: the French map of *Arctic Lands* (Les Terres Arctiques) with Hokkaido marked 'Terre de Iesso' (that's the map Lapérouse used); the Japanese map by Ishikawa Ryûsen, the *Honchö Zukan Kömoku*, on which you see to the North a cluster of islands under the name *Ezogashima*; Francis Caron's *Perfeckte Kaert van de gelegentheydt des Landts van Japan* that presents Hokkaido (*'t Vaste Landt van Iezzo*), not as an island but as an uninterrupted passage between Japan and Tartary . . .

And old Japanese books, their pages soft to the touch as cobwebs, showing black steamships in red sunset harbours, or tea-houses under the moon, or some old city street. And prints, coloured blue, pink, deep red, with all the shades of black the mad and marvellous Hukosai speaks so well about: ancient black, fresh black, brilliant black, flat black, the black of light and the black of shadow . . .

One print particularly took my fancy: 'Englishman doing the dance of Yokohama'. It shows an Englishman with a very long nose doing a wild jig in front of a geisha with a shamisen on her knees and a puzzled expression on her face. This is one of those famous 'Yokohama prints' made soon after the arrival in Tokyo Bay of U.S. Commodore Perry's ships, an arrival that meant the reopening of Japan to the world after its more than two centuries' practically total isolation.

7. In Yokohama

It was because of that print, but not only because of it, for Yokohama's been part of my personal mythology for years (at age 15, in my little Western village, didn't I daub a weird Surrealistico-exotic fantasmagoria entitled: 'Nights of Yokohama'?!) that I decided to make a little jaunt out to the port through which the West penetrated, very ignorantly, very brutally, into the gentle land of Yamato.

Tokyo station (*Tokyo Eki*) in the morning.

I go to the ticket office:

'*Yokohama made*' (all the way to Yokohama).

'Machine.'

The clerk points to a ticket machine to the right of his office.

I put in the 410 yen indicated, get my ticket, wave with it to the clerk.

'Okay, Captain.'

Track No. 7.

Along comes the little blue rattler of a suburban train.

Crowded — crowded — crowded.

In the carriage I enter, a lot of old people. It looks in fact like an old folks' outing.

There's a distribution after a few minutes of beer and sake:

'*Osake!*' (the venerable sake), exclaims an old man. While an old woman, lifting a beer can (Sapporo beer) to her lips says:

'*Hokkaido!*'

I watch another old woman very carefully unwrapping a little cake and munching it delicately, very, very delicately . . .

Shimbashi.

Shinagawa.

Shin-kawasaki.

Kawasaki . . . Kawasaki . . . Wasn't that a print by Hiroshige, one of the 53 stages on the Tokaido (blue waters, and a ferry boat being poled across them)? This morning, factory stacks belching white-grey smoke, a drizzle of rain, red brick buildings and a huddle of blue zinc roofs.

At Yokohama, I go up up to the Bluff, from where you get the best view of the Bay, and wander through the Foreign Cemetery (*Gaïjin bochi*), among the British, American, Russian, Portuguese, Dutch and German tombs: '*Hier ruht Kurt von Seebach, geb. d. 14 September 1859 in Erfurt, gest. d. 21 September 1891 in Yokohama*'; '*In Memory of James G. Cullen, born in Scotland, died in Yokohama Aug. 20th 1881*'; '*A saudosa memoria de Querina Filomena Farias da Silva*'; '*Hier rust Wessel de Vos vermoord te Yokohama*'; '*Hier ruhet in Gott der Oberheizer der kaiserlichen Marine Eduard School*'; '*In Memory of John Hope MacDonald, 1st officer of the N.Y.K . . . a native of Stornoway Scotland*';

'Herbert Boan Jr. Florida 1922–1957, AD2, U.S. Navy, World War II, Korea' — on the stone of that last tomb, somebody had deposited *in memoriam* a can of beer.

After this little walk with death up on the Bluff (it's an old habit of mine, do it everywhere I go), I go down to the harbour: out there in the green waters, a little fleet of Uraga Channel Pilot Boats, a great red hulking brute from the company *Chargeurs Réunis* (C. R. Douala), and a Japanese boat, the *Kuwana Maru.* I stroll then through Yamashita Park, where there's a schoolchildren's painting competition going on (the favourite subject seems to be the Marine Tower), walk along the Nakamuna River, go into a little print shop on Motomachi where I buy another *gaïjin-e* ('foreign people print'), then go visit the Silk Museum and the History Archives.

There I see photos of the little Jap flappers of the twenties, those dot-pattern dresses of the thirties (my mother wore one in the only photo I have of her young), the New Look of 1949 and the so-called Hot-Pants skirt (half-way up thigh) of 1967. And read the history of the Silk Road, so named by the German geographer Ferdinand von Richthofen, all the 10,000 kilometres of it, that Hiuan Chuang travelled, known in Japan as Sanzo-hoshi and who became the hero of the Chinese *Hsi Yu Chi*, translated by Arthur Waley as *Monkey*: that long long road from China to the coastal cities of the Mediterranean through vast expanses of drifting sand and desolate hills. And there's the silk of Yokohama — the ten million dozen of 'Yokohama scarves' exported every year, and those absolutely beautiful stretches of cloth — that one with the wave pattern; that one, blue, with the flight of wild swans . . . In the history archives I pore over maps and photos of whaling and see Commodore Perry meeting the Imperial High Commissioner at Yokohama; read through the commercial treaties and the customs regulations; consult a page of Hepburn's Japanese-English dictionary printed in Shanghai, 1867 . . .

Evening in Yokohama.

Walking around from place to place, from piece to piece, taking notes.

Yellow light, big rainy night, heart of Autumn.

On the evening of September 2nd, 1879, the ship *Vega* anchored off Yokohama. On board was the Swedish scientist and explorer

Nordenskiöld, who had just completed the North–East passage, linking the Atlantic to the Pacific along the coast of Russia and Siberia. Despite a few tempests, the last stage of the trip, from the Bering Straits to Yokohama, had been fairly easy, especially when, once out of Northern waters, the *Vega* had entered the wide-flowing mass of the Black Stream.

At the close of the official ceremonies to celebrate this event, the governor had his secretary deliver a scroll to Nordenskiöld on which could be read a haiku by his hand:

As far as the sea can stretch
the Autumn moon
sheds its beneficial light

As I sat in a bar on the edge of Chinatown in Yokohama, drinking an undefinable whisky and watching the falling rain, I was thinking of the North–East passage . . .

I mean the mental one.

How may thinkers and poets make it?

When I took the train back into Tokyo, there was red sky and rolling raincloud over Yokohama, and a sad-looking, beautiful-looking thirty-year-old woman was reading in the yellow murky light of the carriage a novel.

I could just make out the title.

Sumida River.

8. East of the River

There's a print I love. It's not by one of the great *ukiyo-e* masters, Hiroshige say, or Hokusai, or Utamaro, it's by the man who's said to be the very last master of Floating World painting, Kobayashi Kiyochika. It shows a man and a woman walking along the Mukojima dyke. You see the thin cherry trees on the Sumida River embankment, the lights of Imado on the other side reflected on the waters, and in the distant background, not the great Fuji, but little Mount Matsuchi. It's all in black, grey and yellow, crepuscular and nocturnal, maybe the end of a rainy day — you can almost *smell the rain* in the print.

Nagai Kafû wrote nostalgically about this part of Tokyo: 'In the Meiji Period,' he says, 'there were not a few people who loved Mukôjima and had their houses and gardens there. After the flood of early August 1910, however, almost everyone left. In the changing times since, as the outskirts of the city have moved on, the cherry trees along the river bank have died one by one.'

Nagai Kafû — Kafû the Scribbler, as he called himself — sang the swan-song of old Edo, which he knew foot by foot, especially the low town (*Shitamachi*): 'Ever since I was a child, I have loved to walk about the city'. Nobody better than he can evoke rainy days in a house on the river-bank, the pleasant bitterness of well-brewed tea, the quiet delight of leafing through old coloured prints or turning the pages of old books in a study redolent with the faint smell of incense. In *Quiet Rain*, he writes: 'I had been to the Kyûkyodô to buy fifty of the writing brushes I like best, those known as "A Thousand Words from the Heart", and two packets of joss sticks, and to the Kameya to buy two bottles of white wine . . .' And in *News from Okubo*, he evokes 'all of the dear things in Japanese life — reciting from memory an appropriate old poem while enjoying the special foods and drinks of the four seasons in unexceptionable dishes, walking along a river bank to visit an old friend while the snow of Winter or the rain of Spring falls on a Japanese umbrella, watching tree shadows on a reed blind at the window of a quiet house.'

All of these things were to be approached and enjoyed 'in a free, light, uncomplicated mood', a mood which Kafû found in the plebeian poetry of Edo with its close attention to the beauty of what is simple, ordinary and plain. He sought for that mood also in the prostitutes he frequented, preferring their company to that of citizens and citizenesses more highly placed in the phoney, cheaply modernistic society he saw encroaching on what was left to love and cherish.

At one point, to get away from the tinseldom, Kafû decided to settle East of the river: 'My longing to take refuge in Fukagawa was irresistible', he writes in *Song of Fukagawa* (1909).

East of the River . . .

To that notion 'East of the River', with its deep poetic resonance, Kafû was to devote one of his most beautiful books.

In it, that *Strange Tale from East of the River*, he quotes (quotation is part of this intimate mental geography) a work by the 19th-century scholar of Chinese, Yoda Gakkai, *Twenty-four Views of the Sumida*:

'The Long embankment twists and turns. It bends in an arch from the Mimeguri Inari Shrine on toward the Chômeiji. Here the cherry blossoms are at their thickest. And here, in the age of Kan-ei, Lord Tokugawa released his falcons. Seized with stomach cramps, he drank of the temple well, and was cured. Thereupon he said: "This is the water of *chômei*", of long life. So it was that the well came to be called the Well of Long Life, and the temple itself the Temple of Long Life. Some years later, again at this spot, Master Basho wrote a poem praising the snow. It has remained in men's mouths . . .'

Because of Basho's poem, that temple, the Chomeiji, the Long Life Temple, became so popular among haiku poets that it came to be known familiarly as *Haikudera*, the Haiku Temple. Basho's poem about admiring the snow from the banks of the Sumida is engraved on a stone in its grounds.

'Remaining in men's mouths,' and in men's minds . . .

There are few cultural vestiges in Tokyo, and there are practically no literary monuments (those that exist are discrete in the extreme), but memory goes back far, the past is always there in the mind, so that to know Japan, and to know what Japan knows, I'm coming to see, you have to *travel cerebrally*. An example. The poet Ariwara no Narihara, in exile from Kyoto (the story's told in the ancient *Tales of Ise*), saw a seagull on the River Sumida, and he asked it, in a poem, for news of the capital. That's why the seagull is sometimes called in Japanese poetry *miyako-dori*, 'bird of the capital'. But that is not all. In 1928, a bridge was built across the Sumida. It was baptised Kototoibashi, 'Asking-for-word-Bridge', which takes you right back eleven centuries.

We're still asking for word.

There's one bridge-poem by Basho I know. He wrote it crossing the New Great Bridge (*Shin Ohashi*) that was built over the Sumida when he was living in Fukagawa. The haiku goes like this:

How grateful I feel
stepping briskly over
the frost on the bridge

9. Master Basho

It was in 1680 that Basho took up residence in Fukagawa, then in the far reaches of town. He'd been living in Edo (old Tokyo) for eight years, but he wasn't born there. He was born, in 1644, in the little town of Tsuge, about 15 kilometres from Ueno, where his father taught calligraphy. His mother was from the samurai family of Momachi, and it was as a low-caste samurai that Basho (boy's name, Kinsaku, adult name, Chuemon, early art-name Tôsei), after the death of his father when he was thirteen years old, served in the house of the local lord, Tôdô Takatora. There, he was the servant-companion of the young prince Yoshitada, and they studied haikai poetry together, taking lessons from the master of the Teimon School, Kitamura Kigin of Kyoto. When the young prince died in 1669, Basho decided to leave for Kyoto, where he continued to follow the teaching of Kigin. It was in Kyoto, three years later, that he published his first book: *Kai-ooi* (Mussel Shells), and in that year, 1672, he left for Edo, intending to make his living as a haikai teacher, while continuing the Zen instruction which he had just begun following under master Bucchô.

So we can imagine Basho giving his lessons, attending poetry-parties organised by *nouveau riche* Edo merchants eager to perfect themselves, or their sons, in the arts. Basho would be invited as haikai-master, he'd set the theme of the poetry-meeting, probably in the course of a courteous conversation with his host (the themes? — say, 'Spring in the country', or 'Winter in the city', or 'Autumn Moon' . . .), and he'd sit in with the participants on the appointed evening, make his comments, suggest improvements, and even give grades ('sky-high', 'earthy', 'human'). Haikai literature was light literature, not like the serious and even solemn *waka*; the elegant joke, the witty reference was the thing. Basho was expert at it. He made a good living.

But with the passing of time, he wanted to get out of the city, at least away from its centre. Maybe the Zen instruction was having an effect on his mind, and his own haikai practice was deepening. He probably had had enough of those poetry-parties too. Not that he was going to give up teaching. He was to earn his living as a poetry teacher all his life. But if he could live more cheaply, maybe he would be able to teach less often, and maybe he could do it in a different way? He was well-enough known now for pupils to come to him, instead of his having to be at the beck and call of clients.

Around 1679–80, he must have spoken about his growing desire for more seclusion, more peace and quiet, to one of his pupils, Sampû, a timber merchant. Sampû said he had something that might be suitable: a little hut over in Fukagawa, where his timber was stocked alongside that of all the other timber merchants of Edo. It was just a little place, on the banks of the Sumida, at the mouth of the Onagigawa salt canal . . .

Basho was delighted to accept. One of the first haiku he wrote at and about his 'brokendown little house' as he called it was this:

Shiba no to ni
cha o konoha kaku
arashi kana

— 'to make tea in the hut, the raw winter wind gathers fallen leaves'.

Conditions were Spartan enough at times. He speaks in one text of 'a night icy enough to freeze the bowels', but he liked it there.

Making his tea, watching the snow on the river, listening to the bells of time chime over Edo:

Through clouds of blossom —
Ueno's bell?
or Asakusa's?

And pupils came to visit him. One of them brought a banana-plant, and planted it in front of his door. The poet, with his changed life, was feeling like a change of name. As soon as that little tree (*Bashô*, in Japanese) was planted, it was pretty obvious what it had to be: which is why Basho's been known by that name ever since.

There's a story, probably apocryphal, but it deserves to be true, concerning the origin of Basho's most famous haiku:

Furu ike ya
kawazu tobikomu
mizu no oto

which was to become the passport to the new poetry, gateway to the new depth-space in haikai poetry that Basho was after. The story goes like this:

Bucchô, the Zen master, came to visit the poet in his hut, along with a man named Rokuso Gohei, also a Zen adept.

Basho opens the door.

As Gohei is crossing the threshold, he calls out:

'How is the Buddha-law, in this quiet garden with its trees and its grasses?'

'As you see,' answers Basho, 'the big leaves are big and the small ones small.'

'How have you been lately?' says Bucchô.

'Like green moss after rain.'

'How was it with the Buddha Law before the green moss grew and the Spring rain fell?'

Just at that moment, there was the sound of a frog jumping into the water.

That gave Basho his answer:

'Frog jumping, the sound of water.'

Bucchô was pleased with his pupil.

This was real Zen.

But it was also two-thirds of a perfect haiku. It was a haiku with the first line missing:

a frog jumping in
the sound of water

The three of them got together to supply the first line.

The evening twilight?
Nah. Too romantic.
In the loneliness?
No. Too obvious. Too human.
It was Basho who came up with the solution that deeply satisfied them all.
The old pond.
That frog poem was the beginning of a whole new world of poetry.
The Basho style was born.
Here's one more example of it — a poem almost as famous as that old pond poem, considered to contain all the new feeling and the new tone that Basho put into haikai literature:

Kare eda ni
karasu no tomaritaru ya
aki no kure

(On a leafless branch
sits a crow
Autumn evening dusk)

10. North Road Travelling

There weren't many gulls on the Sumida that October morning when I went to visit Basho's hermitage, but *there was one*, which was the occasion for me to write this little haiku:

That Autumn morning
on the waters of the Sumida
one lone gull

After what I said about the essential, in Japan, being *in the mind*, it will come as no surprise if I say that I had a hard time finding Basho's hermitage.
No indications on the road, no monument on the spot.

You could walk past it without being aware of it.

For the site of Basho's little house is now a shrine to Inari, the rice god, who likes bean curd — which is why there's a piece of *tofu* on the stone ledge there. It's only when you look closer that you see a rock on which are inscribed four characters: *Ba shô an ato* ('This is the site of Basho's house').

Basho's house isn't there.

Where is it?

In the mind, in the mind.

He himself talked about his 'unreal dwelling' . . .

There's a little tin box, like a letter-box, at the side of the shrine. In it, I find a school jotter. That's the Visitors' Book.

I take it out and flip through the pages:

'I have often wondered what Basho's house was like. Very small, I see. That is the real spirit of Basho. How much I agree.'

'I wanted to see the banks of the Sumida. And by chance I came upon the Basho-an. I am very glad.'

'I have just begun to study haiku. What I would like to do now is go for a journey on the roads of the North.'

Ever since Basho wrote that book *Oku no hosomichi* ('the narrow road to the deep North'), this quiet little site on the banks of the Sumida has been inseparable from the idea of roads and travelling, specifically in the direction of the North.

A haiku of Basho's goes like this:

First Winter shower
from now on my name will be
'traveller'

Basho's first trip was a pious one, to his hometown, to visit his mother's tomb — she had died the year before. That was in 1684. He travelled with his disciple Chiri. He wrote up the travel notes and the haiku written on the way when he got back. That lead to the little book *Nozarashi kikô*, called variously in European languages 'Though my bones whiten', or 'Travels of a weather-exposed skeleton'. His second trip was to Kashima, just North of Edo, to see the Autumn moon, and pay a visit to his old Zen master Bucchô. That was in 1687, and the manuscript that came out of it he called *Kashima môde* ('Notes on a journey to Kashima', or 'A Visit to the Kashima Shrine'). That same year, 1687, he made a much longer trip, to visit sites famous in poetry, and do a series of poetry lessons and lectures. The manuscript resulting from that journey was entitled *Oi no kobumi*, 'The Records of a Travelworn Satchel', or maybe something like 'rucksack notebook' (the *oi* was the travelling-box of those mountain ascetics known as the *yamabushi*). The year after, 1688, he paid a visit to the village of Sarashinô, which gave rise to *Sarashinô kikô*, 'Notes of a journey to Sarashino'. But the journey that Basho is most known by, and the one that gave rise to his most complete book, is the one he undertook to the 'deep North' in 1689, just five years before his death.

Why did Basho, at the age of 40, when he'd already worked out an apparently satisfactory way of living, feel that he had to get out on the road?

Sometimes the reason for the trip (or maybe just the pretext) was obvious enough: visiting his mother's tomb, going to contemplate the moon at a particular spot. But the motivation went deeper than that, and it had, I think, several strands, the main one being Zen-buddhist.

Basho still had in mind the examples of Saigyo and Sôji, who had moved about Japan, and before them, there was Ennin, who had travelled in T'ang China. Maybe he felt he was ready to follow in their path now, knowing that he would be able to do it *to some effect*, that is, not just cover kilometres, but open up mind-space. He'd already made a lot of progress in poetry, and in Zen practice. If, in earlier forms of Buddhism, poetry was considered as a profane, if not frivolous activity, it came to be recognised that, deeply practised (Bucchô had seen this happening with Basho), it could itself constitute 'a way', just as travelling was seen as a worthwhile contemplative exercise, complementary to 'sitting meditation' (*zazen*).

The idea of the Zen-journey, or, let's say, meditative travelling (*tabi*: travelling without aim or purpose), was to 'let yourself go with the leaves and the wind', drifting along, attached to nothing (*hoge*). It meant living in *fuga* (*fu*: wind; *ga*: the beautiful), that is with a sense of fleeting beauty. It meant 'carrying in your heart the play of heaven' (*yu*, or *asobi*), while enjoying the world, able to see it as interesting, lovely and bright.

But Basho was no Zen monk in any orthodox sense of the word (he dressed in black, and was often taken for a monk, but he never was one). So that to this 'religious' motivation, you have to add others. Maybe there was a fundamental anxiety in Basho that no mere religion, even an enlightened one, could allay, and maybe he felt that simply getting out on the road could relieve that anxiety. Then there's a literary motivation: wherever he went, Basho carried writing materials. He was, I think, working his way towards a new type of book, let's call it a 'way-and-wind book', more than a narrative account, more than a collection of haiku, *something else*. We can see him groping towards it, with earlier models in mind (the travel diaries, the *michiyuki-bun*), from the first journey on. In fact, the four earlier trips look like preparations for the 'deep North' journey, which was by far the longest, and which lead to the most accomplished book.

Add to all this, a growing curiosity — geographical, ethnological, as well as psychological — for that 'deep North'.

The North has always had a peculiar connotation in Japanese culture.

If the first licensed quarter, the Yoshiwara, was situated within the City bounds, the authorities pretty soon exiled it North, to a region of paddy fields North of Asakusa. Yoshiwara was in fact familiarly known as 'Hokkoku', the North Country, and up in that quarter today (around Senzoku 4-Chôme — Yoshiwara itself was abolished in 1958), there are still some restaurants where you can hear North Country folk songs. The same thing happened to the Kabuki theatre. Considered as too wild, it also was exiled North. So also with everything lawless, wayward — it was 'North'. When a certain artist felt that he was getting so 'far out', so 'high' (like some North Star deity) he needed a change of name, he called himself 'Northern Study' (Hokusai).

Of the roads leading out of Edo, the busiest and the best known was the Tokaidô, the 'East Sea Road', leading to Kyoto and Osaka. Much less frequented, much less well-known was the Oshû Kaido, that headed North out through Asakusa, the Yoshiwara district, Senju and Sôka. It led to what were called *oku no kuniguni*, 'the distant provinces', the traditional name for what is now designated Tohoku, the 'North-East'. These regions were also known as Michinoku — 'the land at the end of the road'.

It was of these that Basho was thinking, and dreaming, in the winter of '88 — these roads, the 'strange sights of the North Country', and 'that shore where the seabirds cry and the Thousand Islands of the Ainu can be seen in the distance . . .'

11. On the Expressway

Samurai crossing the bridge, pedlars bargaining round a tub of fish, straw-roofed boats on the blue waters of the river — that's how Moronobu, the Floating Life artist ('Resident of Edo in the province of Musashi') depicted the Nihonbashi district three centuries ago in Kinko Entsu's twelve-volume guide to the city, *Edo Suzume* (the sparrow of Edo).

Nowadays the river here is more a sludge-grey canal, and the Bridge of Japan, the Bridge of the Rising Sun, is overshadowed by the massive and metallic Tohoku Expressway that whines and roars with traffic morning, noon and night.

The rain was pelting down when we got out, Kenji and I, in his Volkswagen, early that October morning on the Expressway, and I was glad of that. It was the rain that put me in touch with the old Bridge of Japan, for the old *ukiyo-e* painters loved rain, Hiroshige at their head (that famous 'Hiroshige rain'!). Hiroshige — 'He studied hard all by himself, he climbed many mountains and went down into many valleys, in order to sketch Nature' . . .

There were about a million other vehicles getting out of Tokyo that morning — all hissing and fuming and honking North: Bedlam on wheels. No talk in the Volkswagen. Kenji seemed preoccupied. And I was excited about getting out on the road again, that high Japan road, so full of images for me, that's going to take me up through the Musashi plain to Shirakawa, and from there to Sendai, Matsushima, the three mountain country, the Mogami River, Sakata, Kisagata . . .

Musashi, the Musashi plain: *Musashino*. The name (probably of Ainu origin) given to that wild area of moorland in which Edo started up. A poem in the old anthology, the *Manyoshu*, talks of 'the reeds of the Musashi', and so many other poems were to evoke its weird emptiness and its savage beauty, 'the spirit of the Musashi plain', before it was gradually covered. Last Musashi poem I know of, the elegiac text by Kunikida Doppo, at the beginning of the 20th century, lamenting its disappearance.

Elegy, nostalgia, it's strong here, in Tokyo. The last refuge of the soul — you can drown in it. Which is why I want to go North, maybe to retrieve something, maybe to lose something, with a hundred poems in my head:

Once again, once again
here I am crossing
the Hamana Bridge
people must be thinking
I move all over the world

Over the land
misty cloud
over the sea
hordes of gulls
it's a fine country
this country of Yamato

From the cape of Naniwa
marvellous in beauty
where I'm standing now
I look out over the country:
there's the island of Awa
the isle of Onogoro
the isle of Ajimasa
and the isle of Saketsu

At Suminoe
while the Autumn wind
blows through the pine
you hear the roar
of the white-waved sea

High tide, low tide
shores and bays
oh, I want to go and see them
the hundred islands
the thousand islands!

I love the geographic sense of these poems, I love the freshness of the senses you feel in them . . .

Suddenly Kenji blurted out:

'We have betrayed the real world.'

'What's the real world?'

'I don't know. But it's not that' — and he made a gesture with his hand at the Expressway.

'Well, maybe we'll get back to it. This Bedlam thing can't last long. There'll be a big crash some day soon.'

'Too big and too late.'

'Not if we keep some other roads open.'

'Other roads open?'

Kenji started brooding again. I myself was less optimistic than I'd sounded.

Eight o'clock, on a rainy October morning, on the Tohoku Expressway . . .

12. *Shirakawa*

We pulled in out of the traffic at Shirakawa.

Shirakawa (White River) marks traditionally the beginning of the North. Maybe poems, travel-poems at least, were first written, and spoken, as propitiatory offerings to the 'spirits of the road'. What's sure is that it was the established custom to write poems at Shirakawa. In fact so strong was the tradition of the Shirakawa poem that some people wrote their 'Shirakawa poem' without ever setting foot in the place. The most famous example is the poet down in Kyoto, who appeared one Autumn in the literati tearooms declaring that he had made the big trip and here was his poem. In fact, wily gentleman, he'd spent the whole summer holed up in his house getting sunburned at the back window. So he had the tanned face of the traveller, but what he didn't have, as one astute observer remarked, was callouses on his feet . . .

Basho, a real travel-poet with sore footsoles, didn't write any poem at the White River gate. Nothing came to him, and he didn't want to force it. But in the fields nearby he'd heard a young girl singing a rice-planting song, and that simple song seemed to him to contain elements of the kind of poetry he wanted, so that he wrote this haiku later:

First signs
of deep North poetry
a rice planting song

All along the road, I had had my eyes on the signposts. The sign for 'river' seemed to get more and more frequent, as well as the sign for 'mountain'.

Here at Shirakawa, I look at the old frontier map and read the historical notice that goes with it. But mostly I just try to feel my way into the depths of the country and the depths of Autumn, watching leaves, salmon-red, sun-red, blood-red, flutter in the rainy wind. I finally write this kind of half-haiku:

At Shirakawa
no poem, no rice-song
only the rain

And we get on to the road again.

13. A Little Haiku Party

Kenji was keen for me to visit a paper-maker's place he knew at Shiroishi, just off the Expressway, about 50 kilometres south of Sendai.

OK.

But before making for Mr Noguchi's atelier, we sought out a noodle-shop, for we were hungry. It was when we had come back out of the noodle-shop that I saw the travelling monk: a black statue in a temple yard. He had a wide hat on his head, a solid staff in his hand, sandals on his feet, and his eyes were on the horizon — looked as if he was out to go to the end of the earth, and farther. Beside him was a living monk in rubber boots, with his robe tucked up, fiddling at the engine of a Vespa: he didn't look real.

There was a thin rain falling over Shiroishi, just enough to bring out the fragrances of the flower shops and the smell of wood smoke . . .

The paper-maker lived and worked in an old wooden house, with a large courtyard, on the edge of town. The first thing I saw was women washing what looked like bits of root in a trough. This, as was later explained to me, was the plant *nire*, broken into fragments, from which a mucus is drawn. The other initial part of the process concerns mulberry: the mulberry is steamed, the outer bark is peeled off and the white bark thus revealed is exposed to snow before being boiled, beaten and reduced to fibre. This *kozo* fibre is then added to the *nire* mucus, with water, and the whole is filtered through bamboo till it forms a smooth paste, which is then laid out in layers. It seems that Michinoku paper (paper from the North-East) was much prized in the heydays of Kyoto, with a very fastidious writer like Murasaki Shikibu declaring that it was 'the softest'.

After showing us round the workshop, Mr Noguchi offered us tea with little cakes called 'ginger flowers', and it was then I learned he was a great admirer of Basho. When Basho set out for the North, he said, he was wearing a coat (*kamiko*) made of a type of paper which he himself still produced, waterproofed thanks to glue derived from the vegetable *kon-nyaku*, probably dyed brown with persimmon tannin. I said I'd always thought Basho's coat was white, because Chora, in his haiku on him, describes him as a crane:

In travelling clothes
a crane in the Autumn rain
the old master Basho

Mr Noguchi said that maybe his *kamiko* was white after all, undyed, and he was very pleased to hear I knew Japanese poetry so well. After that, we swapped Basho poems, with Kenji joining in:

Red the sun
indifferent to time
but the wind knows the promise of cold

Whiter far
than the white rocks
the Autumn wind

Through the cold rice-fields
on horseback —
my shadow creeps below

The sea darkens
the voices of the wild duck
are faintly white

The Winter storm
hid itself in the bamboos
and grew still

Yes, Mr Noguchi loved and admired Basho — his poetry was like paper, as compared to the 'satin' (more artificial) poetry of other poets — but he had a soft spot too for the more homely Issa, the farmer's son from Kashiwabara who loved his old village so much he was always referring to it in his poems and who was so full of compassion for all things in the world, from bugs to beggars, all 'floating weeds'. Oh yes, undoubtedly, Issa was a great poet too:

Hakidame e
tsuru no sagarikeri
Waka-no-Ura

(The crane comes down
right on the rubbish heap
at Waka-no-Ura)

Nete okite
O akubi shite
neko no koi

(Sleeping, waking
giving great yawns —
a cat on the love path)

When I left Mr Noguchi, it was with a sheet of beautiful paper on which I promised to try and write a dozen North Country haiku.

14. A Lone Guy from Yamaguchi

We were sitting in a bar in Sendai, and the rain was still falling. This was to be the parting of the ways. Kenji was going to pay a visit to his folks, and I was going to set off on my own, first to Matsushima, then into the Yamagata.

'To the new Basho!' said Kenji and raised his cup of sake.

'No, no. Let's just say, quietly, with Issa: today also.'

'To the old Back Country then,' he said, and I raised my cup in acquiescence.

Kenji was really thinking of leaving Tokyo, and going back to Sendai, if he could find a job there. It was something, he told me, more and more Japanese like him were thinking. They call it the U-turn. As if progress had gone far enough, and now it was time to recover and develop what had been lost. No hysterical and theatrical reaction like Mishima's, just a quiet turning back.

You wonder if humanity couldn't just stop for a while, and take a cool look round, and say, OK, it's time to try and remake the circle.

But where is humanity?

Where are the human beings?

There's this nation and that nation, and within each nation, there's this clan and that clan, this party and that party, this sect and that sect, this person and that person.

All with different identities that they want to stick to, and ready to fight for them at the drop of a hat.

What chance has the world in all this moody maniac madness?

They're burning the trees and the grasses.

Covering the earth in concrete.

All in the name of Something or Other.

Only hope is in an emptiness, a namelessness.

There was another young fellow in the bar with us. He was wearing a leather jerkin and on its back you could read: ‘A lone guy from Yamaguchi’.

There are a lot of lone guys from Yamaguchi in this present time of the world.

Wondering where to go and who with.

15. The Pine Islands

The sun had come out from behind the rain, and it was hot when I got down to Matsushima, so hot that when I went into a shop to buy some biscuits, the woman at the counter leaned over to touch my thick, waterproof jerkin (I was dressed for North Country travelling) and said:

‘Samui, desuka?’ (It’s cold, isn’t it?)

I told her I was going to Hokkaido. She gave an exaggerated shiver:

‘Ahhh, sodes’ (Ah, so that’s it).

It was the tail-end of the tourist season in Matsushima, but there were still a lot of people milling about, and a cluster of sightseeing boats in the harbour, with megaphones blaring out folksongs like the ‘Saïtaro air’, a good fishing song, that goes something like this:

From Matsushima to Zuiganji
no temple can bear the comparing
hey ho, good fishing!

There by the mountain, facing the sea
there’s a little pine wood growing
hey ho, good fishing!

From West to East, what a sight to see
Matsushima and its isles a-gleaming
hey ho, good fishing!

Matsushima (the pine islands) is one of the principal beauty spots in Japan, and has long been reputed as such. I was glad to see they were still there, still beautiful, though you had to forget the red stack of a factory in one corner of the scene. But if you were doing an *ukiyo-e* picture, maybe you would just stick it in, as an element among others of 'the floating world'. You might even get a nice effect, with its frank red against the dark green of the pines . . .

When Basho came down here three centuries ago, he sat in an inn listening to North Country ballads sung by a blind minstrel (he liked their 'rustic savour') before going to see the moon above the islands. When he did see the moon, and the clouds scudding across the sky above those piney islands, he says he was conscious of 'another world'. The beauty of Matsushima could only be compared to the most divinely beautiful of female faces, said Basho, while his companion, Sora, wrote this poem-exclamation that makes no attempt at description:

Matsushima, ah
ah, Matsushima
Matsushima, ah . . .

I spent hours in the grounds of a temple, where there were stones with Basho poems engraved on them, which is OK — so long as you keep in mind, as I've already said, that Basho himself was no Zen monk. He studied Zen, right, learned a lot from it, but he was never totally zennified. He simply tried to deepen some general notions, without knuckling down to any prescribed discipline. Too much a man of movement for that, too desirous of staying 'a man of the wind and of the clouds'. The general notions he lived with were maybe these: a sense of the impermanence, the transitoriness of every single thing; a floating sense of personal identity, the mind being a play of moments (no place to fix it — 'like the tracks of birds in the sky'); and a clear perception of the things of nature. It was a way of poetry (deeply founded and grounded) he followed and propagated ('planting the seeds of haiku') rather than the pure way of Buddha.

I sat on in the temple grounds writing up my notebook, then, with evening coming on, walked along the 'Basho path' to Phoenix Hall (*Zuihogaoka*), where I intended to spend the night.

Among the pines up there, I found a school book (subject: mathematics) and a lurid porno magazine showing on its cover a naked woman in chains, one of the chains being deeply (voluptuously?) embedded in her vulva.

The sun went down over the islands . . .

Evening on the coast
lighthouse light coming on
at the tip of a pine twig

When I came out of my wood in the morning and went again to the heights of the hill to have a look out over the bay, it was a clear, crystal-clear morning and everything was neatly etched, from the islands themselves to the huddle of buildings that was the town to the temple grounds with its lines of maple.

Into my head came another little haiku, something which was hardly worthy of Mr Noguchi's paper, but which got put down in my notebook anyway:

Green pine
growing on the heights
century after century

16. Mountain Country

Out of Matsushima, striking West into the Yamagata, via a bus and some foot-slogging, with the intention of hiking for a while around the three-mountain country.

Redgold on the hills, rivers smoking in the morning sun, a little snow on the heights, crows everywhere . . .

For Basho, the three mountains of the Yamagata: Haguro, Gassan, Yudono, were 'full of miraculous inspiration'. As he walked among them in the Autumn wind, the air 'smelt of snow', and his mind was open. The people he met up with mainly were *yamabushi*, those wanderers and ascetics who lived in the mountains in order to achieve physical and mental vigour. Their 'sacred text' was the natural text:

'The sound of the wind in the treetops, the roaring of waves, all these are sacred voices.' Basho could only approve of such an attitude. He wrote haiku after haiku up there in the mountains. Here's one:

> *How many clouds piled up and broken*
> *before, silently, the moon*
> *rises over Mount Gassan . . .*

Mountains give refuge to all kinds of asocial characters, and since everybody needs a little asociality now and then, the 'mountain pilgrimage' has for long been traditional.

When Noda Senkô-in Narisuke, in the 19th century, made his 'pilgrimage to the nine peaks', he met several eccentrics who had also 'made their pilgrimage', though not necessarily in an orthodox manner. There was one man, a doctor, about fifty years old: 'At the age of twenty, he lived like a vagabond. Then he spent seven or eight years in the capital. After that he decided to travel round the country, and he only got home three years ago. He likes strange stories from the different provinces and when he tells stories himself, he mingles truth with fantasy. He's even written a book, that goes in all directions at once.' Then there was the poet Keigetsu Tankyu, whose pen name was Anpu: 'I went to visit him. He really is a very extraordinary individual, with lofty views, that ordinary minds can't reach: a real mountain-mind. When I mention haikai, he says he's no poet. And when I bring up the tea ceremony, he says he makes tea when he likes. With his wild head of hair, he looks like a Dutchman . . .'

I was crossing a red bridge one morning, making for a Shinto shrine on the heights of Yudono, and there was a strong wind blowing, making the long *susuki* grasses sway and hiss and the red-leaved trees lurch and rustle. Tremendous movement everywhere. Why go out of my way to visit a Shinto shrine? Well, because with Shinto, we're on the primal soil of Japan. Here's a religion with no dogma, no metaphysical system, no moral code, just a field of bright energy governed by the sun ('breathe the spirit of the sun') and a mythopoetic world in which the principal rôles are played by the sea, the wind, storm, thunder, lightning, rain, rocks and trees. That it later became a national and nationalist religion has everything to do with politics and nothing to do with its original energies and insights which are concerned with something a lot more fundamental. Those red portals, *torii*, you see dotting the Japanese landscape indicate sacred space, that is, they invite the mind both to expansion and to concentration. The word *torii* may have originally meant: bird perches. Bird symbolism is strong in Shinto. Its propitious colour is white, its propitious direction: North. You still wonder why I'm attracted to Shinto? One of my favourite haiku goes like this:

> *Winter wind*
> *a Shinto priest*
> *is walking in the forest . . .*

I'd seen a lot of priests at the mountain resthouse I'd passed that morning, as well as a lot of pilgrims, or maybe just sight-seers, buying straw sandals at the shop ('The pure land is far away. Ten thousand miles, they say. How can I hope to reach it with only a pair of straw sandals?') But now I was all alone with the wind. I continued on up to the shrine nonetheless.

I pass one compound, where there's a priest on guard, who just lets me pass: some wild Dutchman . . . But at the second compound, higher up, another priest tells me to take off my shoes, bow twice and clap my hands. I do it, feeling a bit phoney. I'd rather just have looked at the sacred thing (*kamui*) in my own way, which would have been closer to the real thing than my doing this act. It's a great red boulder, with a hot spring flowering over it: paleolithic sex symbol, cosmic cunt. I stay with it a long time, then put on my shoes again and go back downhill.

This time, at the lower compound, seeing a booth selling photos and books, and an old priest in it, I go up to him:

'Konnichi wa!'

'Good morning! Very chilly.'

'Yes. Can you show me the way to Gassan?'

He points to a narrow path that skirts a mountain torrent.

'Over there. Nine kilometres.'

'Thank you.'

And I move off.

But I've only taken a few steps when the old priest calls me back. He has a card in his hands with a piece of calligraphy on it, and he hands it to me, bowing his head at the same time with one hand over his heart:

'From me to you.'

From no one to no one.

I went away into the wind.

17. The White Path

In 1974 there appeared in Tokyo a book entitled *Hyohaku no Haijin*, 'the haiku-man of the white path'. It was about a wandering Zen priest and haiku poet called Santoka.

Santoka (it's a pen-name, meaning 'burning mountain peak') was born in 1882, in the village of Sabare, in Yamaguchi prefecture. His father was a dissolute kind of character and his mother committed suicide when Santoka was eleven years old, so he was raised by his grandmother. He started to write haiku very early, when he was about fifteen years old, but he really struck his own vein when he became aware of the new openings in poetry made first of all by Shiki and Hekigodo, then by Seisensui Ogiwara (1884–1976), the founder of the *jiyuritsu*, 'freestyle school' of haiku. This school gave up the traditional 17 syllable (5–7–5) pattern, as well as other traditional obligations, like the 'season word'. Seisensui put forward five new concepts: *jiyu*, freedom; *jiko*, self-expression; *shizen*, naturalness; *chikara*, strength; and *hikari*, brightness. This was revitalising haiku, which, like every other art tends in time to the artificial, unless some powerful renewal-bringing individual rises up from the inside or cross-fertilisation comes from the outside. It was revolutionising haiku, while still adhering to what was essential in the practice, qualities like *wabi* (simplicity) and *sabi* (solitude).

I was at a tea ceremony one afternoon in a garden up in the Aoyama (Blue Mountain) district of Tokyo, and a young Japanese was trying to tell me, in French, what *sabi-wabi* was: '*Quelque chose très simple — profondeur . . . Très difficile expliquer . . . Pas fini, pas de nom . . .*

On dirait rien, mais, profond, il y a quelque chose. Jardin anglais, jardin français, jardin italien — magnifique. Jardin zen, rien — nature, rien.'

How Santoka became a monk and how he set out on his haiku-path was like this. After a year at university in Tokyo, during which he took pretty heavily to drink and suffered a nervous breakdown, he returned home at the beginning of the Russo–Japanese war in 1904 because his father could no longer pay the tuition fees. After selling off most of the family land, Santoka and his father opened a sake brewery and, some time later, at his father's instigation (the old man thought a wife would keep Santoka off drink), at age twenty-five, Santoka married, and a son, Ken, was born. But things went from bad to worse. The brewery failed, and the marriage deteriorated. Santoka left to do a series of odd jobs in Tokyo. But in 1924, there were still no prospects, and he decided to commit suicide. He was standing in the middle of the railway tracks facing an oncoming train when it came to a screeching halt and Santoka was dragged out of the way. A Zen temple in the neighbourhood took him in. The head monk told him he could stay there as long as he liked.

Santoka had studied Buddhism in Tokyo, and he had attended Zen lectures. Now he worked in the temple, did meditation and chanted sutras. In 1925, he was ordained. For a while he thought of continuing his studies at the head temple of the Soto school but, not too keen to find himself at forty-three among a crowd of fledglings, he decided to take to the roads, like the oldest of the old. For the next few years, till his death in 1940, he was going to spend his time between a cottage-hermitage friends offered him, the *Gochu-an*, and the road. He travelled about southern Honshu, Kyushu and Shikoku, then at one point, he followed the Basho road North . . .

All the time he was writing essays, travel journals, and haiku such as these . . .

Well, well
which way should I go?
the wind blows

Walking
in the brightness, in the darkness
of the wind

Going deeper
and still deeper
the green mountains

Aimlessly, flowingly
drifting here and there
tasting the pure water

Peace for the heart
this
living in the mountains

The long black hair of the joy-girls
dishevelled
by the salt sea breeze

Squatting on a sand dune —
today also
there's no seeing Sado Island

This is some inn:
mountains to right and left
and a sake shop in front

Tonight, no sake
just sitting
staring at the moon

Santoka said he knew three joys: the first, study; the second, contemplation; the third, haiku. If there's a word that comes up again and again in these haiku, it's 'mountains'. Westerners want to conquer them, he wrote in one of his essays. Orientals want to contemplate them. What I want is to *savour* them . . .

18. Fields of Force

Clear Autumn along the Gassan trail, torrent tumbling ridge to ridge, crows cawing, North wind blowing, one foot after another, breathing three to three, haiku-walking . . .

> *Sun*
> *shining in a waterfall*
> oshara shonara

About a month ago, over on Haguro, the *yamabushi* were swarming all over the place sounding their conches, but this morning, all I can hear is a crow, *kraa kraa, kraa kraa*, in the bright-blue sky.

And that's the way I like it.

> *All alone*
> *with an old crow*
> *in unfamiliar country*

I get my bearings: Akita to the North, Miyaga to the East, to the South, Niigata, and to the West, a great chain of dunes and the Sea of Japan.

That cluster of sacred mountains: Haguro, Yudono, Gassan all around me, and at my feet a tumbling torrent.

I strip off my clothes and footware, step into the torrent, and splash water over my body. Then I have a little meal: soya bean cake, pickled plum, and some sake:

> *In the mountains*
> *on the banks of a torrent*
> *drinking sake*

All this North-East territory, with its rough climate and its archaic ways is part of *Ura-Nihon* (back-country Japan), and in the old days, the mountain area, Gassan ('moon-mountain') in particular, was the home of the *powers*. There were festivals in the villages to bring the powers down from the heights of their wintry retreat into the rice-field, to ensure good seeding and a good harvest. Festivals with dances:

> *I beat my foot on the great earth*
> *at the birth of the year*
> aru-ô-i
> *I beat my foot on the golden earth*
> aru-ô-i
> *the place wherever I beat my foot*
> *is the pure land*
> *the paradise*
> aru-ô-i

There was ancient agrarian ritual, full of religious belief, then there was Nô theatre that played down the religion, but still kept the *aura* and the sense of sacred place, and can put a shiver down the spine and light in the brain.

'Here I am on the moors of Nasuno . . . Here I am on the beach at Sumiyoshi.'

In the local mountain Nô, the old man, the old traveller, comes wandering on to the stage murmuring incomprehensible words: *'Dodotarari tarari akari rari dô'*, and the chorus answers back: *'Chiiya tarari tararira tarari akarari raridô'*. Then the old man says: 'We've been following the roads right into the back of the back-country.' And the chorus says: 'Blessed lands!' And the old man says: 'Rare places, of great reknown.'

Old festivals, Nô plays — then what?

Walking along the mountain path, with my eye on Gassan's great snow-covered lava dome . . .

19. *Along the Mogami*

Mist had come down, Gassan had grown ghostly, and rain was falling on the river Mogami as I followed it down to the sea.

The great river Mogami crosses the rice-fertile Shônai plain and plunges into the sea at Sakata. Walking along its banks on Route 47,

I saw fir forests drenched in misty rain, green waters pitted by raindrops, and flat-bottomed boats nosing and jostling at their moorings.

One boat had just come in from crab-fishing:

'Fishing good?'

'No, too much water.'

Kaki in the mist, a duck flying over the river . . .

Into my mind come Basho's two Mogami river haiku:

May rains gathered
the river Mogami
rushes down to the sea

The river Mogami
has drowned deep in its waters
the burning summer sun

As I come near to the village of Yunohama (hot water beach) on the coast, I take out my note-book and, under the rain that blurs the ink, and gives me right away a kind of shot-silk manuscript, write this:

Coming down to the coast
mind empty —
the sound of waves

The Sea of Japan, after all the heat of the roads, was unbelievably cool and blue. I went straight down to the shore of grey sand with a little chaos of sulphureous rocks, and sat there on a rock dangling my feet in the water. A few fishing boats were bobbing at anchor, and to my right rose, sturdy and bright, a red lighthouse . . .

After an hour or so, I decided to go and look for a room. I found one in a run-down little *ryokan* that had *shoji* paper on the windows, giving subdued white light, and I was kneeling there in front of the table, getting out my notebooks, when a young girl came in with fragrant green tea and a cake:

All afternoon
in the white flower room
listening to the silence

I spent a very quiet night, an utterly quiet night, with the Japan Sea *sho-sha-shooing* round the moon.

And in the morning moved on to Sakata.

20. Back Country Mist

Sakata, big port, important Northern port: in a café, I heard somebody speaking Russian. Up in the city park where they have one of Basho's haiku inscribed on a rock, I sat beside the stocky white wooden lighthouse, relic of bygone old-style navigational days, and looked down at the harbour with its *chug-chug-chug* of boats and the Mogami River, under a grey sky, approaching its opening and its end. Then went down town again where a truck was moving around slowly and methodically megaphoning something I couldn't understand and, hungry again, looked for something to eat — found it, rice curry, in a snack where the waitress, good-looking girl, had printed on her apron, which I read aloud: 'American rabbit getting ready for the big race'. She gave me a little hip-and-arse movement in reply.

Late evening in the streets of Sakata, I go into this place where they sell sake, all kinds and brands and prices of sake (Sakata is sake-town, kept some of the rice that came down the river to be taken away on boats for making drink) and taste all the stages, from early clouded milky thickness to crystal-clear quintessence. But what I really like is in the middle, a brew called Back Country Mist. Drinking that, I really feel I'm in old North Japan, really feel all the conjugations of rice and ice and the presence of the thick-thatched snowcountry houses, with the faraway swish of the North Pacific full of salmon and whales and with wide-eyed lighthouses shining watchfully on its rim.

I get myself a room in a Western-style hotel, scribble a few scrabbly pages, and fall, still slightly drunk, into sleep.

Next morning I'm up early, prowling round the streets of Sakata, just to see how the town wakes up: quiet rain falling on willow-lined streets, insomniac oldsters taking a morning stroll and doing a little garbage-hunting on the side, school-girls giggling by on bikes, and in this temple-ground with its grey-green gravestones, smoke from an incinerator drifting across the dark-green foliage of pinetrees . . .

I took my time walking from Sakata to Kisagata, since it's just a few miles along the coast.

It was at Kisagata that Basho, whose ghost is always with me, had to turn back ill, as his death-poem written years later puts it:

Fallen ill on a journey
my dreams wander
over withered moors

He sat there in a temple, looking back at the mountains he'd passed through, looking at the movement of the waves with land's end melancholy, enjoying, with a quiet sadness, what he felt to be Kisagata's peculiarly sad beauty. I sat in a café, maybe looking lonely for the owneress gave me a black bunch of Yamagata grapes, for free, then went down to the beach.

The coast-line has changed here since Basho's day, so today's Kisagata is no longer where his Kisagata lay, but no matter, I salute him as I stand there on the twilight dunes before making farther North along the edge of the sea, trudging in the sand with the sun setting round and red.

I slept that night on the beach.

Next day I got on to the roads again, intending to make my way over into the Hakkoda country.

Rice paddies, like a brush with the bristles cut.

Mountain tops floating in cloud . . .

21. At the Limits

So, three hundred kilometers from Tokyo, having said farewell to Basho, I was making over via Honjo, Lake Asawi, the Hachimantai region and Lake Towada, into the Hakkoda mountain range.

The Hakkodas, that's the home of the wind. Red leaves, fast moving cloud, *sssh-sssh* of the wind in the pampa grass.

I'm told (lorry-driver who brought me over from Hachimantai) that the winters here can be very tough. A squad of Japanese soldiers lost their way years ago in the blinding snow, and they were found weeks later, frozen in their tracks like something out of an arctic Madame Tussaud's.

Cold wind today and clear light up on the heights.

In a hill restaurant, I eat a meal of soup, rice and pickles, and an apple, accompanied by wheat tea. Then out again into the wind.

Pinetrees with rough, gnarled, cold-gold bark.

So many crows.

A thousand crows.

A million crows.

All cawing in the wind, and the wind, the Hakkoda wind, carrying their cries into the still high Autumn suspended-in-time emptiness . . .

In Japan, to indicate the limits of the country, like Land's End and John o'Groats, they say: from Kagoshima (on Kyushu island) to Aomori (at the tip of Honshu).

Aomori (means 'blue forest') is where my lunch apple came from. It's apple country up there. As I come into town, I see a big hoarding: *You Me Apple Juice*. And there are piles of big, red, juicy apples everywhere.

Coming closer into Aomori: *Tokyo Tyre; Nitto Tire; Megane nike; Miniminipub; Jealousy Queen; Bar Ber* (classic red and white pole recalling whiskery yesteryear) . . .

After a little meal in a snack bar ('Coffee and Foods'), I go to the museum where there's a display of Stone Age Culture: bones, shells, stones; and a bird room full of naturalised birds with bird sounds; and another room with swans, bears and white monkeys. I also see a suit of shining black fierce bristling samurai armour, and a set of dolls like Siberian shaman figures. Then there are displays on logging and on bear-hunting. And a diaporama that starts up with the stellar cosmos revolving and exploding, then takes you through a world of stone, with storm, sea-thunder, snow, ice, water, galloping horses and to finish shows you a festival with ancient, sun-cult drumbeats and weird wailing flutes out of some dionysian dreamland.

I liked that museum so much, I headed straight for another one, the *Keikokan*, where I saw a display of wonderful Ainu costumes (again, that blue, with those strange wavepatterns) and where there was a room devoted to the writer Dazai, who was born up here, with his books laid out along with their European translations: *Soleil couchant, La déchéance d'un homme, No Longer Human, Lo Squalificato, Ya no humano, El sol que declina, Il sole si spegne, Die sinkende Sonne* . . .

Seeing me so absorbed in Dazai, the guardian comes up to me and asks me where I come from. In such situations, I have a choice between America (which is expected), France (which is respected), and Scotland, which I always see is situated very vaguely on my interlocutor's mental map. This time I decide to go the whole hog, so I say:

'Sukottorando.'

'Sukottorando!' he repeats, slapping himself on the backside, *'Sukottorando — oh, desuka!'* (as if somehow with that one word, Scotland, I'd just explained everything), and he calls over his colleague to meet the man from *Sukottorando*. They then ask me where I'm going, and I say *'Hokkaido'*. At that, the first guardian slaps himself on the backside even harder: *'Hokkaido! — so desuka!'*, and the second guardian brings out one single ominous, omnific word which is:

'Snow.'

In the bar tonight they'll be telling their pals about the foreigner who was going away to get lost in the big impossible snowfields of the far land Hokkaido . . .

22. The Other World

Next morning, along the wild Aomori coast. The sea's rough and greeny-blue, crashing up against the rocky shore while farther out the strong-blowing wind skims and spins off from it fins and fumes of spray. In Asamushi Town, I see a huge advertisement: OCEAN WHISKY. And sure enough I'm drunk with all this oceanic presence: sand, sea, wind, sky — open road, wild emptiness. At Noheji, I go into a sushi-bar where I eat salmon and tunny on layers of clear cold rice, taking in the vase of chrysanthemums, rough gold, and the plastic bear head nailed to the wall (plastic maybe, but the totem there), as well as the flickering images of Variety on TV from lewd and lowdown Tokyo.

On the road again. On one hand, the sea: on the other, rice-paddies shorn, the rice in sheaves neatly stacked left open for the wind to dry. By this time, a half-moon thinly visible in the sky. At Yokohama

Station, little huddle of houses, main street festooned with telephone wires, I find myself an inn *echt japanisch* and settle in for the night, listening to the wind rattling the roof, and looking out the thick storm-windows at a patch of cabbages, the redgold cloud in the evening sky, and a ghost of a rainbow arched over the fast-running sea.

Up then, by route 279, through the forest, where yesterday's tempest has taken its branch-breaking toll, to Osorezan, the Mountain of Fear.

It's like another world, up there. You walk among yellow-white rocks that smell of sulphur, and alongside little cairns of stones sometimes dressed in coloured rags with white cloth hoods. For 'dying', in this whole region, they say 'going up into the mountain', which is what the old people did when they felt their time had come. It's a religious atmosphere that goes back not only beyond Buddhism, but also beyond Shinto. We're in shaman territory: on this mountain, among these stones, female mediums, blind mediums, invoke the spirits of the dead.

Walking there among the sulphur-smelling stones, some with windmills like Tibetan prayer-wheels and big crows wheeling over them — they seem bigger there than usual — calling, calling, calling in the blustery sky, I come to a little temple, in the middle of which sits a bell, a metal bowl-bell, and beside it a hammer. I take the hammer and knock out a sequence of strokes (a sequence that's been obsessing me for the last few years): 5–3–1. Then I go down to the lake, and walk along the edge of its still green-yellow waters, my feet crunching in the thick white gravel of the shore. I see, far off, a statue, of what or who I don't know, its red robe blowing in the wind.

Back in the forest, its cryptomerian silence, mushroom gatherers, red leaves on the torrents, play of light and shade on the whitesplashing waterfall water. I get a ride on a logginglorry on the earth track leading down to the coast, reading: Yo no kama, 18 kms. Track lined with *susuki* grass, and dragonflies darting over it. Gradually the crows give way to gulls: Yakeyama, and a blacksmith repairing anchors. Wooden houses, roofs red or blue or black, sea blue and green whiteflecked.

On to Omazaki, at the tip of the Shimokita peninsula, where I'm going to take the Ferry for Hokkaido.

23. In the Straits of Tsugaru

I like the look of this little restaurant down by the harbour, with its blue *noren* on which are written the two characters *ka-ki*, meaning Joy. Cool and clean inside, the man behind the counter with his set of nine gleaming knives cutting up calmar. No scallops (*hotategai*) today because of the tempest, but he has mouth-watering fritters of shrimp, lobster and aubergine. While I'm eating, and drinking a Sapporo beer, I notice another bear head, not in plastic this time, but in wood — and through the window, I can see the blunt nose of the *Taikan Maru* that does the crossing between Omazaki and Hakodate.

Not many people on the ferry this October afternoon. In the saloon, where you can stretch out on tatamis, an old woman sleeping with her head on her folded arms; a bunch of youngsters drinking and smoking; and an adolescent girl, very beautiful, sitting quiet and collected, her eyes focussed straight in front of her. Up on deck, three lads from Osaka, motorcyclists, out to spend a couple of weeks on Hokkaido.

'Why Hokkaido?'

'No special reason.'

'Not many cars.'

'And you?'

'Don't know yet, I'll see.'

'Where you come from?'

'France.'

'Not many Paris restaurants on Hokkaido.'

'I like my fish raw.'

One of these lads had a word printed on his jetblack jerkin: Nordica, the third stroke of the N being an arrow pointing upwards . . .

'To know true happiness,' says somebody somewhere, 'you have to travel in a distant country, and even out of yourself.' This time, my 'distant country' is Hokkaido, that island in the shape of a giant skate (some say, a kite, but since the Hokkaido is a fishy place, I prefer skate) that stretches between the sea of Japan (*Nihonkai*), the Pacific Ocean (*Taisheixa*) and the Sea of Okhotsk (*Ohotske*).

Late Autumn in the Straits of Tsugaru, thunder-mist, a low growling emerging from the greyness, the spirit of the island moving in the sky.

24. In Hakodate

Coming in to Hakodate harbour on the ferry, the first thing I see is a huge red-painted crane, looming large over the town, for all the world like the bird-perch door to some shinto shrine. But that impression quickly fades as I trudge on into the city centre over greasy cobbles, past a McDonald's, past a massive flashy advertisement for Kirin Beer, past a shop called ominously *Last Scene*.

Last scene . . .

There's somebody I can't forget here: the poet Ishikawa Takuboku, born in 1886 at Morioka in Iwate province, who was up in Hakodate around the turn of the century, earning a living as teacher and journalist, writing haiku like this:

With the sea roaring
on Hakodate's beach
I'm remembering so much

On the salt-smelling dunes
of a northern shore
the polygonum will flower again this year

Grown old travelling
when drunk he recites
a poem he wrote ten years ago

In the waveless bay in February
painted all white
a foreign ship moves forward slowly

Ice on my lips
like a long travelled man
I talk only to ask my way

Just a little salutation in passing to this haiku-man who, after a sad, troubled life, died back there in 1912.

Last scene, last scene . . .

But the polygonum will flower again!

25. Ainu Night

Lightning flashing over Hakodate, heavy rain in the streets, tramcars cling-clanging.

In a food shop I renew my rucksack provisions, packing in dried salmon and dried seaweed (*kombu, wakame*), and lay in too a couple of bottles of Sapporo beer before making for the Ocean Hotel where I get myself a room for the night.

There's a full moon shining in through the window, and I sit watching it, drinking my beer and chewing salmon before going to bed with a heavy blue book of Ainu songs published by the University of Tokyo and bought down there in Jimbocho for reading up here on Hokkaido:

I saw the calm sea
stretching out smooth
right to the ocean's Western edge
far at the Western edge of the ocean
a multitude of whales
were playing about
were splashing about . . .

The first mention I ever saw of the Ainu was in a little known work of Anton Chekhov's called *The Island*, which was based on his stay on Sakhalin from July to October 1890. In that book he says that, when asked who they are, the members of the native population of Southern Sakhalin do not respond with the name of a tribe or nation, but answer simply 'Ainu', meaning 'man'. Chekhov describes them as being 'dark as gypsies', with long beards and moustaches, and thick, wiry black hair, their eyes expressive and gentle. Almost all those who have described the Ainu, he says, refer to their characteristics in the best possible light. The consensus is that they are a quiet, modest, good-natured, trustworthy, loquacious, courteous, respectful, intelligent people. He wonders where they're placed in the racial scheme of things, and mentions 'two opinions which may be fairly accurate': first, that the Ainu belong to a special race which formerly populated all the eastern Asiatic islands; second, that they were a paleo-Asiatic people which was squeezed out of Asia onto the neighbouring islands by Mongolian tribes, the course of the migration from Asia to the islands being through Korea. What seems sure to him is that the Ainu moved from the South to the North, from a warm climate to a cold one. He doesn't know how many Ainu there are on Sakhalin, but it is obvious that the race is dying out rapidly. Before Southern Sakhalin was occupied by the Russians, the Ainu were virtually Japanese serfs. It had been easy to subjugate them, because they were meek and mild, and because they were hungry. The Russians brought them freedom, but unfortunately, they didn't bring rice along with it, so the Ainu began to starve.

In *The Island*, the Ainu are only incidental to the main narrative but ever since perusing that book in a fog-bound Glasgow, many many moons ago, I've read everything on the Ainu I could lay my hands on, along with everything I could find on paleo-Asia and the North Pacific rim, all this concentrating these recent years, with Basho's vision coming in, on Hokkaido.

The Ainu settlements on Hokkaido would be on the shore, or at a vulvar river mouth, with the mountains in the back and the sea to the front: two big forces, and in between them a *field of force* in which the humans try to live a good life, taught by the bear and the whale, the owl and the salmon. This is what the owl said:

It was me who
taught the humans
in their sleep
in their dreams
that some things
they must never do
and suddenly
one day
they understood . . .

That was the day they became Ainu.

26. *At the Edge of the Map*

What we're calling here Hokkaido was only named so (North Sea Road) in 1869, when this whole 'edge of the world' territory was integrated into the central Japanese administration under Meiji. Before that, it was known as Ezo (barbarian country), which you find written in old European maps of Japan in various forms: Yeso, Terra de Iesso, Land van Jedso, Land of Jesso — so far away in the mists that it was almost mythological.

In a very early Japanese map which is part geography and part imaginary topology, you find mention of two fabulous lands, one to the South of central Japan, one to the North. The South land is *Rasetsukoku*, 'the place of female demons', the North land is *Gando*, or *Kari no Michi*, 'the route of the wild geese' . . . That may be the first reference to Hokkaido.

The geography is vague up to about the end of the eighteenth century. Not only is the actual location and delineation of the Northern territory hazy and floating (mapmakers would avoid the issue by showing only its southern tip at the edge of their sheets), but there was little real interest in it. Before the Nara period, not only Hokkaido, but the whole of North-Eastern Japan was known as Koshi, its inhabitants, *Koshibito*, 'people from *the other side*'.

Europeans knew about it only by hearsay. In Vietnam, Father Nicholo Lancilotto heard from a Japanese named Yajiro about the inhabitants of 'Gsoo', to the North-East of Japan. According to his informant, they were 'white-skinned, with whiskers' and fought 'fearlessly, one against a hundred'. Father Luis Frois, in 1565, speaks in a letter of 'a spacious land of wild people and bears'. The first European actually to set foot on the Hokkaido, Girolama de Angelis, who was up here in 1618 and 1621, having to decide in his report if Ezo was an island or not, came to the conclusion that it was, and made a manuscript map showing Ezo as a huge expanse of territory totally dwarfing Japan. When Francis Caron brought out his *Perfekte Kaert van de gelegentheydt des Landts van Japan* in 1661, showing *'t Vaste Landt van Iezzo*, he wrote (I'm quoting the contemporary English version) this:

'The countrey of Japan is supposed to bee an island, though there bee no certainty of it, this vast territorie not beeing yet wholy discovered to the inhabitants themselves. I have often enquired and been informed that Travellers have come from the Province of Quanto wherein the Imperial Citie and Palace of Iedo are situated 27 daies North-East wards, before they could reach the utmost point of the land of Sungaly-Tsugaru bordering upon the Sea. Being come thither they passed over an Isthmus of thirty-three English miles broad, leading into the Countrey of Iezzo abounding in skins and furrs of price. This teritorie is very great, mountainous but little inhabited. The Jappaners attempted its discovery severall times but in vaine, for though they entered to and fro, far into the Countrey, yet they could never find its end, nor any certainty concerning it . . .'

Was it attached to the Asian mainland, was it an island or was it (the presence of so many promontories, gulfs and bays could easily lead to this conception) a multitude of islands, as Basho thought?

If you look at Abraham Ortelius's map of 'East India', *Indiae Orientalis Insularumque Adiacentium Typus*, which came out in Antwerp, 1570, you see Japan as a big oval-shaped island set between China and America with myriads of islets to the south and to the north. These are Basho's 'thousand islands of the Ainu'. But it's highly unlikely Basho ever saw that map. What he might just have seen is Ishikawa Ryûsen's Outline Map of Japan (*Honchô Sukan Kômoku*), where you get intriguing glimpses of the Ezogashima (the Ezo islands) in several places of the map's right-hand border.

Maps were few, and maps were vague, because of lack of knowledge, because of lack of interest. But also because there was an element of risk owing to the harsh reclusion policies in vogue. When Hayashi Shihei of Sendai brought out his map of Ezo in 1758, the map was suppressed, the blocks destroyed and the mapmaker flung into prison. If a mariner was blown off his normal course and shipwrecked on some distant shore, he risked the same fate if ever he managed to get back home. Unwillingly or no, he'd infringed the law.

The first Japanese to go up into the Hokkaido and stay there for any length of time were people on the fringes of central and centralised Japanese society. In the 12th century, there were refugees from the Minamoto-Taïra wars in scattered settlements on the Oshima peninsula. To them were added people banished for whatever reasons to the ends of the earth. And gold-hunters (maybe also silver-seekers: on some maps I've seen Hokkaido marked *Terra de Plata*) — as many as 80,000 of them, according to Girolama de Angelis, during the gold rush of the 17th century. And fishermen, out for anything from herring to whale. All of these people tended to be grouped together under the generic name: *wataritô*, from the verb *wataru*, 'to pass' — those who had passed (as I did yesterday) the straits of Tsugaru.

In the 15th century, the Takeda family, who came to be known as the Matsumae, set up a fief on Hokkaido and in time established 85 trade-places in the territory. The Ainu brought in kombu, herring, salmon ('the three products of Ezo', *Ezo no sanpin*), along with eagle feathers, falcons, trout, bearskins and sealskins; in exchange, they got swords, sake, pipes and tobacco, dishware and jewellery.

In a volume of the *Transactions of the American Philosophical Society*, I've seen a lay-out of the exchange rates which gives an idea of what was going on. If the Ainu could bring in 6 bundles (120) herring or 5 bundles (100) salmon or 15 bundles (300) trout or 6 bundles (120) cod or 3 barrels of dried herring roe or 500 sea cucumbers or 600 dried mushrooms or 3 sealskins or 3 pieces of elm bark cloth or 6 bamboo blinds or 3 rush mats, he'd get a sack (8 *shô*) of rice. For a barrel of fish oil, he'd get 3 8-*shô* sacks of rice; for a bear liver, 14–20 sacks, depending on its size; for an outfit of brocade cloths, 9–10 sacks of rice; for every 5 feet of brocade cloth, 6 sacks; for a Karafuto (Sakhalin) pipe, 5 cups of sake . . .

When, in the 18th century, China opened the 'Nagasaki bundles' it imported in great quantity, they were full of Ezo produce. What began as ceremonial tribute to Lord Matsumae gradually turned into commerce, and to more and more exploitative commerce. It became common practice for the merchants to get the Ainu drunk before making a deal, and if you add to the cheating and the alcoholism the diseases to which the Ainu were not immune, you can see a typical process such as went on in other parts of the world. The Ainu, normally a quiet people, revolted in 1457, again in 1669, and again in 1789. But their race, as well as their original way of life, was on the way down and out.

To the Japanese colonisers, coming up in greater and greater numbers, Hokkaido was an 'empty' land. All they saw were little groups of Ainu living here and there in tiny settlements — *kotan* — of at most ten fires, totally incapable of exploiting the resources of the land. What they didn't, and couldn't, see were the invisible lines that crossed and criss-crossed the emptiness and which connected the Ainu with that land, 'their' land, the 'human beings'' land.

It's those 'invisible lines' I'm interested in, it's those I'm going to try and follow out. Which is why I'm travelling here in the Hokkaido with that blue book of songs in my rucksack.

Here's the song of the Thunder god:

I wanted to see
the human land
and so I came down
to the human country
I came down first
to the top of the country
the sea-folks' country
then I came down
to the land-folks' country
I came forward, shoreward
heading toward
the mouth of the Shishimuka
after that I went upstream
along the Shishimuka river
I moved along
slowly and leisurely
looking over
the face of the land
the human land
I'd come down to that land
because I wanted to see it
and now my heart leaped
in pleasure at its beauty
I looked at the beauties of the country
as I moved on
slowly, leisurely . . .

27. Hoboing in Hokkaido

On the morning of October 15th, a golden, windy morning, I set out on Route 5 along the Oshima peninsula, which is to say, the tail of the skate.

As I come out of the suburbs on the high road booming and fuming with big Nissan and Isuzu trucks on which I hope to get a ride, the first sign I see is a huge advertisement: DRINK MILKLAND HOKKAIDO. Milk, in Japan? The fact is, Hokkaido is Japan's frontier America. When the Meiji government, deciding to turn the face of Japan to the West, created the new 'Northern district' — at least in part to keep the Russians (the 'red barbarians') off — they brought in foreign experts, 76 of them, among whom were 46 Americans. That meant a pretty solid Americanisation, which is there not only in the cattle and sheep farms, but in the very shape of the houses. If you forget for a moment where you are, you may have the illusion of being on a back road in some old blueberry America . . .

So, here I am hoboing in Hokkaido alongside those farmhouses straight out of Vermont and Connecticut and other new Englands, those Milk adverts, those notices announcing COWPUNCHER HOLSTEINS.

Not finding a ride right away, and feeling hungry, I go into a roadside café for a little extra breakfast.

I'm sitting quietly at a table covered with a red-and-white checked cloth, drinking a long glass of milk and munching a doughnut, when a man at another table calls over:

'Amerika, desuka?' (You're from America, aren't you?)

Not wanting to complicate matters, or get this Hokkaido cowboy worried (he's actually wearing a checked shirt and a stetson), I say:

'*Hai.*' (Yes.)

'Oklahoma!'

'Oklahoma!!'

'Gooda ruck.'

'Gooda ruck to you, man.'

— and away I go with my good old lucksack on my back, out again (knowing I'll never know why he did say 'Oklahoma') on to the highroadeos of wild Hokkaido.

Sitting in an Isuzu about a half-hour later, with the radio going full blast, I gather, from one word, *momiji*, that they're talking about the arrival of red leaf Autumn. How can you not have a liking for a country, whether it be Japanee, Ainu, or Japainu, where *red leaves* are every year in the news?

I spent that night at a *kan kokan*, youth hostel, on the banks of Lake Toya.

When I woke, on the following morning, the window was full of white mist, shot through with sunlight — exactly as in the *Song of the Whale*, which I duly quote from my big blue book:

> *Then by and by*
> *I happened to look up*
> *and saw that*
> *the inside of the house*
> *was filled with beautiful white mist*
> *white mist was hovering*
> *inside the house*
> *and flashes of white light*
> *were gleaming, gleaming*
> *a very lovely sight it was*
> *and my heart leaped with pleasure . . .*

Outside, vapour was rising off the lake in the warming sun, people were jogging determinedly and arithmetically round its rim, a man was busy among lakeboats in the shape of swans ready to catch the last lingering clients of the season, and crows were cawing, cawing, cawing by the unholy hundreds.

I got out on the road, making for the central mountains.

Straight on, straight on — *masugu! masugu!* — across the plains. All those trucks: logging trucks, sugar-refinery trucks, brewery trucks, fish-factory trucks . . . Hokkaido seems to be going through a boom, and I'm bumming along on the boom thinking of snowy mountains and empty beaches and swan lakes. Stopping off at some roadside café for an *udong* (noodles, mushrooms, vegetables) or a *ramen* (noodles and soup), or a coffee and *hambargu*, depending on the moment, the appetite, the possibilities. Rolling through the dusky red of Autumn in this big sky country, stubble being burned in the fields, men and women with white cloths wrapped round their heads moving like ghost dancers through the fire and smoke, a crimson little toy-size train rattling by, planes in the sky like fish in an aquarium, volcanic hills smooth and rounded on the horizon, Sobetsu, Bankei, Kônei — hot spring, boulder-filled stream, route 723, Otaki, a clump of very white birches, Kimobetsu, Route 276, Lake Shikotsuku, streaks of snow on still far-off mountain range, road-making and tunnelling, Chitose, salmon culture river, Naibetsu River, coffee and spaghetti ('*Amerikajin?* — *Hai* — Japan good? — Good!'), Three Oaks Farm — Urerotchi Holsteins, Naganuma, Kuribawa Town, Ahirakawa, Naiechyo and a *torii* gate made here hyper-technologically of bright steel tubes.

It was late afternoon when I came into Daisetsuzan National Park. Just beside the roadside restaurant where I've stopped off there's a little Ainu shop and museum: *Ainu kenkyu kai*. I go in there, a little place, shady and obscure, with an old harridan sitting by a fire, an old witch of a brown-skinned woman who lets me move among the swords with their decorated scabbards, the rich embroidered cloths with the thick swirling-sworling patterns, the blue and white pottery, the straw shoes and the snowshoes, the skulls of animals, the bearskins and the huge silver red-gubbed wisdom-eyed salmon . . .

'Where are you going?' asks the old woman as I leave.

'Daisetsuzan.'

Big Snow Mountain.

Bulking there on the horizon.

Ainu holy place, home of the spirits.

28. Big Snow Mountain

Autumn was going into Winter, redyellow into white, leaf into flake, as I went higher up into Daisetsuzan . . .

At one point, with the snow falling thick, I could hardly see the road and began to get worried I might just walk off into the snowy void and bury myself for good in some drift. That's fine sometimes when you think of it, as a way out of all the noise and shit, but when you're on the spot, the body rebels, wants to keep in touch with the rummy, red, rolling earth. So I was worried, while still putting one foot in front of the other. But the sky cleared for a while, long enough for me to come to this little winter resort village where I found an old hostel and in it a room for the night.

What had struck me first was the lump of obsidian that lay in the entrance hall: a huge black lump of solid, gleaming stone. I'd seen a lot of obsidian (paleolithic trade object) down in the Tokyo museum, in the Ainu room, and I'd seen it again in the little Ainu display hut beside the café, but it's only now I really realise my path is going to be marked by that jet-black rock.

Rock paths, salmon lines and swan routes . . .

Snow was clustering thick on the window of my room, with stars shining among the flakes and a moon, a big wild yellow moon, scudding its way across the flurried sky. I liked that wildness outside, and inside the clean neatness: the bare walls, the stove, the green-bordered tatami.

A place of meditation on the top of stormy mountain . . .

First I take out my darkblue Ainu song-book, and read a long poem about the spirits of the mountain, how they rose from the sea and fought on the heights in thunder and lightning.

Then I put the book down and put out the light, and lay in the darkness watching the snow patterns on the window, and the yellow smudge of the moon, and listening to the mountain wind.

In the poem I'd read at the *kan kokan*, there was another bit about the owl:

While all this
was going on
old owl
sat still
with his eyelids
shut tight
the one over the other . . .

All that was left for me to do was to turn myself into that old owl. In the meantime, I did it the easy way — by falling asleep.

29. *Pilgrim of the Void*

When I left the little *onsen* in the morning, it was to find myself in a bright snow-world, with Asahi, the highest peak in this central massif (indeed the highest in the whole of Hokkaido), looming up there at

2520 metres, and the others clustered around it: Eboshi, Akadake, Hakuun, Hokkai, Hakuchin.

I'd just left a little restaurant where I'd got some breakfast, when I met the American, looked about thirty years old, one of those wandering, almost inarticulate Americans I seem always to come up against in out-of-the-way places: pilgrims of the void. I don't think he expected to find another big-eyed Caucasian in that place, at that hour, any more than I did, so our meeting provoked first a surprised look, then a smile, then a quiet hi-hallo, before blossoming out into a little dialogue of the type 'Where have you been?', 'Where are you going?', 'What have you seen?'. He was making back to Sapporo and then to Boston after a fortnight spent around Daisetsuzan and Akan. I told him I came from Glasgow and that I hoped to make it up to Wakanai on the Soya or Lapérouse straits (I didn't want to talk about my real desire, the swans) . . .

'Well, have a good trip'

— that's right: good dreams, good roads.

Breathing in air that felt as if it was mentholised, I struck out on the road to Matsuyama.

It was there I saw a wonderful waterfall which I was told is known as *Hagoromo*, the feather mantle, and which reminded me of a Nô play translated by Fenollosa and worked out poetically by Ezra Pound.

It's a play — one single act — about the losing and the re-finding of a way.

We're on the shores of Miho, a barren pine-waste, close by the 'windy road of the waves'. A fisherman leaves his boat, walks up the beach, aware of 'an empty sky with music' and 'a beauty to set the mind above itself', before he sees an amazingly beautiful feather-cloak hanging on a pinetree. He's taken it when the 'spirit of the air' whose mantle it is, asks him what he's going to do with it. Take it home, says the fisherman, maybe put it in a museum, so that people in the 'downcast age' may have some sense of how things were when spirits moved about the world. The spirit pleads with him. Without that feather-mantle, there is no flying for her, already she feels lost, with the 'knowledge of the road' fading in her mind: the voices of the world are already fewer, the wild geese that travel the highways of the air are fewer. The fisherman sympathises, and says he will return the mantle if only she will do a dance, the dance of the air-spirits. She says, yes, she will do a dance, a dance to live in the memory of sorrowful people. So she dances: 'the heavenly feather-robe moves in accord with the wind'. It's like power and beauty coming back into the world: 'Plain of life, field of the sun, true foundation, great power!' And the chorus concludes: 'Only a little time can the mantle be upon the wind that was blown over Matsubara or Ashitaka, though the clouds lie in heaven like a plain awash with sea. Fuji is gone, the great peak of Fuji is blotted out little by little. It melts into the upper mist . . .'

I spent two days up there on the mountainside, listening to the silence, looking into the light.

30. Cat Street

I was moving down to Kushiro, along a birch-lined river, with Old Father Time gathering clouds behind me.

Route 273 was straight and clean, with green prairie stretching on either side.

Just outside Kamishihiro Station, I got involved in Japanese Army manoeuvres, with truck after truck of helmeted men — stolid they were, no sign — rolling by en route to some warlike rendezvous. But pretty soon everything was quiet again, the river Biribetsu shining in the sun.

I was on my usual regime of hitch-hiking and walking. After a few hours alongside the river, I got taken into Ashoro Station, where there was a Liquor Shop, a garage, and a girl's voice singing a nostalgic song — Sayonara kind of thing — over a loudspeaker, this sunny Saturday afternoon in the Void.

On then to Hombetsu, a village street lined with rowan-trees, where I eat a coffee and *hambargu*, before finally getting a ride into Kushiro.

Kushiro — hardworking little town, full of the smell of fish. I follow the smell right down to the harbour, late afternoon, pale moon in the sky, piles of salt here and there, smell of fish now mingled with the smell of engine oil, a line of boats in — *Kaikomaru, Eishomaru, Urangimaru* — gulls caterwauling round them, me standing there feeling a million miles away from anything.

A little man with whiskers and a white bandanna round his head comes up to me and says:

'Amerikajin?'

I say 'yes', he says: 'welcome Japan'.

I ask him if they still hunt whales from here, you know, the big ones, that spout — *spfoo! spfoo!* He says no, no more, ten years ago. They go out for little ones now, little teeny weeny ones (sardines?). And that kind over there, points to a fish on the tarmac of the pier: mackerel.

So they're leaving the whales alone now. Fine. The business gave Melville a metaphor, but at bottom, it was sheer horror. May the great beasts swim in peace.

Kushiro, night falling.

'Gals Nippon Products are especially selected hair cosmetics for Japanese girls.'

Wandering aimlessly from street to street, I note the names of the dives and snack bars:

Plus On
Nice Space
Free Talk
Royal Snack
Mrs Picasso
Playing Space
Meine Liebe
Lalilulelo

Tempted by *Lalilulelo* (all those lovely little vowels!), I went up a flight of stairs to the first floor where it was, but seeing the stairs climbed still higher, followed them up and found myself in the tiniest of restaurants where a girl was frying sardines over burning embers on a grate and where I ate a plate of delicious sardines and another of delectable aubergines, with a Sapporo beer, before going to look for a place to spend the night.

Cat Street, that's where I was lodged in Kushiro. Not knowing much of the language, and unable to read most of the signs, moving about in silence, I'm obliged to re-name places for my own use, and as this was a little alley full of cats . . .

After settling in, I went back out into the streets and started wandering round and round again when I came upon this amazing restaurant I'll call the Salmon Inn, like something straight out of Melville, ancient Nantucket style, with whale bones over the door, a huge fish hanging from the ceiling, and a tremendous wide-eyed salmon in a glass case just beside my table, to which I'd groped my way through the noise and smoke.

I await my fishy meal, thinking of salmon.

31. The Way of the Salmon

Salmon — from *salire* (Latin), to leap.

The leaping fish . . .

The King, the Chinook, the Tyree, the Quinnat, the Cohu, the Silver, the Sockeye, the Blueback, the Nerka, the Humpie, the Chum, the Dog, the Keta, the Cherry, the Masa, the Steelhead . . .

All moving on their lines
from the Sacramento to North Hokkaido
from Monterey Bay to Kamchatka
from the Fraser River to the Kurile archipelago
from the Klamath River to Korea and Alaska
from the river Amur to the river Pusan
totem animal of the North Pacific
at the living heart of all the cultures:
Chinook
Salish
Kwakiutl
Haida
Tsimshian
Aleut
Yukagir
Koryak
Chukchi
Ainu

salmon — moving round the ocean
then, at fixed moments
going back up to the great rivers to spawn
(eggs laid in gravel, orange-red or translucent, with cold water running over them —
up to a thousand eggs from one single female in a redd)
the alevins hatch out, nestle in the gravel till they're an inch in length, quick little blighters, shy of light, feeding at dawn and dusk
stay in lakes and streams two years (except the Pinks and Dogs that start out earlier)
then migrate to salt water
travelling in schools at night
spend then three to five months in bays and estuaries to become acclimatised
feeding on plankton, shrimps and squid
before setting out
onto the great journey
(the Asian salmon travelling clockwise, the North American salmon counter-clockwise)
maybe ten miles a day
thirty miles a day at spawning time
Pinks make the circuit once
Sockeyes do it once each year for three or four years
how do they do it?
are the circuits printed in their genes, do they feel their way through a magnetic field, do they smell their way upstream???
once back
their bodies change
fish that had been fat, sleek, gleaming, leaping
now go soft
now is the time when the Humpies grow their hump
and when the Dogs grow long sharp teeth
now is the time the Sockeye turns bloodred and its head olivegreen
they pair off into male and female

make the nest
the male swinging back and forth over the female
rubbing her and nudging her
as she scoops out the redd from silt and gravel
then she lies rigid
at the centre
while he comes in
curving his body against hers
till the eggs are laid
in clouds of milt
then it is
the fish begin to die
their bodies
thrown up on the banks
food for bear and eagle

the circle, the cycle . . .

When, around midnight, I left the inn and got back to Cat Street, I had a five-minute get-together with a little black-furred, golden-eyed beauty who, seeing me coming, slumped down on her side and started purring.

I must have smelled of salmon.

32. The Clear Coast

Autumn's misty redness, the blue-gleaming Pacific, snowstreaked peaks on the horizon . . .

I left Kushiro early in the morning, making for Nemuro via Akkeshi and Attoko. Kushiro's streets were still bathed in mist, with hundreds of crows roaming and rummaging the streets.

As the mist gave way to sun and blue sky, the coast appeared in all its definition and clarity: boats at anchor, cranes stalking in elegant silence, shell-gatherers busy at work.

At a place called Itoizawa, I came across a café with big windows looking out to sea, and sat there with my blue Ainu book beside a pot of tea, finding this, in the *Song of the Blood-Red Bird*:

A thin path of light
could be clearly seen
going upstream
along the course of the river . . .

When I got on the road again, I was thinking of that blood-red bird following a thin path of light, upstream, updream.

This whole area is like a bird sanctuary, though I don't suppose it bears any such name, it doesn't need any such name. Every now and then I'd see those cranes stepping with incredible grace in the shining quietness. Or a band of grey heron, like smoke made flesh, reflected in the still, clear water.

Thinking of the old Japanese for 'elegance': the teeth of an animal, and a bird in flight . . .

Akkeshi, at the tip of a promontory, takes its name from an Ainu word meaning 'place of oysters'. Its harbour was full of *kombu*-boats, that go to gather seaweed over by the Habomai Islands, which aren't Japanese, but Russian.

More cranes, rising from a sea of yellow grass. Wild duck flying over a marsh. A beach of black sand.

I came into Nemuro on a bus.

33. At Nemuro

When I went into the station at Nemuro to enquire about trains to Wakanai (if I wasn't to see the swans I'd go up there), I was preceded by a guy with this phrase emblazoned on the back of his jerkin: 'Too fast to live, too young to die.' If you keep your eyes open for the backs of jerkins in Japan, you can get any number of lessons in psycho-sociology.

But what intrigued me in the Nemuro railway station was the huge crab suspended over the ticket office window. This one didn't *move*, like the mechanical one down in Shinjuku, Tokyo, but it was very much *there* nonetheless. Is the Japanese mind naturally surrealistic?

I met live crabs just down the road, in Crab Row (its street map name may be Generale Watanabe Avenue or something), one long line of steaming cabins in which crabs — lusty-coloured, blind-groping crabs — are cooked while the customer waits. I was waiting there for nothing in particular when a little woman in a thick rubber apron came out of the steam right up to me and stuck a huge red crab in front of my face.

'Hanasakigawa,' she said, and screamed with laughter.

I must have looked as if I didn't understand a word — which was exactly the case.

She pointed to me.

Then to herself.

Then to the crab.

And went into another scream of laughter, joined in this by another steam-cookie who stood close by with her hands on her hips.

'Hanasakigawa!' she said once more.

And pointed to herself.

And to the crab.

'Ah, sodes!' I said, and laughed too, still not understanding what it was all about, but beginning to surmise there were some fishy sexy allusions in the air, and not wanting to spoil the fun.

So I pointed to the crab.

And pointed to myself.

'Hai!' she cried, thrust the crab into my hands as a gift, and ran away laughing to get on with her job.

I later found out *hanasakigawa* meant something like 'flower-opening'.

With my big red crab in my grateful hands, I went down to the harbour and, sitting with my back to a capstan, broke the crab open and had a little feast to myself.

By this time, the sun was setting red, very red, and a big, round, cold moon was beginning to crawl over the town.

I was in no hurry, though. Later, I'd find myself a place to sleep somewhere. But for the moment I was quite content to sit there all alone on the pier, even though it was a little chilly — Winter coming on, when so much of Hokkaido freezes up, including Nemuro Bay.

I was thinking of the swans, imagining them on the plains of Siberia, now that extreme cold had seized the air up there, gathering for the great migration, flying into the sun, crossing over the regions of the Ienissei, Lake Baikal, Manchuria . . .

And under the big moon of Nemuro, in the cold loneliness of the North Pacific night, I renewed my allegiance, in light and in darkness, to the still, despite everything, so beautiful terraqueous globe.

34. Philosophy of the Swan

Later that night, in my room at the North Sea Hotel, I was thinking of how, in the eighteenth century, the last time deep questions were put in a *public* way, the swans were at the centre of the debate concerning wildness and domesticity, the civilised and the primitive, the rude and the cultivated.

Buffon was all for nature ordered and decorative: 'How beautiful is cultivated Nature, enhanced by the hand of man!' But at the same time he recognised that men can at times over-do it, and, while demonstrating how great an advance to civilisation was brought by the domestication of animals such as the horse, the ox, the dog and the sheep, he has a sneaking admiration and liking for indomitables that live in faraway wildernesses, burning deserts, ice-cold mountains.

Like the swans.

It's this that comes across in that revealing text contained in the *Histoire Naturelle des Oiseaux*. In the big 18th century folio edition of this I consulted at the Sorbonne library in Paris, the only image it has is the engraving of a tame swan (maybe even with clipped wings) floating in an artificial pond at the foot of a monumental flight of stairs in the Jardin du Roi. But the text apologises for this, and goes in another direction, opens out into a space that is a lot more interesting, a lot more exciting than this 'art scene'.

If most Western minds only have an image of sitting swans, says Buffon, it's because they've forgotten what a wild swan is. When they think of the swan, they see it swimming in some confined space, graceful and decorative, but no more than that. Whereas, Hesiod knew, who calls the swan *altivolans*, a high flyer, and Homer says that, along with geese and cranes, the swan is one of the great travellers of the world. Pindar declares that Jupiter set loose two eagles from the opposite ends of the earth, so as to be able to designate as 'the middle' the place where they met. Plutarch says baloney: those eagles were swans.

Buffon then goes into the multiple kind of nomenclature I like, going round the world in words.

Swan is *kuknos* in Greek; *olor* in Latin; in Arabic, *baslak* or *cinnana*; in Italian, *cygno, cino*; in Spanish, *cisne*; in Catalan, *signe*; in German, *schwan*; in Saxon and in Swiss, *elbsch* (supposedly derived from Latin *albus*, white); in English, *swan*, the little one being called *cygnet*; in Swedish, *svan*; in Illyrian, *labut*; in Polish, *labec*; in the Phillipines, *tagac* . . .

Thereafter, he insists on the sheer physical beauty of the bird, both its form and its movements, quoting Virgil, Ovid and a dozen other poets to prove his case. Adding that the swan is also intelligent ('to catch fish, it is full of ruses') and strong ('it could break a man's leg with its wing'). It also lives a long life — some say even 300 years ('which is no doubt exaggerated').

On to geography:

Since the swan often feeds on marsh grass and seaweeds, it likes to settle on quiet rivers and lakes. The Ancients spoke of the swan populations of the Meander, the Mincio, the Strymon and the Caystre (called by Propertius 'swan river'). Venus' island, Paphos, was full of swans. Strabon speaks of the swans of Spain and there's even mention of them on the sea of Africa. But if the species can exceptionally be found in the South, it's mainly a Northern bird, to be found on the shores of Western Europe only in very severe winters.

So the bird is a wild 'traveller of the world', and it is beautiful — but it is also a political model: 'It lives in peace with all Nature. Among the many populations of water birds who look to it as leader and law-giver, it behaves as a friend rather than as a king. It is the first inhabitant of a quiet republic.'

You can tie that in with the evolution of thought in prerevolutionary France. You can also tie it in with Buffon's notion, derived from a report by Peter Simon Pallas, that this swan-territory of North-East Asia (in particular Southern Siberia and Tartary) had once been the home of an ancient civilisation with a very high culture that had later been diffused to China, Atlantis, Egypt, Greece, Rome and Europe . . .

Buffon comes finally to the famous 'swan-song'. He says quite categorically that it's a fable, which he salutes in the by-going as 'poetic', but goes on to give a detailed description of the bird's throat and vocal organs:

'Other shore birds, such as the crane, have the same folds and curves in the windpipe, and it is no doubt this that gives their voice that great raucous resonance . . .'

Why should I be carrying around in my rucksack these photocopied pages of an old 18th century text instead of some modern book on ornithology? It's simply that, as I've suggested, back there in the 18th century, you had that general discipline called 'natural philosophy', before all the specialisms, a discipline in which poetry, science and philosophy come together, and where an *overall* questioning is to the fore, and the search for a global comprehension, a global conscious experience.

That questioning can still be ours — though the answers, no doubt, can't be the same. There's probably no global answer. What there *can* be is a *field of correspondence*.

And somebody, some *body*, trying to co-ordinate and concentrate that field, keeping the sense of wild signs — and flying.

35. Around the Lake

Another dawn, mist rising over the Pacific waters, and in the yards of the fishing smacks in the harbour, clusters of silent crows.

I was making for the Notsuke peninsula.

After an initial ride on a truck, I'd started walking when a big van passed me bearing on its side the bizarre inscription: SPIRIT COOPERATION COMPANY.

God only knows what that could mean.

I'd heard down in Tokyo about this lake, down at the tip of the peninsula, where you could see the wild swans coming in from Siberia to hibernate.

My dates were about right. I had the ghost of a chance . . .

Towards the end of the day, I came to this place where there was a lake on one side of the road, and on the other an inn, beside it a telephone booth with a metal swan on its top.

This must be it.

The Swan Inn, which had a big lump of obsidian at its door, had two storeys, the lower one being a restaurant, the upper one a kind of swan gallery, with large photos of swans all round the walls: swans cleaving the air, sleeping in the snow, fishing in the lake, accompanied by printed texts of information.

I sat in the restaurant eating a meal, with a middle-aged couple doing the same a few tables away, and lingered on a while when they'd left, before going to ask the inn people if there was any place I could spend the night, and succeeding nights, as I'd come to see the swans. They said (the cook spoke English) they didn't take in guests, but there was a camping and caravaning site down the road. I said I had no tent, no caravan, no car, and asked if they'd let me sleep in the swan gallery. Hardly keen at first, they finally accepted.

Maybe that was the Spirit Cooperation working . . .

I laid out my sleeping bag, showed how I wouldn't make any mess, and that I didn't smoke, and that — bringing out my big blue Ainu book — I was a student of nature and the mind, and they seemed reassured.

Before laying me down to sleep, I took a walk round the room, shining light on the swan-images with my torch.

Like some paleolithic Plato.

36. The Arrival

For the next few days, I haunted that lake.

It was all so beautiful on the lakeside: the reeds, the quietness, the clear air. I walked round it, or lay out under a tree, and just waited.

A couple of days passed, then three, then four, with nothing happening, as in the Ainu *Song of the Crow*:

> *This is the way*
> *I continued to live*
> *on, and on*
> *uneventfully . . .*

I just kept walking round the lake in silence.

Then, on the evening of the fifth day's attentive waiting, with twilight coming down blue and rose, there was a great cry in the air, a great

whoo whoo whoo

and then a rushing sound of wings.

It was like the cry heard once on the Mediterranean: *Great Pan is dead*, only the other way round.

Suddenly the emptiness was full of clamour and beating wings.

They came in groups of five to ten.

First one group.

Then another.

Then another.

I waited till there were about ninety birds on the lake, then went to the inn to sleep, intending to be up before dawn.

Well before dawn, I was lurking among the frosted reeds of the lakeside — up to my knees in marsh at one point — waiting to see the beginning of the day.

It was the ducks that wakened first, skimming over the waters agitatedly, while the swans still slept. A shimmering and a quivering over the darkblue waters, wind on the golden grass . . .

Only when the sun rose did the whiteheads wake, spreading their powerful wings, and beginning to raise a cry, now here now there.

I crouched there among the reeds, watching them, listening to them — then one rose into the air, followed by a band of others, all whooping in chorus.

Round and round they circled.

Round and round they circled in the clear bright air.

I followed them with my eyes and with my mind.

On the empty lake
this morning of the world
the wild swans

37. Epilogue

It was a bright Autumn morning, and I was riding in the express train, the *shinkansen*, from Tokyo to Kyoto. *Da-ra-da-da, da-ra-da-da*, it had said, before it really picked up speed, and thereafter it was *dara-dara, dara-dara, dara-dara*: a smooth gliding along the tracks over the territory separating the Eastern Capital from the ancient capital of the West.

Dara-dara, dara-dara
dara-dara, dara-dara

If that ground-note had been the only one, I'd have been completely glad. In fact, I was slightly less glad than that, because the carriage I was in was packed full of school-kids, little boys and girls in uniform (grey jacket, red tie), giggling, shouting, playing with SNOOPY cards, fiddling at transistors, delving into their lunch-boxes. Not that they weren't pleasant, they were, very. One youngster leaned over his seat to me and asked:

'What your name?'

'Ken.'

'Hidote,' he said, pointing to himself, then, 'where you go?'

'Kyoto.'

'Nagoya.'

Blue sea shimmering.

Lighthouse.

Tunnel.

I was seated beside an elderly, dignified gentleman who might have been a cultured businessman, or a university professor.

Realising I didn't know how long this journey was going to last — all I knew was we'd left *Tokyo Eki*, Tokyo Station, platform 17, at 10.24 — I turned to him and said:

'Excuse me. When do we get to Kyoto?'

He searched for his words, and then came out with:

'One — and half.'

What I knew then, apart from the time of arrival, was that this man was not a Professor of English or a man who did a lot of business with the US. I liked him all the more for it, and wished I had put my question to him in Japanese (my knowledge of the language did go as far as that).

Suddenly the uproar in the carriage ceased, and in its place there was just one big *Ahhh*. I looked up and saw Fuji, perfect, dark-blue, with a white cap and white streaks down its sides.

'Won-der-ful!' cried a little girl, stretching out her arms, somewhat for my benefit, while the elderly gentleman, in a low tone, said:

'Fujisan.'

I didn't say anything, but I was thinking to myself that probably no other people in the world has such a relationship to a mountain. Thinking also I was lucky to see it so clearly this first time.

At Kyoto, I found myself a room in the Shimabara quarter, near the Nishi Hongan temple, had a meal, and a bath, and a sleep (I'd just spent two sleepless nights in Tokyo), then went out into the Kyoto evening.

There was a golden, fuming light in the sky, that was later to turn into red dusk. I saw a tower, painted rosy and white, rising up out of the city centre, strangely unreal — like a lighthouse in an ocean of dreams. Then a girl passed by, with a face like something out of a Nô play. And at the edge of the Kamo River, I saw a white heron stalking in the twilight.

Evening in the ancient capital
on the grey waters of the river
a lone white heron

In the Colorado Coffee shop, I was sitting quiet, enjoying my Blue Mountain Blend, when a Japanese with dark mafia glasses leaned over from the neighbouring table and said:

'Amelika?'

Getting used to this kind of thing, and always willing to ring the changes on any kind of nationality (within reason), I answered:

'Yeah.'

He then said: 'Good.' At that, I just smiled. His next question was: 'Doctor?' (why, I'll never know). I said: 'No,' and made ready to move off. *'Adios, amigo,'* he said. I gave him a little John Wayne salute and went back out into the night.

Red lips
in a rainy street
the face of Autumn

Five in the morning
a waterfall
tumbling through the dark

Next day around nine, I was crossing Shijo Bridge among the crowds. The big department stores were just opening: the Daimaru, the Takashimaya, the Hankyu, rolling up their shutters. I left the main thoroughfares, and moved away along the Pontochodori, where you could hear the cheepering of birds and, across the greygreen waters of the river, the green trains trundling into the city: *Cha-yata-ka-chak, cha-yata-ka-chak*. Seemed to be an awful lot of little dens and bars and clubs down that way: *The Zen Pub, Bon Aloi, Château Puff, New Rug, Joy Box, Second House, Penny Rain, Boomerang, Rubicon, Funky Babe* . . . I went into one place for a coffee, *Coffee House Nemu*, it was called (sub-title 'Something Typical Space'), and sat there for a while watching the misty flow of the river. Then came back into the city, where I went into a junk-shop, an amazing junk-shop, packed with all kinds of bric-a-brac, where the conversation between me and the owner went like this:

'Where from?'

'France.'

'Français?'

'Oui.'

'Vous êtes typiquement français!'

'Ah, bon.'

'Où vivez-vous?'

'Paris.'

'Où, à Paris?'

'Montparnasse . . .'

— and there was another little identity-play that left everybody happy and did not disturb the emptiness.

That afternoon, I paid a visit to the quarters of the EFEO, that is, the *Ecole Française d'Extrême-Orient*, the French Far-Eastern School.

I had a job finding them. What I had scribbled on a piece of paper by a man in Tokyo was the name of the temple grounds in which the School was situated, but I couldn't read the words too well, and hence wasn't sure of the pronunciation. After an enquiry or two, I finally got to the temple, but still I could see no school, so I stopped somebody else:

'Excuse me, do you speak English?'

'A little.'

'The French School, the *Ecole Française*, where is it?'

— he made a tremendous grimace, like an actor in an *ukiyo-e* print, to indicate he hadn't a clue. I continued walking, looking for a sign. Stopped somebody else again:

'Excuse me, speak English?'

'A little.'

'Where is the *Ecole Française*, the French School?'

— he thought for a while, and I was sure I'd missed yet once more, when he looked as if he'd had an illumination, and said:

'*Hai!* Turn light.'

So I thanked him, and turned right. There I found a secluded court-yard, went in back of the yard, and saw, lying on a door-step, a really *huge* pair of shoes, real bath-tub brogues, and for a Japanese, absolutely impossible. I knew I must have arrived. So I knocked, not too loud, and a man came to it, smoking a fat cigar in a fat holder. He turned out to be a Belgian, and sure enough, this was the EFEO. I apologised for barging in on him and said I hadn't realised the presence of the EFEO in Kyoto was so discrete. 'Oh, yes,' he said, *'on vit comme un ver dans sa pomme'* (we live like a worm in its apple). Inside their apple, the main task, he told me, consisted in the elaboration of a dictionary of Buddhist vocabulary. They'd been at it about twenty years, and were nothing if not thorough: at present, they were somewhere around the letter C . . . And there was I breezing in with my wild swans . . .

During the next few days, I visited some of the celebrated places of Kyoto:

Here I go
walking through Important Cultural Property
with holes in my socks

while visitors
photograph the Imperial Villa
maple leaves soak in the sun

Who was here
before the emperor?
the grey heron

Watching
while the guide does his talk
the hovering of the hawk

Also went to some of the temples, contemplating more than one dry garden:

Empty bamboo
and water trickling
Ryoan-ji, early morning

On the clean-raked sand
a heedless bird
has left its tracks

Kennin-ji (supposedly the oldest temple in Japan), early morning: cloud moving slowly in blue sky, a dog, pigeons, a little school-girl with big satchel on back walking hen-toed, pine-trees, three men with white head-kerchiefs sweeping the grounds . . . Soami's dream at Ginkakuji, a garden of silver sand to catch the moonlight . . . The breasts of emptiness (so I read the sand piles that day) at Daisen-in . . . A yellow butterfly fluttering in the silence above Sesshu's garden.

Another place I spent at lot of time in at Kyoto, was 'the house of the poet-hermits', the hermitage built in 1641 by Jôzan Ishikawa, samurai, scholar and landscape-gardener who, having incurred the wrath of the Shogun of Edo, had retired to Kyoto, there to associate with men of culture, practise the tea-ceremony and write poems. In one of the rooms of that hermitage, the *Shisen-do*, Ishikawa had painted the portraits of 36 famous Chinese poets, among them Li Po

(Rihaku) and Tu Fu (Toho), and for every portrait, he'd written a poem. I looked at the portraits, pretty sure the likenesses were no more than approximate, if not purely imaginary, and examined the poems, unable, alas, to decipher them. All I could read were the red leaves in the garden (what the poems were probably about anyway), where I sat contemplating the leaves and the stretch of white sand, and listening to the *suzu*, that little bamboo contraption which, thanks to the presence of a rock and running water, produces a regular *clunk*, Jôzan's favourite sound.

But if I was in Kyoto, it was still mainly for Basho. That northern trip of Basho's, his 'way to the innermost', had ended in the Autumn of 1689. When he was forced to turn back because of illness, he'd come South along the Sea of Japan, finishing up at Ogaki. From there, he'd gone to Ise, then to his native town, Ueno, and from there to Nara, Kyoto, Otsû and Zeze, on the shores of Lake Bika. It was in that latter region he had found an abandoned cottage, the *Genjû-an*, 'the unreal dwelling', where he spent the Summer of 1690:

'I have burnt my face in the hot sun of Kisagata in the Northern provinces and worn my heels out on the rough shores of the Northern Sea whose high dunes make walking difficult, and now here I am, nearing fifty, rocked by the waters of this lake.'

A little later, after some other moves around Omi and Iga, we find him settled in the 'villa' of one of his pupils, Kyorai, a place to the north-west of Kyoto called *Rakushisha*:

'In the fourth year of Genroku (1692), I went to Saga, to Kyorai's place, the villa Rakushi . . . I was given a room in a corner of the villa whose partitions had been redone and its garden cleared of weeds. I had a writing table and a shelf of books containing *Master Haku's Book*, the *Poets of the Empire*, the *Story of the Generations*, the *Tale of Genji*, the *Tosa Journal* and the *Pine-needle Collection* . . . The Rakushi villa had stayed the way its old owner built it, and parts of it were falling in ruins. But in its wildered state it was even more attractive than in the days of its splendour. Exposed to wind and rain, the sculpted timbers had become worn, the strange shaped rocks and the bizarrely gesturing pines were overgrown with scratch-weed, but alongside the bamboo path a flowering lemon-tree shed its perfume.'

In the Rakushisha garden today there are several rocks on which poems have been inscribed, like the one Basho wrote when he left this place:

Samidare ya
shikishi hagitasu
kabe no ato

(Summer rain
poems ripped off
traces on the wall)

There's also a *gorinto* (a monument of five stones, representing earth, water, fire, wind, sky) called *haijin to*, dedicated to all haiku-poets past, present and to come.

In passing, I came out with this little thing:

Autumn rain
earth and sky here
haiku salutations

and it was there my journey ended.